PRAISE FOR *TWO MEN FROM BABYLON*

"While working together at the White House, both Wallace Henley and my late father developed a spiritual, more comprehensive lens that allowed them to see how God's ultimate plan is played out in history through improbable leaders and nations. In this book, your spiritual eyes will be opened to see how God works in human history."

—GINNY DENT BRANT

"In this book, author Wallace Henley, with his background in the White House and in pastoral service in the church, writes about 'the Lord of History,' who raises up and tears down whom He will—ultimately for the furtherance of His kingdom. That includes King Nebuchadnezzar, ruler of ancient Babylon, and Donald J. Trump, 45th president of the United States. The overall point of this important new book is to explore what Christian historian Christopher Dawson calls 'the overruling purpose of God.' I recommend it highly."

—DR. JERRY NEWCOMBE, AUTHOR; SENIOR PRODUCER, ON-AIR
HOST, AND COLUMNIST, D. JAMES KENNEDY MINISTRIES

"A powerful, thought-provoking read that brings into perspective how God uses unlikely leaders to bring about His plans and purpose. You won't just read the book, you'll reread each chapter; write in the margins, and lean back and say . . . WOW . . . God really is in control!"

—PERRY ATKINSON, CHRISTIAN MEDIA LEADER, PRESIDENT
AND GENERAL MANAGER OF THE DOVE RADIO AND TV

"Wallace Henley has written one of the most insightful books I have ever read. God is the Master of history and chooses the leaders who shape it. Man looks at the outside and questions why many leaders fill the seats they do, not under-standing God's bigger design and how He uses the most unusual to accomplish the sometimes unexplainable. Honestly, this is a book that will challenge you greatly and help you understand God's ways better."

—STU JOHNSON, RETIRED US AIR FORCE COLONEL; EXECUTIVE
ADMINISTRATOR OF GRACE INTERNATIONAL CHURCHES AND MINISTRIES

ALSO BY WALLACE HENLEY

The White House Mystique
Globequake
God and Churchill
Call Down Lightning

TWO MEN
FROM
BABYLON

Nebuchadnezzar, Trump, and the Lord of History

WALLACE HENLEY

EMANATE
BOOKS

Published in Nashville, Tennessee, by Emanate Books, an imprint of Thomas Nelson. Emanate Books and Thomas Nelson are registered trademarks of HarperCollins Christian Publishing, Inc.

Thomas Nelson titles may be purchased in bulk for educational, business, fund-raising, or sales promotional use. For information, please e-mail SpecialMarkets@ThomasNelson.com.

Unless otherwise noted, Scripture quotations are taken from New American Standard Bible®. Copyright © 1960, 1962, 1963, 1968, 1971, 1972, 1973, 1975, 1977, 1995 by The Lockman Foundation. Used by permission. (www.Lockman.org)

Scripture quotations marked AMP are from the Amplified® Bible. Copyright © 1954, 1958, 1962, 1964, 1965, 1987 by The Lockman Foundation. Used by permission. (www.Lockman.org)

Scripture quotations marked KJV are from the King James Version. Public domain.

Scripture quotations marked THE MESSAGE are from *The Message*. Copyright © by Eugene H. Peterson 1993, 1994, 1995, 1996, 2000, 2001, 2002. Used by permission of NavPress. All rights reserved. Represented by Tyndale House Publishers, Inc.

Scripture quotations marked NKJV are from the New King James Version®. © 1982 by Thomas Nelson. Used by permission. All rights reserved.

Scripture quotations marked NLT are from the Holy Bible, New Living Translation. © 1996, 2004, 2007, 2013, 2015 by Tyndale House Foundation. Used by permission of Tyndale House Publishers, Inc., Carol Stream, Illinois 60188. All rights reserved.

Any Internet addresses, phone numbers, or company or product information printed in this book are offered as a resource and are not intended in any way to be or to imply an endorsement by Thomas Nelson, nor does Thomas Nelson vouch for the existence, content, or services of these sites, phone numbers, companies, or products beyond the life of this book.

ISBN 978-0-7852-3877-5 (eBook)
ISBN 978-0-7852-3876-8 (HC)

Library of Congress Control Number: 2020933130

Printed in the United States of America
20 21 22 23 24 LSC 10 9 8 7 6 5 4 3 2 1

Dedicated to the memory of
Harry S. Dent,
"Boy Scout"

*The pursuit of discovery is guided
by sensing the presence of a hidden reality
toward which our clues are pointing.*
—MICHAEL POLANYI

CONTENTS

PROLOGUE

Before the Golden Age of Greece, and long before the Roman Empire, there was Babylon.

Long after Greece and Rome, there is still Babylon.

The founder of what would ultimately be literal Babylon was Nimrod, a man described in Genesis 10:8–9 as "a mighty hunter before the LORD." In his commentary on Genesis, Matthew Henry described Nimrod like this:

> Nimrod was resolved to lord it over his neighbours. The spirit of the giants before the flood, who became mighty men, and men of renown . . . revived in him. Nimrod was a great hunter. Hunting then was the method of preventing the hurtful increase of wild beasts. This required great courage and address, and thus gave an opportunity for Nimrod to command others, and gradually attached a number of men to one leader. From such a beginning, it is likely that Nimrod began to rule, and to force others to submit.[1]

Centuries later in 620 BC, Nebuchadnezzar, a successor to Nimrod, became the ruler of Babylon and would demonstrate that founders of a nation inject their spiritual DNA into their offspring. Nimrod himself bore the DNA of the "giants," the "mighty ones" who descended from the

Nephilim (Genesis 6:4). The Bible reveals that at the core of the Nephilim spirit was self-pride and a passion for self-exaltation. This is the essence of "all that is in the world, the lust of the flesh and the lust of the eyes and the boastful pride of life" (1 John 2:16).

This also is the essence of Babylon in all its forms. Nebuchadnezzar, in his time as Babylon's ruler, would pursue these lusts extravagantly—until, in a chaotic period in his personal life, he discovered the Lord of History.

TWO MEN FROM BABYLON

In vision, style, and personage, many view Donald Trump as a type of Nebuchadnezzar, a child of ancient Babylon. In AD 2016, he, a child of modern Babylon, became the president of the nation at whose gates she sits. Thus, even though the ancient city of Babylon became a desolate desert ruin, the Babylon image will not go away. It appears in several varieties across history. Under Nebuchadnezzar a desert waste became a city of splendor. Its very name, *babilu*, means "gate of god." Nebuchadnezzar himself laid the spiritual foundations of the great city in his embrace and propagation of idolatry. One of the spectacles on the streets of Babylon was a gleaming image of Baal made of fifty thousand pounds of gold.

The Greek historian Herodotus (480–429 BC) wrote of the impressive nature of Nebuchadnezzar's Babylon.[2] The city was a huge square, each side spanning fourteen miles, with a walled enclosure fifty-six miles long, anchored by 250 towers, each 450 feet tall. The wall itself, according to Herodotus, was 300 feet high and 25 feet thick, backed by another wall of 75 feet. A moat surrounded the entire complex. Eight huge gates, including the spectacular Ishtar Gate, were embedded in the walls. Nebuchadnezzar's famous hanging gardens bloomed lavishly, irrigated by hydraulic pumps bringing water up from the Euphrates.

CITY OF SPLENDOR, EMPIRE OF TERROR

Nebuchadnezzar himself lived in the world's most spectacular palace. To provide for all this splendor, Nebuchadnezzar turned Babylon into a terroristic state, raiding many other cities, including, in 589 BC, Jerusalem. It was here that the Hebrew exile Daniel would spend many of his days early in his captivity.

Then Babylon, the city of splendor that was also the empire of terror, became a conquered city. In 539 BC, Cyrus the Persian, in a sneak attack, diverted the Euphrates and invaded Babylon. Ultimately, the site of Nebuchadnezzar's glorious city became a desolate desert ruin.

MODERN BABYLON

But Babylon did not disappear. In the Revelation visions of the apostle John, centuries after Nebuchadnezzar, it became the primary symbol of the world system organized without God and in defiance of the Lord of History, just like Nimrod.

Mighty cities are sometimes characterized in modern times as "Babylon," but none as much as Donald Trump's hometown—New York City. Peruvian author Mario Vargas Llosa gets the connection, and wrote:

> In New York City I have always felt I was at the center of the world, in *a modern Babylon* . . . from which, as from a giant heart to the extremities, there circulate to the globe all fashions and vices, values and nonvalues, usages, customs, music, images and prototypes resulting from the incredible mixtures in this city.[3]

What we seek to show here is not that Trump is a reincarnation of Nebuchadnezzar but that the president bears a resemblance to a type of leader that recurs across history, seen graphically in Nebuchadnezzar. By the same token New York is no more a reincarnation of ancient Babylon than Donald Trump is a reincarnation of Nebuchadnezzar, but the city is yet another version of the spiritual characteristics of ancient Babylon.

Trump is a type in time and history of Nebuchadnezzar, as New York City is a modern-day manifestation of the spirit and character of Babylon. Rash, dominating, quick-tongued, and, at one point, crazy . . . such was a fitting description of Babylon's king Nebuchadnezzar. Those characteristics would also seem to fit Donald Trump, especially in the eyes of his critics, many of whom believe Trump to be as crazy as Nebuchadnezzar at his blathering worst.

Nebuchadnezzar hailed from and presided over the greatest city of his time—"Babylon the Great." Donald Trump is from what many call the modern "Babylon," New York City, and presides over a mighty nation that has dominated modern history just as Nebuchadnezzar's Babylon overshadowed the ancient world.

Nebuchadnezzar both reflected and set the tone of the viciousness of his world. Donald Trump both reflects and contributes to the tone of coarseness in our age.

BOASTING AND HUBRIS

When it comes to boasting, the "two men from Babylon" show much resemblance. Both Nebuchadnezzar and Trump suffer bouts of hubris, evidenced by egotistical bragging.

The hubristic pride of Nebuchadnezzar was evident one day when he strolled in his spectacular palace, admiring his city. Gloating, he said to himself, without realizing he was speaking to God too, "Look at this, Babylon the great! And I built it all by myself, a royal palace adequate to display my honor and glory!" (Daniel 4:30 THE MESSAGE).

When it comes to boasting, Donald Trump is as good at it as

Nebuchadnezzar was. "Actually, throughout my life, my two greatest assets have been mental stability, and being, like, really smart," Trump tweeted on January 6, 2018. Such attributes, he continued, "would qualify as not smart, but genius . . . and a very stable genius at that!"

People who criticize Trump's boasts often don't understand his personal history, and the background from which the self-glorifying statements come. Trump says he's not boasting, but just stating the facts. What many don't understand is that he is speaking from a worldview engrained in him from youth by two powerfully influential people in his life—his own father and their pastor.

One of the most disturbing of Donald Trump's early statements as a presidential candidate was that he had never felt the need to ask for God's forgiveness. David Brody and Scott Lamb described how Trump had been brought up under ideas from "power of positive thinking" preacher Norman Vincent Peale, who later regretted that he had neglected "the traditional Christian emphasis on repentance."[4] Asked to elaborate on his own belief about repentance and forgiveness, Trump said that "when we go in church and when I drink my little wine, which is about the only wine I drink, and have my little cracker, I guess that is a form of asking for forgiveness. And I do that as often as possible, because I feel cleansed . . . to me that is very important."

Trump's boasting likely comes out of that "think positive" mindset proclaimed by Peale. Stripped of religious garments, the "think positive" philosophy morphed into a secular version of the "positive confession" movement in contemporary elements of Christianity. As he was steeped in the teaching of Peale early in his life—then reinforced by his own father—the president may not see his bragging as pride and hubris, but as an assertion that leads to positive outcomes and success.

However, that does not cancel the proverb that says pride leads to a "fall." Nor does it erase the truth of 1 John 2:16 that the essence of sin is not only the "lust" of the "eyes" and "flesh," but also "the boastful pride of life."

A GRAND ENIGMA

The presidency of Donald J. Trump is therefore a grand enigma, so enigmatic that powerful opponents—and even some supporters—thought he must have had outside help to win the Oval Office. The Mueller investigators spent more than $30 million over two years searching for Russian collusion and produced almost 450 pages trying to solve the Trump enigma but found no collusion. Impeachment proceedings then feverishly sought reasons to remove Trump from office.

The maddening (to some) mystery remained: *What power made Donald Trump the president of the United States of America?*

Victor Davis Hanson recognized the strangeness of Trump's victory, and wrote that "according to conventional electoral wisdom, Trump should not even have had an outside chance of winning the presidency (he was occasionally polling 10–15 points behind Hillary Clinton in the weeks after his campaign announcement). That he did still astounds—or perhaps shocks—that so many could be so wrong about his chances."[5]

When we drill down into the word *enigma*, we see just how enigmatic *President* Trump is. A thesaurus search reveals some of the related words:

Paradox

Victor Davis Hanson wrote of a paradox that might have been "the key to the Trump enigma." It is, thought Hanson, Trump's "ability to make his poorer and more middle class rivals seem abject snobs and inauthentic snarks, as if populism was a state of mind and attitude rather than preordained by class."[6] Hanson sees "paradox" everywhere in the Trump phenomenon. Hanson finds a huge paradox in the fact that a man who is so uncouth "can change the lives of 330 million."[7]

Daniel Henninger, writing in the *Wall Street Journal*, described the "Trump paradox" as well. "This era's most disliked president has produced a successful first year in office."[8]

However, the paradoxical was apparent in Trump prior to his election to the White House. "Paradox" can also signify an absurdity. Michelle Bachman, a Republican congresswoman from Minnesota and Trump supporter, drove at least one writer into near hysterics. George J. Bryjak read a statement in which Bachman said that Trump "is highly biblical," and that "we will in all likelihood never see a more godly, biblical president in our lifetime." Bachman's statement probably went too far even for some of Trump's supporters, but it shoved Bryjak close to the edge. "One would be hard pressed to find a more absurd statement," he wrote.[9]

Several years before anyone imagined Trump as a contender for the presidency, let alone the winner, syndicated columnist George Will called Trump a "bloviating ignoramus."[10]

Such opinions deepened the paradoxical aspect of the Trump enigma, and excited Trump-watchers of all types to try to figure out the man, his presidency, and whatever forces lurked mysteriously in the background to boost him to that high office.

Perplexity

The enigmatic is perplexing, sometimes to the point of almost driving people insane. "Trump Derangement Syndrome" is the way some Trump supporters and other conservatives describe the craziness of the anti-Trump establishments—especially academics and media.

Elaine Wilson-Reddy said she "had to take a step back" when a friend told her of a question she had posed on Facebook to her Republican acquaintances: *Was there anything Donald Trump could do that would make those Republicans stop supporting him?* The perplexing answer was no. "I guess I have to believe that with all Trump's done since he began his campaign, there probably isn't anything he can do that will harsh their mellow," wrote an apparently bewildered Wilson-Reddy.[11]

Conundrum

The conundrum, or "riddle," of Donald Trump was captured in a statement published in 2015 by the Center for Politics at the University of Virginia:

"Friends, there is no way on God's green earth that the Republican Party hierarchy is going to allow Donald Trump to be their nominee for president."[12]

Professor Stephen Hawking believed he had the answer to how Trump did just exactly that: Trump "appealed to the lowest common denominator." Emily Shire, commenting on Hawking's "solution" to the Trump conundrum, expanded on its complexity when she said that "a bombastic reality TV star with zero political experience, a noted record of flip-flopping, and an eagerness to insult women, minorities, and people with disabilities defied the Republican establishment in one fell swoop. How?"[13]

Mystery

"How?" is indeed at the heart of the Trump enigma.

Journalists, academics, celebrities, members of Congress, and a multitude of others are searching for a contemporary "Alan Turing," the British savant who solved the Nazi "Enigma" code in the Second World War. The mystery of the covert code consumed Turing and his team, working in Bletchley Park in Buckinghamshire, England.

However, no cryptanalysts have been able to decipher the mystery of Trump, because they are looking in the wrong places.

Since the Democrats' 2018 takeover of the United States House of Representatives, there has been a near-frantic attempt to turn the House into a political "Bletchley Park," where money and energy are being spent on trying to wrest the Oval Office from a man they believe should not, by all logic, be there at all.

Who put him in office? How was it possible for a person many prognosticators said could not win the presidency to do just that? Did Russia somehow bring about the Trump victory? Were there mysterious forces at work beyond the capacities of the "deep state" to put Donald Trump in the Oval Office?

The Mueller investigation found no collusion with Russia. Thus, the enigma remained. Among its most bewildering riddles is, *How did a thrice-married casino owner and womanizing New York dandy who said he had never felt a need for God's forgiveness win the support of serious Christians and committed conservatives to become the leader of the world's most powerful nation?*

In addition to Michele Bachmann, some of the nation's leading evangelicals believe that God put Trump in the presidency. They include people like Franklin Graham, son of Billy Graham; Liberty University president Jerry Falwell Jr., whose father was the founder of the Moral Majority; and Robert Jeffress, pastor of Dallas First Baptist Church—a flagship for Southern Baptists, America's largest evangelical denomination.

Nikki Haley infers that both the permissive and intentional will of God (an idea we will discuss in chapters ahead) could be applied to Trump's election to the Oval Office. "I think God sometimes places people for lessons and sometimes places people for change," she told David Brody, White House correspondent for the Christian Broadcasting Network. Donald Trump, she believes, was put in the president's chair "for such a time as this."[14]

How could she and others believe God chose Trump as president? Why would such noted leaders put their reputation on the line for a man like Trump?

Could it be that God really did select or at least permit Donald Trump to occupy the Oval Office in this critical season for the United States? If God, who is perfect in His holy character, chose Trump, whose character is regarded by many as flawed (to put it generously), why would the Lord of History grant him authority?

To answer that question, we must turn to the Bible.

THE HEART OF THIS BOOK

There are two Scripture passages at the heart of this book. One is from the Old Testament, and the other from the New. The Old Testament Scripture was written by the Hebrew prophet Daniel, who was captive in Babylon during Nebuchadnezzar's reign. In fact, Daniel had much interaction with the king, who himself was such an enigma. Inspired by the Holy Spirit, Daniel wrote:

> Let the name of God be blessed forever and ever,
> For wisdom and power belong to Him.
> It is He who changes the times and the epochs;
> He removes kings and establishes kings.
>
> (DANIEL 2:20–21)

The New Testament text that is joined to Daniel's prophecy records words spoken by Jesus: "This gospel of the kingdom shall be preached in the whole world as a testimony to all the nations, and then the end will come" (Matthew 24:14).

In these pages we take these passages literally, resulting in five beliefs that frame the content of the book:

1. God has grand purposes for time and history: the coming of the King of kings and Lord of lords, the advance of His kingdom in the world, and ultimately, at His return, the establishment of the kingdom globally.
2. There are manifestations of the kingdom that appear throughout finite time and history, giving hints of how the world will look when the kingdom comes fully.
3. The biblical church established at pentecost is the primary agent for the expansion of kingdom ministry in the world between Christ's ascension and His return, and through it all institutions are to be impacted by kingdom principles.
4. Nations are of strategic importance in the fulfillment of God's plan.
5. It is God who establishes and removes the leaders of those nations either by His intentional will or by His permissive will, with His purposes for time and history in view.

Human observers can only speculate about the resolution of the riddle that is Trump. However, the thesis of this book is that the answer to the removing and establishing of any national leaders, whether Barack Obama,

Donald Trump, or any others, can be found only in the kingdom purposes and plans of the Lord of History. In fact, if Hillary Clinton had been elected in 2016, someone could have written the same book, exploring the same questions and topics.

Therefore, the Lord of History is the focus of this volume, not President Trump or any other human leader.

DEEP HISTORY

We have heard much in the age of Trump about the "deep state," the term used by many to describe the cluster of Washington bureaucracies dealing with intelligence, spying, and secrets. However, this book will seek to expose "deep history." In the lives and positions of the "two men from Babylon," we see how "deep history" works.

Important thinkers, since at least the Golden Age of Greece, have seen patterns in events, personalities, and nations that have made them think there is much more going on in time than we realize. Christopher Dawson, the twentieth-century Roman Catholic philosopher of history who taught at both Oxford and Harvard, was strongly influenced by Saint Augustine, whom Dawson considered "the founder of philosophical history," and who believed that "history itself had a spiritual meaning."[15]

Dawson's study of Augustine, coupled with his own research into history, convinced him that there are "moments when the obscurity of history seems to be illuminated by some sign of divine purpose."[16] In agreement with Augustine, Dawson thought the existence of the Jews and their role in biblical history was a perfect example of the insertion of divine purpose into the historic flow. "That God chose an obscure nomadic tribe to be His 'Chosen Nation' proves the point," said Dawson.[17]

Further, wrote Dawson, "the Christian believes in the purpose of history as God's sacred instrument."[18] For Dawson, each "phase of history has its singular role within time, within the Divine Economy itself." The West, "especially in its classical and medieval phases, served as 'the vehicle for the world diffusion of the Church and the Christian faith.'"[19]

Christopher Dawson also expressed concern about historians who focus their attention merely on the personalities and events that constitute "the raw material of history" and "lose sight of the deeper spiritual forces that make history intelligent to us."[20]

Dawson is telling us that studying history without seeing those "deeper spiritual forces" is like looking at Michelangelo's Sistine Chapel ceiling and focusing only on the ingredients that went into the mix of the paint rather than the magnificent artistic work they produced.

"The whole world, all human life, is one long story," said Isaac Bashevis Singer, a Jewish philosopher.[21] The search for the Author of the grand story of history takes us beyond the pillars of the earth, into the greatest depths of reality.

Thus, the idea of "deeper spiritual forces" underlying history and helping us understand its meaning is not simply the belief of fundamentalist religious people but that of some of history's deepest thinkers. In the Judeo-Christian worldview, these thinkers line up across the doctrinal-expressional spectrum, from evangelicals, to charismatics and pentecostals, to Roman Catholics and Orthodox Christians, to Jews, especially the Orthodox.

CHRISTOCENTRIC HISTORY

As Christopher Dawson brought Augustine's view of time into focus, so Protestant theologian Oscar Cullmann reached back to Irenaeus, a second-century scholar. According to Cullmann, the earliest Christians had a "Christocentric" view of history.[22] Irenaeus, according to Cullmann, "clearly" recognized "that the historical work of Jesus Christ as Redeemer forms the mid-point of a line which leads from the Old Testament to the return of Christ."

Other individuals in diverse streams of life, some not so traditionally religious, also veer toward the providential view of history. In *God and Churchill*, Jonathan Sandys and I traced Churchill's belief in what Dawson called "the deeper spiritual forces" behind history and the way it shaped his crucial leadership in the Second World War.

Jonathan told me that as he researched his great-grandfather's life,

> I began to realize the weighty reality of Churchill's belief that he was guided by "Destiny," and that "Providence" was watching over and guiding his every step. Initially, I dismissed my great-grandfather's use of such terms as nothing more than a man driven by circumstances to a desperation-faith rather than true faith in God as the Creator of the world and Author of history. But as I deepened my research, evidence of an outside, perhaps Transcendent influence began to materialize. Evidence appeared that Churchill had been protected from the start, and that he indeed had a mapped-out destiny.[23]

The "deep history" I write about here can also be called *providential history*. That is probably the term Churchill would have preferred; nevertheless, the meaning is the same. Though it's unlikely Churchill knew of *The London Baptist Confession of Faith* (1689), in principle he probably would have agreed with its definition of the providential view:

> God, the good Creator of all things, in his infinite power and wisdom, upholds, directs, organizes and governs all creatures and things, from the greatest to the least, by his perfectly wise and holy providence, to the end for which they were created. He governs in accordance with his infallible foreknowledge and the free and immutable counsel of his own will, to the praise of the glory of his wisdom, power, justice, infinite goodness and mercy.[24]

Alexis de Tocqueville, the Frenchman who came to America early in the nineteenth century to seek understanding of the new nation, spoke of both providential history and exceptionalism. He discovered a commonality of purpose on the part of Americans in the pursuit of true democracy. Without knowing it, said de Tocqueville, they were "blind instruments in the hands of God. . . . The gradual development of equality of conditions is therefore a providential fact."[25]

Tocqueville contemplated the development of "national character" and wrote that with regard to "the destiny of certain peoples . . . an unknown force seems to carry along toward a goal of which they themselves are ignorant."

Oscar Cullmann, the twentieth-century Lutheran theologian who taught at Basel, Switzerland, as well as the Sorbonne in Paris, shed light on the nature of providential history. "The terminology of the New Testament teaches us that, according to the Primitive Christian [first century] conception, time in its unending extension as well as in its individual periods and moments is given by God and ruled by him."[26]

DEEP HISTORY MADE VISIBLE

Evidence of the reality of deep history becomes visible in what many have identified as historic cycles. Will Durant may not have been in full agreement with historic cycles' theory, but he believed, as Dr. Al Mohler stated, that "civilization begins with order, grows with liberty, and dies with chaos." Mohler pointed out that Durant, along with his wife and coauthor, Ariel, is describing "the process of civilizational decline, as order gives way to a corrupted view of liberty that finally dissolves into chaos." Mohler, the president of Southern Baptist Theological Seminary, believes that in the contemporary era, "our civilization is standing at the brink of chaos."[27]

The Bible and the lessons of history generally illuminate our understanding of deep history. We encounter such a cycle in the experience of Old Testament Israel, as recorded in the Bible's book of Judges. Throughout the history of the Hebrews' settling in the promised land, they cycled through definite stages:

Ratification

This is a period in which there is a wide consensus of both citizens and their leaders around the importance of God and His Word as the foundation of the nation.

Relapse (of Memory)

There is a slow breakdown of the ratified consensus as the old generation dies and a new one emerges that loses memory of the historic values based on God and His revelation, until finally there is a drastic separation between the new generation and the principles that brought forth their nation.

Rebellion

The new generation now actively revolts from the God-centered values and principles and attempts the creation of a new society without God, frequently with gods of their own making.

Refiner's Fire

As the consequences of rebellion intensify, the nation moves into periods of mounting crisis in which all the institutions that sustain civilization begin to crumple, and antinomianism (lawlessness) sweeps the society.

Remembrance

A remnant within the general population begins to wonder what has gone wrong, what was lost to have brought on the destruction of society and culture. Prophetic voices arise to call people back to the original ratification of God and His Word as the true foundation. The prophets are persecuted through an intensifying effort to marginalize them, caricature them, vilify them, criminalize them, and then eliminate them. Yet there are still those in the societal remnant who embrace the call of the prophets.

Repentance

People among the remnant take seriously the need to repent of their own sins and those of the society of which they are a part. As God promised in 2 Chronicles 7:14, He hears their prayers, forgives their sin, and begins the healing of their land. This inspires others to repent, leading to the next stage.

Revival

God does not hold back His blessings until 100 percent of the people repent, but He sees the remnant as representing all in the society. Thus, He sends revival, and spiritual renewal spreads as many others in the nation repent and turn themselves and their institutions back to God.

Ratification

The full circle is reached as a critical mass of repentance and return to God is reached, bringing widespread transformation to the nation, new vitality, and a period of rest for at least a generation, until the cycle begins all over again.

All this occurs as interactions between the sovereignty of God expressed in His will, and the freedom of human beings to receive or resist God's intended purposes for human history and the people within it.

And to achieve His purposes, the Lord of History will use unlikely, complex, and powerful leaders like Nebuchadnezzar and Donald Trump—the "two men from Babylon."

ONE

THE LORD OF HISTORY

and Unlikely, Complex, Powerful Leaders

Behind the weak power and the blind science of man, there is the overruling purpose of God which uses man and his kingdoms and empires for ends of which he knows nothing and which are often the opposite of those which man desires and seeks to obtain.[1]

—CHRISTOPHER DAWSON

Does God have a plan for history and the historic roles of leaders, whether a Nebuchadnezzar or a Donald Trump?

President Ronald Reagan and Pope John Paul II thought so.

Paul Kengor and Robert Orlando wrote about the partnership between the pope and the president in ending the Cold War.[2] Kengor and Orlando explored the similarities in the men's lives—especially their miraculous survival of assassination attempts aimed at each. "The pope and the president both saw their mission as to try to do God's will according to a Divine Plan," said Kengor and Orlando.[3]

God is sovereign in and over history, and not only do Ronald Reagan and Pope John Paul II offer evidence to prove it, but so do Nebuchadnezzar and Trump, along with all those men and women across time who have been elevated to national leadership, in accord with the prophecy of Daniel.

The point of it all is the manifestation and victory of Jesus Christ and His kingdom in the fallen world, for the sake of all humanity.

PARABLE IN TIME AND SPACE

The Second World War is a vast parable in finite time and space of the struggle in the cosmos between the kingdom of God and the kingdom of darkness. No national leader understood the nature of the conflict more than Sir Winston Churchill, the British prime minister during the war. Better than any, he saw the threat to civilization itself brought on by Hitler and the Nazis. In his "Finest Hour" speech delivered on June 18, 1940—the eve of the Nazi Blitz against Britain—Churchill said, "I expect the battle of Britain is about to begin. Upon this battle depends the survival of Christian Civilization."[4]

As we will see, the highest form of civilization is the kingdom of God. Satan's attempt to oppose it and impose himself and his tyranny over the universe would result in the destruction of all order. Churchill believed that the Sermon on the Mount delivered by Jesus Christ was the finest expression of "Christian Civilisation" in which "resides all that makes existence precious to man, and all that confers honour and health upon the state."[5]

In a much larger sense, this is what Satan and his principalities and powers (Ephesians 6) seek to bring down. The Bible gives us a stark picture of this cosmic war in the Revelation visions of the apostle John, who wrote,

> And there was war in heaven, Michael and his angels waging war with the dragon. The dragon and his angels waged war, and they were not strong enough, and there was no longer a place found for them in heaven. And the great dragon was thrown down, the serpent of old who is called the

devil and Satan, who deceives the whole world; he was thrown down to the earth, and his angels were thrown down with him. (Revelation 12:7–9)

Churchill may not have had precise, direct knowledge of this reality, but he did have an intuitive sense of the deeper meanings. More than any other leader at that time, Churchill voiced concern about the urgency of preserving what we now might call Judeo-Christian civilization. Every decision, every leadership appointment, every strategy had to be weighed on the scales of victory over the Nazis, whose aim was the imposition of the tyranny of the Third Reich in the place of Judeo-Christian civilization. For Churchill, there was no other option than winning the war. Churchill made it clear when he told Parliament, the nation, and the world: "Victory at all costs, victory in spite of all terror, victory however long and hard the road may be; for without victory, there is no survival."

The stakes are even higher in the battle for God's kingdom. If the kingdom of God is "righteousness and peace and joy in the Holy Spirit" (Romans 14:17), then what the evil one wants to bring is the opposite: evil and injustice, conflict and misery.

INTERSECTION WITH THE CHURCHILL FAMILY

In 2014, the mystical personage of Sir Winston himself swept into my life in the form of Churchill's great-grandson, Jonathan Sandys. The intersection of our lives would be too brief: in 2019, I conducted the young man's funeral. Death had come through lung disease. Jonathan was only forty-three.

Much of Winston Churchill was embedded in Jonathan's personality. A zesty exuberance buoyed him. Jonathan, like his great-grandfather, had a plucky wit and large vision. He reflected the temperament the world saw in Winston Churchill.

But more than anything else, Jonathan revealed something of the God-conscious soul of Winston Churchill. In fact, Jonathan asked me to coauthor a book with him on Churchill's spirituality, referred to above. *God and Churchill* appeared on the scene a year after Jonathan and I met.[6]

Sir Winston once said that he was not a "pillar" of the church, but that he was a "flying buttress." Churchill had a sense of God's direction in his personal life. Once, during the London Blitz, he and his bodyguard, Walter Thompson, had come out from Churchill's underground bunker to survey the damage. Suddenly there was an explosion nearby. Thompson appealed to Churchill to get back to the bunker and take cover. Churchill responded that all was well, that someone was watching over him. "Do you mean Sergeant Davies?" Thompson asked, referring to a soldier nearby carrying a hefty gun. "No," answered the prime minister, as he pointed heavenward.

Churchill's belief in God's providence over his personal life extended to history, and the nations of his era embroiled in the Second World War. In one of his famous speeches, "Never Surrender," Churchill declared,

> Even though large tracts of Europe and many old and famous States have fallen or may fall into the grip of the Gestapo and all the odious apparatus of Nazi rule, we shall not flag or fail. We shall go on to the end, we shall fight in France, we shall fight on the seas and oceans, we shall fight with growing confidence and growing strength in the air, we shall defend our Island, whatever the cost may be, we shall fight on the beaches, we shall fight on the landing grounds, we shall fight in the fields and in the streets, we shall fight in the hills; we shall never surrender, and even if, which I do not for a moment believe, this Island or a large part of it were subjugated and starving, then our Empire beyond the seas, armed and guarded by the British Fleet, would carry on the struggle, until, in *God's good time*, the New World, with all its power and might, steps forth to the rescue and the liberation of the old. (emphasis added)

That was not a platitude. Deep down in his soul Churchill had the sense that God was directing the course of historical events, and that somehow, in a "time" known only to God, Hitler and the Nazis would be beaten.

Thus, though Churchill never used the term, he believed God to be the Lord of History. As Jonathan shared inside family lore about Sir Winston, and as we conducted intense research, Churchill's belief in God's sovereign direction of history became so clear that our book was subtitled *How the Great Leader's Sense of Divine Destiny Changed His Troubled World and Offers Hope for Ours.*

God's providential guidance of history, and the Daniel principle that He sovereignly "establishes" and "removes" leaders in light of His kingdom purposes, did not end with Nebuchadnezzar or Winston Churchill. God has not been dethroned and is still in charge of time and history. His ways are not our ways nor His thoughts our thoughts, and often God's leadership choices are enigmatic. Nebuchadnezzar and Donald Trump are proof of that. The few in Britain who thought of and remembered Churchill's earlier career, and regarded him as a failure, were shocked when King George VI gave him the office of prime minister.

And another of the most enigmatic leaders of modern times was Richard M. Nixon, my boss from 1970 to 1973.

THE RICHARD NIXON ENIGMA

One day in 1972, I bumped into an associate at the White House whose appearance shocked me. The man, in his fifties, had spent his career in Washington, working in Congress, and now as a senior aide to Nixon at the White House. To a young staff assistant, such as myself, just stepping into the swamp, my friend was usually reassuring. He was always calm and steady. However, on this day, he was ghost-pale, agitated, and clearly distressed.

All he would tell me was that he had just returned from meetings at the Committee to Re-elect the President—which became known as "CREEP"—and what he had heard there had disturbed him greatly. He never disclosed what he learned that day, but eventually the whole world knew there had been much to be concerned about when, in 1974, Nixon had to resign the presidency.

Nixon had entered the political big time as vice president under President Dwight Eisenhower. Nixon was an unlikely choice for that position. As a congressman, elected first in 1946 to represent California's 12th District, Nixon rose to national prominence through his work on the House Un-American Activities Committee investigating and exposing Communists who had gained positions in federal agencies, including the State Department. The American Left began to hate Nixon as he pursued Alger Hiss and others.

Whittaker Chambers, who had worked for *Time* magazine, was a key witness during this era. He had been a Communist, but turned, and gave important evidence to the House Committee. In his book *Witness*, Chambers described how influential elites in the media and other establishments viewed Nixon and his fellow Un-American Committee members:

> The Committee's members were the least intelligent in Congress because no decent man wanted to serve on it. They were uncouth, undignified and ungrammatical. They were rude and ruthless. They smeared innocent people on insufficient evidence or no evidence at all. They bullied witnesses and made sensational statements unfounded in fact. When, occasionally, they did seem to strike a fresh scent, they promptly lost it by all shouting at once or by making some ridiculous fumble.[7]

Chambers found this characterization "outrageous."

In 1950, Nixon ran in California for the Senate. His opponent was a leftist, Helen Gahagan Douglas. Nixon waged an intense campaign against her, stoking the Left's outrage.

Two years later, General Dwight Eisenhower, hero of D-Day, was the Republican nominee for the presidency. He and his advisers searched for a running mate and remarkably settled on thirty-nine-year-old Nixon. This was the period of the beginnings of the Cold War rivalry between the United States and the Soviet Union, and Nixon "was best known for Red hunting and the conviction of [Soviet spy] Alger Hiss," noted *U.S. News & World Report* writer Brooke Berger.[8]

Ironically, two decades later, I would watch Nixon pursue détente with both the Soviet Union and Communist China. As a member of the White House staff, I fielded many phone calls from irate conservatives who felt Nixon was going soft on Communism.

In 1960, Nixon famously lost a squeezer of a presidential election to John F. Kennedy. Nixon bided his time, and in 1962 ran for the governor's job in California. He was beaten again. "You won't have Nixon to kick around anymore," he told the press.[9]

"Barring a miracle, Nixon's political career has ended," *Time* magazine declared in November 1962.[10]

"Miracle or not, slightly more than six years later, the same Richard Nixon stood on the steps of the Capitol in Washington and took the oath of office as the thirty-seventh president of the United States," wrote journalist Jules Witcover in April 1970. The title of Witcover's book was *The Resurrection of Richard Nixon*.[11]

So, one day a year or so later, I stood in a circle in the middle of the Oval Office about to pray with President Nixon and his guest, evangelist Oral Roberts. Based on the howling of the great mass who hated Nixon (Donald Trump may be only slightly ahead of Nixon in the number of establishment elites who loathe him), it seemed as unlikely for Nixon to pray as winning the presidency. But he did win, and that day I heard him pray. His Quaker roots were much in evidence, though in the very office where that sacred moment occurred, the same man uttered the profanities and execrations captured on the Watergate tapes.

Why would God allow, or intentionally raise up, such a man for the presidency?

NEAR THE BRINK

In answering that question many would point to a crisis in October 1973 that could have destroyed a nation and brought the world to the nuclear brink.

On October 6, 1973, the highest holy day in the Jewish calendar—observed even by many secular Jews—Egypt and Syria attacked Israel, hoping to recover what they had lost in the 1967 Six Days War. The death toll in the 1973 Yom Kippur conflict could be even higher. The danger was not only to the Israeli state but to the world, since it brought the United States and the Soviet Union into the most threatening standoff since the 1962 Cuban missile crisis.

Initially, it appeared that Israel, staggering from the surprise attack, would be defeated by the powers backed by the Soviets. Even Moshe Dayan, at that moment the Israeli minister of defense, began to wonder if surrender was the only hope. In the north, along the Golan Heights, more than 1,400 Syrian tanks surged at 180 Israeli tanks. In the south, near the Suez Canal, some 436 Israeli soldiers faced a barrage of 80,000 Egyptian troops.

An urgent call from Israeli prime minister Golda Meir awoke President Richard Nixon at 3:00 a.m., Washington time, telling him that if the United States did not send arms immediately, Israel would be defeated. Nixon's foreign policy advisers in the State Department and the White House–based National Security Council urged caution, fearing a move to arm Israel would complicate the efforts at détente with the Soviet Union, then under way.

Nevertheless, after the plea from Prime Minister Meir, Nixon gave the order to his staff: "You get the stuff to Israel. Now. *Now.*"

Within a short period, US aircraft had flown more than eight hundred sorties that included some twenty-five thousand tons of weapons and other supplies, and fifty-six fighter planes.

Little more than a year later, during the Watergate crisis that would end the Nixon presidency, the public became aware of the existence of a secret recording system Nixon had had placed in the Oval Office. Among the presidential conversations, Nixon's voice can be heard making anti-Semitic remarks.

Why, then, did Richard Nixon immediately order military aid to Israel that would save that nation from defeat?

Perhaps the president heard his mother's voice in Golda Meir's. Nixon may have recalled that day in his youth when his mother had perhaps unwittingly prophesied that in some distant future period Nixon would be in a position of high power, and that he would rescue the Jews from destruction.[12]

History records that Nixon did exactly that. Golda Meir called him "my president."

Nixon's was by no means the last of enigmatic presidencies. In fact, on December 21, 1987, Nixon wrote a personal letter to a man who would become one of the most enigmatic of all the American presidents. The letter read:

Dear Donald

I did not see the program, but Mrs. Nixon told me that you were *great* on the Donahue Show.

As you can imagine, she is an expert on politics, and she predicts that whenever you decide to run for office you will be a winner![13]

THE GEORGE WASHINGTON ENIGMA

"I deal little in politics," said George Washington as he was elected to the Virginia House of Burgesses in 1761. Historian Ron Chernow thought Washington was "feigning aristocratic indifference" regarding his electoral victory.[14] Nevertheless, the prominent plantation-owner-slaveholding-surveyor-frontiersman was thrust into elected office. That small step would lead eventually to the giant step of becoming America's first president.

In between there were enough brushes with death that Washington should not have been alive to lead the Colonists' victory over the British in the Revolutionary War, or to become the nation's first president.

In May 1761, Washington became seriously ill with persisting fever and cold-like symptoms amplified by the malaria that dogged him. "I have found so little benefit from any advice yet received that I am more than half of the mind to take a trip to England for the recovery of that invaluable blessing—health," he told an acquaintance.

Washington did not make the voyage, and the ailment intensified. Later, he would write a relative that he almost died, and that he had "been very near my last gasp . . . but thank God I have now got the better of the disorder and shall soon be restored to perfect health again."[15] As Chernow noted, Washington was probably haunted by the memory of the deaths of his father and two older half brothers before they reached age fifty.

George Washington believed in providential history. He would come to say that he thanked Providence, "which has directed my steps and shielded me in the various changes and chances through which I have passed from my youth to the present moment." Though many have tried to lump him in with Enlightenment deism, Washington never embraced that view of a distant, incommunicable god. Instead, Washington "resided in a universe saturated with religious meaning." God, to George Washington, showed, in Chernow's ironic description, "a keen interest in North American politics." Washington, said Chernow, "seemed to know that he operated under the overarching guidance of a benign Providence."[16]

Washington illustrates powerfully a central contention of this book: God allows or raises up either through His permissive or through His intentional will the right person at the right time for the right place and the right reasons. For example, through Moses, God told Pharaoh: "I have allowed you to remain, in order to show you My power and in order to proclaim My name in all the earth" (Exodus 9:16).

Many books have been written about God's sovereign will and human free will. How can God be truly in control of history and the lives within it, and, at the same time, humans be free to choose for themselves?

In answering that question, we must distinguish between God's permissive will and His intentional will.

To illustrate, consider the Nile River, which stretches more than four thousand miles over eleven African countries. The Nile rises far away from its ultimate destination, the Mediterranean Sea. The current flows inexorably northward, toward its encounter with the Great Sea. The sweep of the waters takes sailors to the Mediterranean unless they have the option of mechanical rudders that will enable them to go against the flow. Further, all along the way, there are tributaries where they can opt to take their boats.

AS THE NILE FLOWS

The inevitable course of the Nile to the Mediterranean is an illustration of the ultimate intentional will of God. The Lord of History has an intended destination for all creation, including human history, and the vast river of time is taking everything and everyone toward it. However, human free will means that individuals can momentarily resist the flow by going up a tributary or plunging into a whirlpool that arcs away from the ultimate destination, even as it is carried toward it.

The permissive will of God allows individuals to choose against God and His ways. Yet the ultimate intentional will of God cannot be defeated any more than one can turn back the Nile and keep it from emptying into the Mediterranean. Therefore, God's circumstantial permissive will operates amid our rebellion to still accomplish His ultimate intentional will.

This is the meaning of Romans 8:28–29: "And we know that God causes all things to work together for good to those who love God, to those who are called according to His purpose. For those whom He foreknew, He also predestined to become conformed to the image of His Son, so that He would be the firstborn among many brethren."

The intentional will of God is that all people "called according to His purpose" be conformed to Christlikeness. Each individual has the freedom to reject the call of God, or to otherwise miss God's intent. The circumstantial will of God means He works through everything that comes into the lives of "called" people to accomplish His ultimate intentional will for them.

The general will of God is that no one "should perish, but that all should come to repentance" (2 Peter 3:9 KJV). But not all will come, despite God's desire. He is omnipotent, and could force the issue, but His love means He will permit us to be free—even if it breaks His Father-heart. The special will of God comes into play in the personal lives of those who respond positively to His call and enter relationship with the Father through the only begotten Son—Jesus, the Christ.

TRUMP: NO AND YES

Was it therefore God's will that in 2016 Donald Trump would defeat Hillary Clinton and become president of the United States?

The answer is both *no* and *yes*.

It is *no* since God's ultimate intentional will was that no human being would ever rule over another. "There is a time in which one man rules over another to his own hurt," wrote Solomon in Ecclesiastes 8:9 (NKJV). God's desire was that all individuals, as Adam and Eve before the fall into sin, be in perfect relationship with Him, and hence at peace within themselves and one another. In that condition, men and women would govern themselves, and no external government would be necessary. The fall alters that ideal state, and government becomes an urgent necessity in the fallen world.

Thus, said Edmund Burke,

> Men are qualified for civil liberty in exact proportion to their disposition to put moral chains upon their own appetites . . . in proportion as they are more disposed to listen to the counsels of the wise and good, in preference to the flattery of knaves. Society cannot exist, unless a controlling power upon will and appetite be placed somewhere; and the less of it there is within, the more there must be without. It is ordained in the eternal constitution of things, that men of intemperate minds cannot be free. Their passions forge their fetters.[17]

James Madison also understood and wrote:

> If men were angels, no government would be necessary.
>
> If angels were to govern men, neither external nor internal controls on government would be necessary. In framing a government which is to be administered by men over men, the great difficulty lies in this: you must first enable the government to control the governed; and in the next place oblige it to control itself.[18]

Thus, God's perfect intentional will would have been that Donald Trump is not president, nor any other, not even Washington or Lincoln. But in a fallen world, there must be governments and presidents. Thus, in that sense, we will argue here, *yes*, it was God's will that Donald Trump be elected as president of the United States in 2016, just as it was for Barack Obama to occupy the Oval Office before Trump.

Why, then, did God "promote" George Washington to the presidency?

This imperfect man was perfect for the moment. God's eyes search the earth for those whose hearts are His and whom He can strengthen (2 Chronicles 16:9). George Washington refused to allow himself to be exalted almost like a monarch—as some in the Philadelphia Constitutional Convention wished. He never lost sight that he was a farmer-soldier. Washington resisted the deistic spirit of the age and believed in the relational God revealed in the Bible.

He may not have been an evangelical in the present understanding of that word; nevertheless, George Washington was a man of faith who understood his country's need for God, and his own. While "one cannot be dogmatic about the details of Washington's personal piety, he certainly believed in a personal God who is sovereign over human affairs," wrote historian John G. West Jr.[19]

So, again, *Why George Washington?* In what ways was he the right person in the right time in the right place for the right reasons?

"Washington was very cognizant of the fact that his actions as president would establish the office and have consequences for his successors," wrote West. In that sense, George Washington played the crucially important role of infusing the aborning presidency with the healthy spiritual, philosophical, and political DNA that would shape it through the centuries.

Among his initial communications as America's first chief executive, Washington said that "it is devoutly wished on my part that these precedents be fixed on true principles." Holding the presidency to those principles has proven a daunting task. The problem is that humans hold the post, with all the weaknesses of human nature as well as the gifts, talents, and skills they bring to the Oval Office.

THE ABRAHAM LINCOLN ENIGMA

For the boy Abraham Lincoln, the technology in Gordon's Mill may have been the equivalent of the latest computer gadget to a young person today. The mill was just two miles from the log cabin he occupied with his family in a shrinking forest.

The mill consisted of a hefty grinding stone, a long pole to which a horse was hitched, and a surface for scattering corn kernels. The boy delighted in his new assignment in the Lincoln household of hauling bags of corn to the mill to be ground up into the stuff of feasts. "Raw corn could be ground into cornmeal, and then cooked into corn pone, corn grits, corn bread, and corn griddle cakes" resulting in "culinary delicacies," wrote Lincoln historian William Freehling.[20]

On a certain day the future Great Emancipator came happily to Gordon's Mill with his bags of corn, eager to watch the horse trod the circle, moving the grinding wheel over the kernels. But also on that day, America almost lost the man who would free the slaves and go down in history as one of its greatest presidents—if not *the* greatest.

The horse was reluctant to walk the circle that day and moved too slowly for young Abe's eager preference. The boy whipped the animal onward, irritating the horse, who kicked at him. Suddenly a hoof struck young Abe's head, delivering such a blow that the boy collapsed, in his own words in later years, "apparently killed for a time."

The hoof just missed by inches rendering Abraham Lincoln dead before he reached the purpose for which God had put him in the world.

That escape from death was but one of the riddles surrounding Abraham Lincoln. Who had spared Lincoln's life that day, and why? For that matter, who had kept young Tom Lincoln—the man who would sire the future president—alive many years before when he was almost shot dead during a fracas? And why?

"Coincidences as well as deep causes do drive human epics," wrote Freehling in considering Abraham Lincoln's life.

But there are other enigmas: How can a man who lost jobs, failed in business, suffered bankruptcy, was defeated in elections, was crushed through great personal loss because of the deaths of loved ones, including the woman he loved more than any other and hoped to wed, a person who seemed consigned to spend his career drifting from one menial job to another, a man given to depression (to name a few obstacles), get elected as president of the United States and have strength left to guide the country through its greatest national crisis—the rending of the Union?

Lincoln was derided and mocked as Trump is today. One newspaper even called Lincoln "Honest Ape." For that reason and many more, Lincoln could easily vie with Donald Trump as the poster boy of presidential enigmas.

THE CALVIN COOLIDGE ENIGMA

Coolidge, America's thirtieth president (1923–1929), is an enigma who has been underrated in history, as he was in his own day. In fact, when he was elected to his first office in the Massachusetts Legislature, a colleague, Richard Irwin, wrote a letter of introduction to John N. Cole, the Speaker of the House, that reveals how young Coolidge was regarded initially:

Dear John,

This will introduce the new member-elect from my town, Calvin Coolidge . . . he is better than he looks.[21]

Coolidge is enigmatic because he did not fit the profile that popular culture expects of a president of the United States. It is doubtful Coolidge would have spent valuable time on Twitter had the medium existed in his day. He proved that a president does not have to have the charisma of a Kennedy, the tough hide of a Lyndon Johnson, or the bravado of a Theodore Roosevelt.

After serving in various political offices in Massachusetts, including governor, Coolidge was recruited by Warren G. Harding as his vice president. Harding, whose term was scandal-ridden, died, and Calvin Coolidge became president of the United States. Coolidge brought dignity to the Oval Office after the Harding scandals. Further, Coolidge "embodied the spirit and hopes of the middle class" and could "interpret their longings and express their opinions," wrote biographer Claude Moore Fuess in 1940, the year after Coolidge's death. "That he did represent the genius of the average is the most convincing proof of his truth."[22]

Coolidge, in contrast to Donald Trump and most presidents, was noted for his economy of speech, earning him the moniker "Silent Cal." His wife, Grace, displayed a sampler on the couple's living room wall, reminding every visitor of the nature of the person they were visiting:

A wise old owl lived in an oak
The more he saw, the less he spoke
The less he spoke the more he heard
Why can't we be like that old bird?

Why would God elevate such an "old bird" to the presidency of the United States?

Calvin Coolidge was a stabilizer in the era just after the First World War. He also revealed the type of character that could be trusted with such immense power. "It is difficult for men in high office to avoid the malady of self-delusion," Coolidge wrote in his autobiography. "They are always surrounded by worshippers. They are constantly, and for the most part sincerely assured of their greatness."[23]

Few warnings regarding the hubris that can consume occupants of the Oval Office are clearer than that. Coolidge's attitude was shaped by his understanding of God's transcendence and the accountability to God of those He has entrusted with authority. "It is hard to see how a great man can be an atheist," Coolidge told a Boy Scouts group. "We need to feel that behind us is intelligence and love."[24]

Coolidge was important in a nation still bristling with racism. At one point he received a communication from an irate citizen because an African American was contemplating a run for Congress. Coolidge, revealing that his quiet temperament did not mean a lack of conviction, replied: "I was amazed to receive such a letter. During the [First World] War 500,000 colored men and boys were called up under the draft not one of which sought to evade it. A colored man is precisely as much entitled to submit his candidacy as any other."[25]

Just six years before Coolidge came to the presidency, Communists seized power in Russia, under Vladimir Lenin. Leftists in the West watched eagerly for the successful implementation of socialism there in the hopes that Europe and the United States would embrace or be forced into accepting the philosophy.

Coolidge saw through it all. As a US senator prior to becoming vice president and then president, Coolidge was called upon to help settle a bitter strike. Even after the issues were settled, he was concerned by the "violence and cynicism" he had noted on the part of the strikers. In fact, "Silent Cal" was "exasperated." He wrote his stepmother a letter expressing concerns sharply relevant for today: "The leaders [of the strike] are socialists and anarchists, and they do not want anybody to work for wages. The trouble is not with the amount of wages; it is a small attempt to destroy all authority, whether of any church or government."[26]

Calvin Coolidge was one of those enigmatic presidents who seem un-expected and unlikely, but who appear at the right time at the right place for the right reasons. The list of America's chief enigmatic chief executives would be long.

THE HARRY S TRUMAN ENIGMA

Harry Truman was serving as Franklin Roosevelt's vice president when, in 1945, Roosevelt died. Truman was loathed by the establishment, and, like Donald Trump, was considered an outsider.

In fact, Donald Trump may be more like America's thirty-third president than any other. Had Twitter existed in Truman's day, he may have been offending people with ad hominem characterizations as bitingly as Trump does now.

Victor David Hanson caught the similarity, and wrote that when Trump entered the presidency, he "was replaying the role of the unpopular tenure of loudmouth Democrat Harry Truman," who "miraculously won the 1948 election against all expert opinion and polls."[27] Truman would leave office in 1953 "widely hated," noted Hanson. Scandal seemed to whirl around Truman constantly because of his close relationship with a dark Kansas City political machine led by unsavory characters.

Yet, like Trump, Truman surprised people with his accomplishments in the seven-plus years he was in office. There was fury when Truman fired popular general Douglas MacArthur. Then there was the problem of Truman's personal behavior, which involved cursing and drinking and gambling. "Truman, in short, did things other presidents dared not do," said Hanson.

Why would God, in accord with Daniel 2:20–21, elevate such a man to the presidency? Perhaps it was because Truman had the pluck to stand against the mighty and lofty Washington foreign policy establishment and extend US recognition of the state of Israel in 1948.

"HIS ACCIDENCY" AND OTHER PRESIDENTIAL ENIGMAS

There are many other enigmatic presidents about which we could write. John Tyler, the nation's tenth chief executive, was called "His Accidency" because he became America's first unelected president. As vice president he ascended to the office upon the death of President William Henry Harrison after only one month in office. More than a century later, there was Barack Obama, the nation's first African American president, whose middle name is Hussein and whose government experience was limited to a three-year term in the United States Senate.

In the United States the electorate selects its leaders. However, there is a strong hand guiding the choices in light of a much larger plan—the Lord of History.

TWO

PERFECT GOD, IMPERFECT PEOPLE

*God uses imperfect people to accomplish His perfect will.
He always has and always will.*
— James Robison, evangelist and
Trump spiritual adviser

Mary Todd knew what she wanted in a husband. She was the daughter of a notable family and was determined to have a spouse whose breeding and prospects were every bit as erudite as the family whose blood flowed in her own veins.

Mary's grandparents were Robert Parker and Levi Todd. Both had played significant roles in founding Lexington, Kentucky. Parker and Todd relished what William Freehling, in his book *Becoming Lincoln*, called the new city's "most pretentious motto," which was, "Here thrives Transylvania University, 'The Athens of the West.'"[1] Freehling noted that Parker and Todd "had built two of the area's most sumptuous brick houses." Mary Todd had spent much time in each of the houses and was greatly impressed with the elegance and her own status. Her father, Robert Smith Todd, had even exceeded her grandfather's accomplishments.

Mary's schooling at Shelby Female Academy and Mentelle's for Young Ladies expanded her refinement. She learned French and studied Europe's classical literature. As the story goes, there was a day when Mary was visiting the home of Henry Clay, a major Kentucky and national political figure who served in the US House of Representatives (where he was speaker of the House), the Senate, and as secretary of state, one of Washington's most prestigious positions. Such was the heady atmosphere to which Mary Todd was accustomed, and it is no surprise that she declared in Clay's parlor that someday she would be a president's wife and live in the White House.

Her route there would be full of surprises.

While Mary was immersed in her lavish surroundings, the man she would accompany to Washington's executive mansion was moving between Kentucky, Indiana, and Illinois in search of a home. His father, Tom Lincoln, had been careless about the boundaries of land where he could settle and hack out a living for his family, which included a gawky son named Abraham. While Mary was enjoying her grandfathers' ostentatious brick homes, there were times when young Abe experienced eviction and dwelled in little more than a lean-to in rugged forests.

The lad's grandfather, the first Abraham Lincoln, had moved to Kentucky in 1782 and made friends with, among others, Daniel Boone. Abraham's son, Tom Lincoln (the president's father), was known as a hard worker, conservative in his habits and behavior, and interested in church gatherings. He ultimately joined a Baptist congregation that took a strong stand against slavery.

It was ironic, therefore, that the man who would take Mary Todd to the White House was a rough-hewn product of these wilderness people. Rarely has there been a more unlikely pairing, and the marriage would be difficult. Abraham Lincoln, son of Tom and grandson of Abraham, was a "social misfit" in the magnificent parlors frequented by young Mary. He was, in fact, "the least formally educated, the most incorrectly attired, the least socially connected, and the most conversationally inept."[2]

Yet Abraham Lincoln became not only Mary Todd's husband but also the president of the United States.

GOD AND THE "FOOLISH THINGS"

Neither the presidencies of Abraham Lincoln nor Donald Trump should be a surprise considering that God is the Lord of enigmas. This is the same God who said to and through Isaiah: "My thoughts are not your thoughts, nor are your ways My ways" (Isaiah 55:8). Even Solomon in his great wisdom would come to the precipice of mystery beyond which he could not pass, and write, in Ecclesiastes 8:16–17, "When I gave my heart to know wisdom . . . and I saw every work of God, I concluded that man cannot discover the work which has been done under the sun. Even though man should seek laboriously, he will not discover; and though the wise man should say, 'I know,' he cannot discover."

Through Isaiah, God declared:

> I dwell on a high and holy place,
> And also with the contrite and lowly of spirit
> In order to revive the spirit of the lowly
> And to revive the heart of the contrite.
> (ISAIAH 57:15)

That revelation beams with sublime beauty. God is enthroned in the "highest heaven," but on earth His dwelling place is with the "lowly" and "contrite."

Jesus carried forward the theme in the Beatitudes:

> Blessed *are the poor in spirit,*
> For theirs is the kingdom of heaven.
> Blessed *are those who mourn,*
> For they shall be comforted.

Blessed *are the meek,*

For they shall inherit the earth.

Blessed *are those who hunger and thirst* for righteousness,

For they shall be filled.

Blessed *are the merciful,*

For they shall obtain mercy.

Blessed *are the pure in heart,*

For they shall see God.

Blessed *are the peacemakers,*

For they shall be called sons of God.

Blessed *are those who are persecuted* for righteousness' sake,

For theirs is the kingdom of heaven.

(MATTHEW 5:3–10 NKJV, EMPHASIS ADDED)

The Lord demonstrates the principle of God's preference for the "lowly" and "contrite" in His dealings with children. When Jesus' followers tried to shoo away the mothers presenting their babies and toddlers, Jesus rebuked His would-be protectors: "Let the little children alone, and do not hinder them from coming to Me; for the kingdom of heaven belongs to such as these" (Matthew 19:14). Further, "unless you are converted and become like children, you will not enter the kingdom of heaven" (Matthew 18:3).

The ideal of the kingdom of God that will someday encompass the whole earth is that

The wolf also shall dwell with the lamb,

The leopard shall lie down with the young goat,

The calf and the young lion and the fatling together;

And a little child shall lead them.

(ISAIAH 11:6 NKJV)

The Holy Spirit, through Paul, shows clearly the types of people God honors when the apostle wrote,

The message of the cross is foolish to those who are headed for destruction! But we who are being saved know it is the very power of God. As the Scriptures say,

> "I will destroy the wisdom of the wise
> and discard the intelligence of the intelligent."

So, where does this leave the philosophers, the scholars, and the world's brilliant debaters? God has made the wisdom of this world look foolish. Since God in his wisdom saw to it that the world would never know him through human wisdom, he has used our foolish preaching to save those who believe. It is foolish to the Jews, who ask for signs from heaven. And it is foolish to the Greeks, who seek human wisdom. So when we preach that Christ was crucified, the Jews are offended and the Gentiles say it's all nonsense. But to those called by God to salvation, both Jews and Gentiles, Christ is the power of God and the wisdom of God. This foolish plan of God is wiser than the wisest of human plans, and God's weakness is stronger than the greatest of human strength. Remember, dear brothers and sisters, that few of you were wise in the world's eyes or powerful or wealthy when God called you. Instead, God chose things the world considers foolish in order to shame those who think they are wise. And he chose things that are powerless to shame those who are powerful. God chose things despised by the world, things counted as nothing at all, and used them to bring to nothing what the world considers important. As a result, no one can ever boast in the presence of God. God has united you with Christ Jesus. For our benefit God made him to be wisdom itself. Christ made us right with God; he made us pure and holy, and he freed us from sin. Therefore, as the Scriptures say, "If you want to boast, boast only about the Lord." (1 Corinthians 1:18–31 NLT)

James wrote that God resists the proud but gives grace to the humble (James 4:6). Yet leading nations requires strong individuals. If God is to use the Donald Trumps of the world, He must first humble them. Trump's upbringing under the "power of positive thinking" message preached by Norman Vincent Peale, along with a childhood of privilege, would not have conditioned him to be "lowly" and "contrite." This requires brokenness.

That brings us to the "two men from Babylon." Neither seems to fit the criteria discussed above. Neither Nebuchadnezzar nor Donald Trump would be viewed as lowly and humble. Why, then, would God use them as leaders? We discover the answer as we look closely at what it takes to bring an individual into his or her personal "Zone of Excellence."

ZONE OF EXCELLENCE

We all have what I call a "Zone of Excellence," but sadly, many of us never enter that special place, and we spend a lifetime without achieving our best. The "Zone" is carefully defined by specific markers, one of which is trials and suffering, the way we react and what we learn in the tough times of our lives, and what we gain from the "hard knocks."

Humility forged through trials that can break a person is a vital part of the "Zone of Excellence" for every human—no matter how lowly. Inside that "Zone," which we discuss below, success is guaranteed and failure highly unlikely. We are all put in the world for God's purposes. "Before you were born I set you apart and appointed you as my prophet to the nations," God told Jeremiah (Jeremiah 1:5 NLT). And the principle of God's foreknowledge and purposes for us all is made clear in Psalm 139:

> For You formed my inward parts;
> You wove me in my mother's womb.
> I will give thanks to You, for I am fearfully and wonderfully made;
> Wonderful are Your works,
> And my soul knows it very well.

My frame was not hidden from You,

When I was made in secret,

And skillfully wrought in the depths of the earth;

Your eyes have seen my unformed substance;

And in Your book were all written

The days that were ordained for me,

When as yet there was not one of them.

(vv. 13–16)

God equips all of us with spiritual gifts, natural talents, and skills. Through the fall, when humanity chooses sin, we are cut off from the Spirit's empowerment of our gifts and severed from the high purpose He has for us. All that's left is the strength of the fallen flesh, raw power. Having lost our sense of the Creator's intention for our lives, we launch out in what Robert McGee called the "search for significance."[3] However, when we receive Christ's life as our own, the Holy Spirit comes to live within our own spirit, we are reconnected with God's high purpose, and we receive the Holy Spirit's empowerment of our spiritual gifts.

The Zone of Excellence is defined by four markers:

Identity in Christ

"Know thyself," urged Socrates and other Greek philosophers. However, *how* we know ourselves and *where* we search for our identity is crucial. If we look strictly to ourselves to know ourselves, we will make one of two—and sometimes both—mistakes. Either we will think too highly of ourselves, or we will underestimate who we truly are in our Creator's eyes. The source of our identity and our understanding of it must therefore be transcendent— beyond us.

Our essential being is that we are designed and made as *imago Dei*, the very image of God. There can be no higher view of the self, but, at the same time, it is one that makes us aware of our need to rise to our best through His power.

Clues to the way Donald Trump sees himself emerge as people probe his personality through their encounters with him, as well as his own words and actions. David Brody and James Lamb wrote that "Trump's true DNA is that of an outsider: fearless, authentic, and free from the shackles of consultants and GOP operatives."[4] This would suggest that Donald Trump is his "own man" in the sense of healthy self-perception (though this trait can deteriorate into narcissism quickly). That sense of self-identity is wholesome and essential for leadership, but to a degree. Unless there is humbling through brokenness, such a self-perception can stoke egoism and pride, which God opposes.[5]

Spiritual Gifts

These are the Spirit-given capacities that enable us to carry out the purposes for which God places us in the world. Paul wrote that "each person has a special gift from God, of one kind or another" (1 Corinthians 7:7 NLT). The Bible provides lists of the spiritual gifts, which include exhortation, giving, leadership, mercy, prophecy, service, teaching, administration, apostleship, discernment, faith, healing, helps, knowledge, miracles, tongues, interpretation of tongues, wisdom, evangelism, shepherding (pastoral), and hospitality.[6]

Until we receive Christ and His Holy Spirit, the gifts are present in us in potentiality. When the Holy Spirit enters the human spirit, our gifts are energized—think of a newly constructed house that has all the wiring, but no power until the switch is turned on.

What spiritual gifts does Donald Trump bring to the presidency, either potentially or operationally, depending on where the president is in his relationship to Christ? Our spiritual gifts form our personality, so observing Trump's personality traits gives us evidences of the spiritual gifts that can operate within him.

Donald Trump's complex personality is as enigmatic as other facets of his character. "Across his lifetime Donald Trump has exhibited a trait profile that you would not expect of a U.S. president: sky high extroversion combined with off-the-chart low agreeableness," wrote psychologist Dan P. McAdams.[7]

Another psychologist, Ryne H. Sherman, sees Trump's personality as adjusted, meaning not anxious or nervous. Trump is ambitious and results-oriented, sociable, characterized by low interpersonal sensitivity, and inquisitive, among others.[8]

While the list of Trump's personality traits could go on and on, we can see from those given here some of the president's spiritual gifts in potentiality or functionality: exhortation, faith, leadership, vision,[9] discernment, and hospitality.

Donald Trump is a gifted man, but these abilities can be used negatively as well as positively. He has great capacities to lead as president of the United States, but also great capacities for doing much harm. What determines good or bad uses of our gifts is the power in which we try to exercise them. The danger is trying to function in our giftedness by the power of the flesh rather than the Holy Spirit. Here Trump's narcissism could be a danger as it has been with other presidents.

Natural Talents and Skills

Donald Trump inherited much from his father, Fred, not only in properties and wealth but also in natural abilities. As an adolescent, Fred, not long after his father's death, partnered with his mother to form E. Trump & Son, the launching of what would become the Trump Organization. The *New York Time*'s obituary for Donald Trump's father called Fred Trump the "Postwar Master Builder of Housing for the Middle Class." This title, as David Brody and Scott Lamb pointed out, was given to Fred Trump for "having built and managed twenty-seven thousand apartments in Brooklyn and Queens."[10]

Donald Trump, therefore, would have been raised in a legacy of can-do vision, entrepreneurship, business acumen, and a follow-through determination without which great visions are mere clouds. From his grandfather and father, Trump inherited the natural skills and talents that would enable him to bring dreams into the hard reality of concrete and steel.

Formation Through Trials and Troubles

Nebuchadnezzar could not become the king God could use until he spent seven years in the wilderness. What about Donald Trump's brokenness? Here is where the "positive thinking" theology under which he grew up could be a hindrance. Donald Trump lived in a protected environment. He might have been shielded from the intense trials that have characterized the lives of other leaders, especially Abraham Lincoln.

Formative troubles came early in Abraham Lincoln's life. He could not have imagined as a child that the hardships, what he was learning from them and the strengths they were building in him, would contribute to his excellence and endurance decades later. For example, at age nine, a plant, the white snakeroot, would take the life of young Abe's mother. The blooming of the plant was deceptive, festooned with milky white leaves and bursts of little flowers. Cattle were attracted to the plant but then became violently ill. Humans who drank their milk would die in agony within three weeks.

One October day in 1818, nine-year-old Abe watched his mother succumb to the "milk disease" and then helped his father make her coffin.

We all have options as to how we will respond to hardships. Some people become embittered, shaking their fist at God, and driven by anger in their human relationships. Others fall into denial, floating through life on fantasies. Some individuals allow their pain to drive them into withdrawal or fatalistic resignation. There are folk who determine that their travails will not conquer them, but that they will go forward in life and work despite the pain. These are the men and women who allow their suffering to sharpen and strengthen them.

The highest and best response to personal tribulation is through embracing in both heart and mind the worldview described by the apostle Paul in Romans 8:28–29: "We know that God causes all things to work together for good to those who love God, to those who are called according to His purpose. For those whom He foreknew, He also predestined to become conformed to the image of His Son, so that He would be the firstborn among many brethren."

Donald Trump did not suffer in his earlier life as did Lincoln, and that might be one of the shortfalls of Trump's formative years. The man who knew immense abundance materially did not have an abundance of pain as did Lincoln. The "positive thinking" worldview may have shoved Trump toward denial. Trump's suffering did come later in life through bad business decisions and failed marriages.

TRUMP'S PERIOD OF TROUBLES

In the 1990s, Trump passed through a period of troubles, a "season of despondency." Trump had overspent on some business investments, and there was turbulence in his marriage. In an interview appearing in *Psychology Today* in 2016, Trump said he made it through that troubling time by drawing from what he had learned through Norman Vincent Peale. Trump told his interviewer that he was "a firm believer in the power of being positive" and that what helped him through the hard time is that "I refused to give in to the negative circumstances and never lost faith in myself. I didn't believe I was finished even when the newspapers were saying so."[11]

Abraham Lincoln, as president of the United States, was an enigma to many, probably including even Mary Todd, yet he is remembered by history as the Great Emancipator. Many now would say that Trump is no Lincoln, but Trump is every bit as enigmatic. That should come as no surprise. The Bible says that "promotion cometh neither from the east, nor from the west, nor from the south. But God is the judge: he putteth down one, and setteth up another" (Psalm 75:6–7 KJV).

The Scriptures show that God is the Lord of the enigmatic, the things and people that "are not" in terms of their reputation and potentialities in the estimation of many in their society. Lincoln and Trump share the "are not" status. Powerbrokers and kingmakers may not have seen them as presidential possibilities, but apparently the Lord of the enigmatic did.

THREE

THE KINGDOM PLAN AND EXCEPTIONALISM

I've always believed that this blessed land was set apart in a special way, that some divine plan placed this great continent here between the two oceans to be found by people from every corner of the earth—people who had a special love for freedom.

—PRESIDENT RONALD REAGAN, JANUARY 31, 1983

Nebuchadnezzar's Babylon was exceptional among the nations of its era in its wealth, its prestige, and the way it was feared, if not respected, globally.

Babylon's unique culture was watched over by an elite, the Chaldeans, definers of Babylonian political correctness. They were sanctioned by Nebuchadnezzar himself and reported directly to him. The Chaldeans demanded allegiance to their worldview, compliance to its cherished beliefs and values, and retribution upon all who departed from it, ranging from lions' dens to fiery furnaces.

Nebuchadnezzar's Babylon demonstrates that exceptionalism in a nation can be negative as well as positive. In a world of exorbitant excruciations, Nebuchadnezzar's tortures were "exceptional" in their brutality and pain. Few of the tyrant's actions reveal this as strikingly as the incident with the golden statue.

Nebuchadnezzar's pursuit of idolatry was extraordinary in its lavishness and determination. Recognizing that the presence of Hebrew captives like Daniel and his friends might "pollute" Babylonian religion, the king took action. He ordered the construction of a gold statue ninety feet tall and nine feet thick. The image loomed over a flat plain. No one could miss it, and no one could fail to be awed at this latest project of the king whose ancestors erected the Tower of Babel.

Nebuchadnezzar, certain he would now expose and destroy the Hebrew spiritual infiltration, which he himself had instigated by conquering Judah and capturing its best citizens, commanded worship of the golden image.

Daniel's fellow Hebrews—Shadrach, Meshach, and Abednego—refused.

Soon they would face Nebuchadnezzar's exceptional brutality. *The Message* version of the Bible reports what happened like this:

> Nebuchadnezzar, his face purple with anger, cut off Shadrach, Meshach, and Abednego. He ordered the furnace fired up *seven times hotter than usual.* He ordered some strong men from the army to tie them up, hands and feet, and throw them into the roaring furnace. Shadrach, Meshach, and Abednego, bound hand and foot, fully dressed from head to toe, were pitched into the roaring fire. Because the king was in such a hurry and the furnace was so hot, flames from the furnace killed the men who carried Shadrach, Meshach, and Abednego to it, while the fire raged around Shadrach, Meshach, and Abednego. (Daniel 3:19–23, emphasis added)

"SEVEN TIMES HOTTER"

"Fired up seven times hotter than usual" captures the essence of the exceptional intensity Nebuchadnezzar visited upon his enemies.

Yet—and here is the enigma—Nebuchadnezzar's Babylon provided a positive impetus for the spiritual cleansing of the Jews, God's covenant people, the deepening of hunger for God's ways, and the passion for a return to the land they had lost. The Hebrew captives, far from their homeland, began to remember, awakening to what they no longer had. Their longing was expressed in poignant outpourings from their aching hearts, like Psalm 137:1–9 (NKJV):

> By the rivers of Babylon,
> There we sat down, yea, we wept
> When we remembered Zion.
> We hung our harps
> Upon the willows in the midst of it.
> For there those who carried us away captive asked of us a song,
> And those who plundered us requested mirth,
> Saying, "Sing us one of the songs of Zion!"
>
> How shall we sing the LORD's song
> In a foreign land?
> If I forget you, O Jerusalem,
> Let my right hand forget its skill!
> If I do not remember you,
> Let my tongue cling to the roof of my mouth—
> If I do not exalt Jerusalem
> Above my chief joy.
>
> Remember, O LORD, against the sons of Edom
> The day of Jerusalem,

Who said, "Raze it, raze it,
To its very foundation!"

O daughter of Babylon, who are to be destroyed,
Happy the one who repays you as you have served us!
Happy the one who takes and dashes
Your little ones against the rock!

THE AMERICA OF TRUMP, ET AL.

That brings us to Trump's America, itself an enigma.

By "Trump's America" we do not mean the nation he has created, but that of his era. It has been a long time coming. It is also the America of Barack Obama, George W. Bush, Bill Clinton, George H. W. Bush, Ronald Reagan, Jimmy Carter, Gerald Ford, Richard Nixon, Lyndon Johnson, John F. Kennedy, and others who have occupied the Oval Office.

This is the same America Seymour Lipset was thinking about when he wrote: "There can be little question that the hand of providence has been on a nation which finds a Washington, a Lincoln, or a Roosevelt when it needs him."[1]

The contemporary version of America was born in the roiling 1960s, when utopianism took to the streets, and mighty institutions surrendered values and principles to the aborning social warrior movements. Reverence for God and respect for human life began to be discarded, and, worst of all, the consensus of the elites shifted from belief in the Lord of History as the foundation of all that is good in civilization, and America's roots in the Judeo-Christian worldview. Instead, idealism and trust in the power and ability of humans to construct the perfect society displaced the vision for God's kingdom. Spiritual and philosophical amnesia erased the memories of the disasters of socialism and statism among important

Chaldean-like consensus-setters. Yet human beings made in the image of God cannot sever themselves from the quest for the transcendent, and they developed their own "spirituality," often embracing New Age religions.

To many in the elites of the entertainment, information, academic, political, and corporate establishments, the idea of American exceptionalism became especially repugnant. In the new egalitarian age, almost all worldviews became equally valid and contributive. I say "almost" because the elites began to believe and preach that the Judeo-Christian worldview was the source of many evils. The opponents of exceptionalism became warriors determined to destroy the convictions that had produced the very freedoms they were now turning into antinomianism and anarchy.

As exiles in Nebuchadnezzar's Babylon stirred a hunger in the Hebrews—especially a remnant among the captives, like Daniel and his friends—so in contemporary America, where the distortions of sexuality, the recasting of marriage, and the slaughter of infants on a level that would vie with and even exceed the atrocities of Nebuchadnezzar's Babylon, there is a stirring of hunger and thirst for righteousness. The remnant in the land especially is beginning to ask: Who or what did we forget? Who or what did we leave behind? Who or what is back there to which we should return? Where is our true home spiritually as well as physically?

Down here in the current version of Babylon, there is hope because Jesus said, "Blessed are those who *hunger and thirst* for righteousness, for they shall be satisfied" (Matthew 5:6, emphasis added). We do not understand or experience true hunger and thirst until we have been deprived. And only those who can remember the good nourishment and refreshment that lie buried back in a lost era or place can really know the extent of the loss.

Only those who have seen and known "Jerusalem" can fully comprehend the destitutions of "Babylon."

ENIGMATIC AMERICA AND EXCEPTIONALISM

Like Nebuchadnezzar's Babylon, America is enigmatic in the eyes of many. It seems to be an exception in principle, if not always in practice. So, the debate rages: *Is the United States truly an exceptional nation, and, if so, in what sense?*

There are multitudes living within the United States who cannot truly see their country and its exceptional qualities and mission. They take the blessings for granted. Perhaps the reason is that the United States of America must be understood not so much politically and materially as spiritually, in the context of its kingdom mission: the role of the country in the advance of the "gospel of the kingdom" throughout the world (Matthew 24:14).

More than anything else, as we argue elsewhere, we must recapture the "city on a hill" vision expressed by John Winthrop in 1630, and the world-view arising from it, if we are to continue to enjoy freedom, security, and prosperity. Already America is veering from its course as restrictions are placed increasingly on biblically based churches and institutions, and free-dom of speech and expression are squelched.

Timothy Carney put numbers to this problem and detailed its conse-quences in his book *Alienated America: Why Some Places Thrive While Other Places Collapse.* He looked intensely at a society, in the words of reviewer Kevin Roberts, "lost in its own cultural and social wilderness."[2]

How did we get here?

THE "UNCHURCHING" OF AMERICA

The "root cause," Carney found, is the "unchurching of America," especially among working-class people.[3] "The woes of the white working class are best understood not by looking at idled factories but by looking at empty churches," Carney concluded.[4] His research showed that "in counties with the highest church attendance, civic institutions are vibrant and jobs are plentiful."[5]

Some would say that America itself has been an enigma among the nations. "There is a Providence that protects idiots, drunkards, children, and the United States of America," quipped Otto von Bismarck, the ruthless Prussian leader who unified Germany in the nineteenth century.

Others speak of "American exceptionalism." But not Donald Trump, the "America First" president. "I don't think it's a very nice term," Trump once said. "I think you're insulting the world."[6] John Gans Jr. wrote in the *Atlantic*, "Obama has talked more about American exceptionalism than Presidents Reagan, George H. W. Bush, Bill Clinton, and George W. Bush combined."[7]

Perhaps Trump simply did not understand the meaning of the term *American exceptionalism.* Maybe the confusion lies in the context of the age. Abraham Lincoln understood the term and was not hesitant to speak of exceptionalism. In a speech to the New Jersey Senate, Lincoln said,

> I am exceedingly anxious that this Union, the Constitution, and the liberties of the people be perpetuated in accordance with the original idea for which that struggle was made, and I shall be most happy indeed if I shall be an humble instrument in the hands of the Almighty, and of this, his *almost chosen people*, for perpetuating the object of that great struggle. (emphasis added)

Trump does believe that America has played a unique and special role among the nations. "The United States of America has been among the greatest forces for good in the history of the world, and the greatest defenders of sovereignty, security, and prosperity for all," said Trump in a foreign policy statement on September 25, 2018.[8]

INSPIRING OR INFURIATING

Depending on which side of the political aisle you find yourself, Trump's mantra, "Make America Great Again"—about which we write in more detail in chapter 12—is either inspiring or infuriating. To some, it is a summons to an age when nations respected the United States for its global leadership, unprecedented prosperity, remarkable freedoms and opportunities. To others, like former attorney general Eric Holder, the slogan is offensive and historically inaccurate. America was never great, he said, pointing to slavery and other low moments in America's past, and, in his view, discrimination against LGBTQ+ individuals.[9]

Eric Holder was right that America has sinned—at times, grievously—but he is wrong to generalize that America has never manifested greatness. Nations need grace just as much as individuals.

The best way to comprehend any nation's role in and value to history, and whether it was "great," is through the eyes of the Lord of History. This means that civilizations and nations must be seen in a spiritual sense, and not merely a geopolitical understanding. This is among the reasons Nebuchadnezzar's Babylon is of such significance. Spiritually, it is the historical "meme" of the world system driven by the Nimrod-antichrist spirit of defiance against God.

Russell Kirk was an important twentieth-century scholar and philosopher of history who understood the deeper meanings. He concluded that "a civilization cannot long survive the dying of belief in a transcendent order that brought the culture into being."[10] Christopher Dawson believed, as did Baron John Dalberg-Acton, that "religion is the key to history.... We cannot understand the inner form of a society unless we understand its religion."[11]

AMERICA'S DNA

The DNA of what would become the United States is a major clue to its purpose in the world. John Winthrop, who in 1630 arrived in the New World aboard the ship *Arabella*, gave utterance to the founding vision of the Massachusetts Bay Colony that he would serve as governor: "We shall be as a city upon a hill." Perhaps his most important words were: "We are entered into *Covenant* with [God] for this work." Winthrop wanted the community he would establish in the New World to be an example of the kingdom of God on earth to other nations. His speech was titled "A Modell (*sic*) of Christian Charity."

Wilfred McClay, an American history scholar, wrote that Winthrop's speech "laid out the settlement's mission and guiding purposes. This speech leaves one in no doubt about the fundamentally religious intentions behind the colony's existence and the hope that the godly community they were creating could eventually serve as a means of renewal for the Old World they had left behind."[12]

The *New York Times* once proposed that America's historical narrative should be revised by resetting the national birth date. The *Times* argued that the "true founding" of the United States should be pegged to August 20, 1619, when the first slaves from Africa were brought to the Jamestown Colony in Virginia. The writers believe that "nearly everything that has made America exceptional grew out of slavery."[13]

When I read about this, I thought immediately of Winthrop, and wrote in the *Christian Post* that if America's birthday was going to be changed (which I don't advocate), it ought to be 1630, when Winthrop spoke of the "covenant" with God.

Russell Kirk, in his important book *The Roots of American Order*, recalled that the Israelites broke the Ten Commandments almost as quickly as they were revealed to them. So, said Kirk, "the principles of order re-affirmed by Winthrop were violated by the settlers in New England not long after their landing in Massachusetts."[14] But the "DNA" was in their hearts and souls—and so was God's grace. Winthrop articulated values that would be foundational in the worldview expressed in the Preamble to the Declaration of Independence, and in the Constitution that would provide the details of implementation.

Winthrop also told his companions that they, as well as he as their leader, must always have "before our eyes our commission and community in the work" and "keep the unity of the spirit in the bond of peace . . . the Lord will be our God and delight to dwell among us. . . . For We must consider that we shall be as a City upon a Hill; the eyes of all people are upon us."

Governor Winthrop took those last words directly from a saying of Jesus, recorded in Matthew 5, the Sermon on the Mount. The context is the lifestyle of the kingdom of God, and those who live by its precepts. Such people, said Jesus, would be "the salt of the earth" and "the light of the world."

When He spoke, the Lord was standing on a slope by the Lake of Galilee. Perhaps Jesus pointed toward the village of Safed, perched on a mount within view of His listeners. Its position was high enough that its light gave direction to night travelers. "A city set on a hill cannot be hidden," said Jesus.

Paul Johnson, in his classic book *A History of the American People*, discussed what those words meant to John Winthrop when he spoke them on the *Arabella*. The New England colony Winthrop would lead "would create an ideal spiritual and secular community" that others across the world— and especially across the Atlantic from the "Old World"—could see as an example of a good society.

If we recommit to making America a "city on a hill," we won't have to worry about making it "great again."

A century after Winthrop, powerful God-sent movements energized the spiritual seed through the Great Awakenings. Through them, the Holy Spirit moved on to the Colonies, preparing the way for independence from Britain and the formation of the new government.

Christopher DeMuth, a scholar at the Hudson Institute, analyzed the Awakenings and their impact on shaping early America. DeMuth said that the First Great Awakening—with its emphasis on personal responsibility and self-rule—was an important antecedent to the American Revolution, the Declaration of Independence, and the Constitution. He wrote that, "as it turned out, the secular consequences of the awakenings were unifying and enlarging, galvanizing the American nation." For example, "they brought back many women and black Americans to Christian practice and belief."[15]

John Witherspoon, president of Princeton University in 1776, member

THE KINGDOM PLAN AND EXCEPTIONALISM

of the Continental Congress, and signer of the Declaration of Independence, had the nation's spiritual core in mind when he prayed: "God grant that in America true religion and civil liberty may be inseparable, and that unjust attempts to destroy the one, may in the issue tend to the support and establishment of both."[16]

DNA IN THE PREAMBLE

So, again, the influence of the spiritual DNA was seen in the Preamble to the Declaration of Independence when it states:

> We hold these truths to be self-evident, that all Men are created equal, that they are endowed by their Creator with certain unalienable Rights, that among these are Life, Liberty, and the Pursuit of Happiness—That to secure these Rights, Governments are instituted among Men, deriving their powers from the Consent of the governed, that whenever any Form of Government becomes destructive of those Ends, it is the Right of the People to alter or abolish it.

Eric Metaxas wrote that in 1776, "a nation was formed in a way that a nation never had been born . . . something entirely new: the nation as *idea*." Rather than being founded around "a group of ethnically or tribally similar people" or one "composed of disparate groups held together by a strong leader," the United States of America was "conceived in liberty."[17]

Historian Wilfred M. McClay believes the early explorations of the American continent, ranging from the first people groups to cross over from Asia to Leif Erikson and the Norse voyagers from northern Europe, point indirectly "toward the recognizable beginnings of American history." Further, McClay said, those expeditions "point to the presence of America in the world's imagination as an idea, as a land of hope, of refuge and opportunity, of a second chance at life for those willing to take it."[18]

There had long been "a mystique about the West," McClay wrote.[19] "The West had long been thought of, in Europe, as a direction offering renewal and discovery," he said. In the sixteenth century Sir Thomas More, author of *Utopia*, envisioned a perfect society somewhere on a western island. As McClay pointed out, even before that the Greeks thought of the Isles of the Blessed and the paradise of the Elysian Fields that Homer theorized as being on the western edge of the world.

Some of the ideals seen in the souls of ancient philosophers would indeed be realized in the West, as if the human psyche somehow sensed it. In a world of kings, lords, emperors, and potentates, the idea that all humans are created equal and deserving of liberty was an exceptional thought. The idea that basic human rights were not granted by the state but ordained by God—and that those rights were therefore inviolable—was remarkable. The notion that even governments were accountable for their decisions and actions was amazing considering the tyrannical systems ruling everywhere else at the time. The Founders did not recognize it initially, but they had also planted in the nation the seed that would abolish slavery. It is regrettable they did not act immediately on the concept of human equality.

Historian William Federer found that a government "of the people, for the people, and by the people" was a rarity. In fact, wrote Federer, such a system was so exceptional it had not been seen in six thousand years of recorded history. Throughout all the previous epochs, governing power had been centralized in one person, or an elite few.[20]

"THE SOUL OF A CHURCH"

G. K. Chesterton, the twentieth-century British journalist and author, was asked, "What is America?" He replied that America is

> a nation with the soul of a church . . . the only nation in the world that
> is founded on a creed . . . set forth with dogmatic and even theological

lucidity in the Declaration of Independence.... It certainly does condemn anarchism, and it does also by inference condemn atheism, since it clearly names the Creator as the ultimate authority from whom these equal rights are derived.[21]

Chesterton echoed Frenchman Alexis de Tocqueville, who, as we have seen, visited America in 1831. Based on his experiences and observations, Tocqueville would write a classic, *Democracy in America*, published initially in 1835. Tocqueville described the exceptional conditions he found in the young nation:

> On my arrival in the United States it was the religious aspect of the country that first struck my eye. As I prolonged my stay, I perceived the great political consequences that flowed from these new facts.... Among us [in France] I had seen the spirit of religion and the spirit of freedom almost always move in contrary directions. Here I found them united intimately with one another: they reigned together on the same soil.[22]

What Tocqueville saw and experienced piqued his curiosity, and he began to search for the "soul" of America. He interviewed people from all walks of life, and concluded: "Religion, which among Americans, never mixes directly in the government of society, should therefore be considered as the first of their political institutions."[23]

Tocqueville said he did not know "if all Americans have faith in their religion," but nevertheless, "I am sure that they believe it necessary to the maintenance of republican institutions." Even more, "in the United States religious zeal constantly warms at the heart of patriotism," he noted.

The Great Awakenings help keep "religious zeal" and "patriotism" from becoming mere civil religion. The revivals had swept some portions of the nation—and impacted all—before Tocqueville's arrival. Those spiritual movements focused on the holiness of God, the tragedy of human sin, and the need for repentance. The influence of such preaching and its theology focused on the kingdom of God ruling over the human heart personally rather than centering on institutions—but institutional philosophy and reform came as the fruits of individuals and their relationship with the Lord of History.

Long after Tocqueville, political scientist Seymour Lipset explored why America was still "the most religious country in Christendom." The United States "has always been considered by analysts from the early nineteenth century [and that would include Alexis de Tocqueville] to our own day as exceptional."

THE GOSPEL OF THE KINGDOM

But why was America so special? Why does God care who leads the United States (or any nation)? These questions can best be answered by looking closely at the sayings of Jesus in Matthew 24.

Jesus and His disciples were leaving the temple complex in Jerusalem one day when suddenly some of His followers became aware of its immensity. They had seen it all many times, but for some reason the size of the enormous blocks that made up the structure caught their attention that day. "Do you see all these buildings?" Jesus asked them. "I tell you the truth, they will be completely demolished. Not one stone will be left on top of another!" (v. 2 NLT).

Jesus and His friends trekked out across the Kidron Valley and toward the slopes of the Mount of Olives. They sat down and looked at the expanse of the temple spread out below them. The disciples were still thinking about what Jesus had said concerning its destruction—then some forty years into the future. "Tell us, when will all this happen?" they asked. "What sign will signal your return and the end of the world?" (v. 3 NLT).

Jesus then described events that will cycle across the line of time in large repetitive themes. These are the "birth pangs" that lead to His coming with His kingdom into the finite world. He gave the men His summary statement:

"This gospel of the kingdom shall be preached in the whole world as a testimony to all the nations, and then the end will come" (v. 14).

It is important to examine the Greek words appearing in the original to experience the amazing implications of this prophecy. *Nations* is derived from *ethnesin*, a word meaning "race" (of people), or people groups. We get the English word *ethnic* from that Greek term. *End* is from *telos*, meaning the aim, goal, or purpose achieved at the successful conclusion of some process. *Strong's Concordance* illustrates the word *telos* by referring to a sailor's telescope "unfolding (extending out) one stage at a time to function at full strength (capacity of effectiveness)."[24]

Therefore, Jesus is saying that the whole purpose of history is the announcement of the good news of His gracious reign on earth. Every age of finite time (*kronos*) will mark an advance of the proclamation until at last, by God's calculation, every people group on the earth will have heard the fantastic news of the coming of the gospel of the kingdom of righteousness (goodness and justice), peace, and Holy Spirit–given, endless joy in the whole world (Romans 14:17).

But how does this process of successive stages happen according to God's plan? It is centered on the "nations," which, in the Scriptures, are clusters of people groups. In every stage of history, therefore, there are advances of this glorious proclamation, sometimes quickly and dramatically, as in the eighteenth-century Great Awakenings in Britain and her American Colonies, or incrementally, as in the ongoing effort now to identify unreached people groups globally, and get the gospel of the kingdom to them.

Make no mistake, the exceptional nature and the greatness of America that Donald Trump and others want to recover is all about the gospel of the kingdom, though they may not know it. This means that no politician, as we will see in chapter 12, can bring the nation to that level of "greatness."

"The mission of the West is synonymous with the mission of the Church," said Christopher Dawson.[25] Though he was speaking in a Catholic sense, Dawson was nevertheless right in the broadest context.

Thus we have the *gospel of the kingdom principle* that gives a deeper understanding of American exceptionalism: God sovereignly raised up a civilization and then a nation of exceptional freedoms, security, and prosperity to become the base in its historic period for the advance of the gospel of the kingdom in the whole world.

The stunning fact is that, in God's plan, *America was all about giving the church the freedom to propagate the gospel of the kingdom and the material resources to advance it in the world.*

Further, Jesus said that "the greatest among you must be a servant" (Matthew 23:11 NLT). What goes for individual human beings applies to their countries and civilizations themselves. Nations that focus on conquest and domination are unexceptional, a dime a dozen throughout history. Exceptional nations are servant nations, richly endowed for the sake of blessing others. America—as with any country—is at its worst when its national policies are exploitative. Portions of America were grotesque in the age of slavery. Even now, if Donald Trump wants to fulfill his goal of seeing America "great again," it will not have greatness if his policies to realize that vision are based on exploitation.

The president's understanding of America as exceptional must arise from the Bible and be expressed in the Judeo-Christian worldview. It must not be a matter of his opinion, but be objective and absolute.

The "greatness" of the United States, despite all its shortcomings, is in living by, promoting, and protecting the standards of that worldview. This is the "track" on which America must remain if it is to continue under God's blessing and fulfill its national destiny. This is not a "religious" form of "manifest destiny," because America has been made great and prosperous, not to be a master, like Nebuchadnezzar's Babylon, but to serve civilization itself and, above all, God's aims in the world He created.

Donald Trump himself apparently believes this. He told David Brody and Scott Lamb, "I am a believer . . . And when you believe, many good things can happen. And hopefully those good things will happen for the nation."[26]

The early church believed in this principle, according to theologian and church historian Oscar Cullmann. As we noted previously, the first-century followers of Jesus Christ viewed all history as "Christocentric," in Cullmann's words. History is moving from its beginning to a point of purpose, with God stepping in all across the line of time. Thus Cullmann said that "the historical work of Jesus Christ as Redeemer forms the mid-point of a line that leads from the Old Testament to the return of Christ."[27] History, to those with the first knowledge of the Lord Jesus Christ, "is means of which God makes use in order to reveal His gracious working."

All the early believers had to do was contemplate the nations around them. Greece was exceptional in its culture and language. Rome was exceptional in the creation of roads for trade throughout the empire, which, cruel as Roman dominance frequently was, nevertheless established a crucible into which the gospel could be poured. And the Pax Romana provided relative security for those who traveled those roads.

Then we come to the modern age and see America's rise in the process of the "extension" of the "telescope." This explains the meaning of the United States and its blessings in the context of God's kingdom mission. God has always blessed the whole by raising up the exceptional so that all could share in those blessings.

This is what I saw in seed form upon leaving the White House staff in 1973. The vision has intensified and sharpened through the years. I concluded long ago that *the state of the church's health in a nation determines the health of the nation.* We will look at this idea more closely in chapter 11.

God's desire is that every nation be exceptional in its peace, prosperity, freedoms, and security. But that requires in the heart of a nation an exceptional church. The following quote is often attributed to Alexis de Tocqueville, and though there is doubt about whether it was he who spoke it, or someone inspired by his writings about early America, there is little doubt about its truth:

I sought for the greatness and genius of America in her commodious harbors and her ample rivers—and it was not there . . . in her fertile fields and boundless forests—and it was not there . . . in her rich mines and her vast world commerce—and it was not there . . . in her democratic Congress and her matchless Constitution—and it was not there. Not until I went into the churches of America and heard her pulpits flame with righteousness did I understand the secret of her genius and power. America is great because she is good, and if America ever ceases to be good, she will cease to be great.[28]

EXCEPTIONAL LEADERSHIP REQUIRED

From the outset, in the context of God's plan for the advance of the gospel of the kingdom in time and space, America was marked as exceptional, and in need of exceptional leadership. This is why God raises up the "right" leaders for specific periods of the nation's history. However, the "right" leaders from God's view might be the "wrong" leaders from the human perspective. Therefore, this by no means suggests that being a leader in American government means being a perfect person. The Oval Office has been occupied by scalawags and scoundrels. But, as we saw in chapter 2, God's pattern seems to always be that of working with people who seem the most unlikely.

There were many prayer meetings as President Barack Obama ran for his second term of office. Groups of churches were praying earnestly for his reelection, believing that he needed four more years to carry out his goal of transforming the United States. Others were just as passionate in asking God for Obama's defeat, concerned that the changes he wanted would produce a socialistic nation.

Mr. Obama won. One segment of intercessors rejoiced that God had responded affirmatively to their crying out to Him, while the other grieved, some of them wondering why God had not answered their prayers.

But God heard and answered the prayers of both groups. Since God, according to Daniel 2:21, both raises up and puts down civil leaders, it was the Father's will, intentional or permissive, that Barack Obama—for the sake of the kingdom—have a second term in office, just as it was God's kingdom purpose that Donald Trump be elected in 2016.

Many of those who sought Trump's impeachment had judged him as guilty before the hearings began in the House of Representatives. However, it is far too early to project how history will judge this "man from Babylon." We can pray and hope that Donald Trump and all who follow him in the presidency will get a heart vision for God's kingdom of righteousness, justice, peace, and transcendent joy, and the role of America in its global advance.

That will contribute mightily to America's being "great again."

Whatever the case, it is time to focus on the attributes of the coming kingdom, and heralding its approach worldwide, in accord with Jesus' teaching in Matthew 24.

FOUR

TIME AND THE TWO MEN FROM BABYLON

All the world's a stage,
And all the men and women merely players:
They have their exits and entrances.
—WILLIAM SHAKESPEARE, *AS YOU LIKE IT*

I f everybody is thinking alike, then somebody is not thinking," said General George Patton. This means that as groups of individuals face seemingly impossible challenges, someone must venture into new territories of thought. They must reach "beyond" the ordinary.

This is what happened in England at Buckinghamshire's Bletchley Park as a team led by computer genius Alan Turing sought the secrets of the Nazi Enigma code. The enemy was able to communicate secret plans for devastating attacks through the ciphered messages. To break the Enigma code Turing and his associates had to plow through some fifteen million million million algorithmic possibilities.

Then there came a "certain day" when Alan Turing experienced an "epiphany" through the discovery of a flaw in the coded messages. He noted a letter in one of the encrypted words that should not have been there. Turing began to search for a phrase that he knew would be included by Nazi operators in every message. Eventually Turing found that phrase at the end of every transmission: *Heil Hitler.* Reasoning outside the box from the encrypted letters in that phrase, Turing was able to discover the flaw in the system and break the code.[1]

He had gone beyond the usual range of logic to crack Enigma.

SEE THE LARGER CONTEXT OF TIME AND HISTORY

The same principle is true in time and history. To understand any phenomenon in finite time, we must go beyond the existential moment and see the larger context in which the event occurs. What we live through and experience in a narrow present moment is part of something much bigger.

Nebuchadnezzar and Trump—along with all the other national leaders who have had their moment on the world stage—cannot be understood apart from their roles in the larger drama. Oscar Wilde borrowed Shakespeare's phrase, and quipped: "The world is a stage and the play is badly cast."[2] Those who suffered under Nebuchadnezzar and those in our time who loathe either Trump or Obama would readily agree.

But to make sense of leaders in their onstage moment, we must pull way back, and have the larger drama in our minds, if not in our views.

"There is no larger drama," says the nihilist. "The only drama that matters is the one on the stage at this moment," says the existentialist. "The larger drama is the beautiful fantasy that plays out in my mind," says the romanticist, at least a trace of which is in all of us.

The biblical worldview of time and history is that the present moment is not an illusion but rather a hard reality that it is part of a larger scheme. Our moment on the stage has a point of origin, an "entrance," but also a point of destination, an "exit" from finite time. The destination is not a "terminal" or termination, but a *telos*—the arrival at a specific goal or purpose, and entry into something beyond the "stage" of existence in finite time.

Nebuchadnezzar and Trump have had their moments on the stage, and just as they had their "entrances," they had their "exits," both actions determined by the requirements of the drama in which they were players.

The only way to assess Nebuchadnezzar or Trump is in the context of the spiritually transcendent.

Centuries ago, Solomon, another man of great wealth with whom both Nebuchadnezzar and Donald Trump could relate, saw the historic in the transcendent sense, and wrote: "To every thing there is a season, and a time to every purpose under the heaven" (Ecclesiastes 3:1 KJV). That principle includes King Nebuchadnezzar, Donald Trump and his presidency, and your own existence in time and space, and mine.

THE SEASON

Shakespeare may not have known New Testament Greek, but in his plays, he often reflected a biblical worldview and used many of its memes in his dramas. The inference of "exits" and "entrances" on the "world's stage" aligns with the biblical doctrine of time, as revealed in the interplay in the New Testament of the Greek words *kairos* and *kronos*.

To grasp the implications of those terms for the present age, we must take a closer look at the biblical doctrine of time.

As we have seen in previous pages, Jesus Christ stated in Matthew 24:14 that the purpose of history is the global proclamation of His kingdom to all "nations," or people groups, so that all persons across time will have the opportunity to hear and respond to His invitation to receive salvation, be reconciled to God, and become citizens of His kingdom. This is the context in which we best understand the biblical revelation of the nature of time and the raising up and putting down of leaders (Daniel 2:21) within the scope of what the Bible refers to as *times and seasons*.

The NASB version of Ecclesiastes 3:1 expands our understanding of the original Hebrew expression: "There is an *appointed time* for everything. And there is a time for every event under heaven" (emphasis added).

The Bible reveals finite time as both linear and cyclical. This is not as impossible as it sounds: think of a train moving along a track. There is linear progression toward the destination, but the train is carried along by the repeating cyclical motion of the wheels.

To dig out the richness of time as revealed in the Bible, we must sift through categories of words appearing in both Testaments. Immediately when we open the Bible, we run smack-dab into one of those vital terms: *Bereshith*, the Hebrew name for Genesis. It means "the start," or "beginning." Genesis 2:4 sums up the whole book of Genesis, when it says, "This is the account of the heavens and the earth when they were created." The Hebrew word for "history" appearing here is *toledah*, "generations." Thus, Genesis is the historical account that measures and reports on the foundational generations of all humanity and the people groups who comprise it.

Genesis, the English term, comes from the Greek word *geneseos*, signifying birth, generation, or the history of origins. The emphasis is on events and circumstances that surround the foundational generations of the human family.

THROUGH THE BIBLE LENS

Therefore, through the lens of the Bible, history is *generational* experience advancing toward a purpose. History must go forward from past to future because it's impossible to reverse direction and go back into the past (unless some of the more exotic implications of string theory, an idea regarding the physical construction of the universe, are true). However, God can step into any point along the track of finite time. In a sense, when we seek forgiveness of sins, He goes back to the moment we committed the sin and cancels the penalty incurred at that point in time. When we repent, God can transform past destructive disasters into blessings in the present and future.

The whole story of Joseph is an example. God took the past evil committed against Joseph when his brothers threw him into the pit and transformed the past event into a redemptive moment in the future. Decades after their evil deed against their brother, they would face Joseph as prime minister of Egypt. They were terrified when they realized the man who had rescued their family from famine was the teenager they had abused. Understandably, they trembled. Reassuring them, Joseph said, "You meant evil against me, but God meant it for good in order to bring about this present result, to preserve many people alive" (Genesis 50:20).

Max Lucado pointed out that in the original Hebrew this passage reads: "You wove evil, but God *rewove* it together for good." So, said, Lucado, "God, the Master Weaver . . . stretches the yarn and intertwines the colors, the ragged twine with the velvet strings, the pains with the pleasures. Nothing escapes His reach. Every king, despot, weather pattern, and molecule are at His command. He passes the shuttle back and forth across the generations, and as He does, a design emerges."[3]

This is in view when Colossians 4:5 speaks of "redeeming" the time. God can get back the good He intends in all things (Romans 8:28–29) and gets that good even from past events in our lives and histories that went bad. So, while we physically cannot go back into time while in our mortal bodies and finite world, there is a spiritual sense in which God can alter the trajectories established in the past and get things back on track.

Forward progression necessitates a track on which history can move, and that is the meaning of time. Maimonides, a twelfth-century Torah scholar, understood the connection between historic movement and time. Time is the outcome, he said, "consequent upon motion."[4] Neither can exist without the other. "Motion does not exist except in time, and time cannot be conceived by the intellect except together with motion," Maimonides thought.

Time is, therefore, like a train moving in a linear direction from a point of origin to a point of destination, on wheels that *cycle* along the *linear* tracks. History is the sequence of events that repeat themselves in broad style in linear progression, and time is the medium in which the motion of history can occur.

Thus, Mark Twain's observation: *"History doesn't repeat itself, but it often rhymes."*[5]

BOTH TESTAMENTS

We see this in both the Old and New Testaments—the Hebrew Bible and the Greek Bible. Both have special words to convey the reality of linear-cyclical time. *Zemdna* is translated as "time" in the Old Testament, as is *moed*. *Zemdna* means time only in the sense of duration, the ticking of the clock. *Moed* refers to "appointed times," those periods in which defining events and directional circumstances arise in the lives of people, their relationships, and institutions.

The richness of meaning emerges in the conjunction of the two Hebrew words. The *Moedim* are the feasts of Israel that mark significant intersections in space and time between the nation and God. *Zemdna*-time's buildup of moments finally arrive at the *Moedim*, in which the Hebrews interact with God through observances by which they move beyond human time. *Passover* takes the Israelites back to the night in Egypt that secured their delivery. *Purim* is a spiritual trip back into the time of Esther and her courageous acts by which the Hebrews were saved from the genocide Haman had planned for them. *Yom Kippur* reaches outside *zemdna*-time, and releases the grace of God within the era of law. Grace is a constant in the eternal continuum but will not appear in earth-time fully until the completion of Christ's work on the cross, yet it is manifest in the *moed* of Passover.

The coming of the Messiah and His fulfillment of the covenant promises within space-time is what makes the linkage of *zemdna* and *moed* extraordinary. All the rescue events in Israel's experience brought about by

God's direct intervention from outside human time (*zemdna*) are "salvific"; that is, they point to the salvation that is a reality in the eternal continuum, the kingdom of heaven, but which is yet to come in earth-time.

The linkage of the Old and New Testaments is what makes the Bible revelation whole and complete. Therefore, it should not surprise us that the Greek language of the New Testament reflects the *zemdna-moed* motif. The parallel Greek word for *zemdna*, sequential time as experienced in the natural world, is *kronos*. Another, *kairos*, expresses the ideas carried in the Hebrew *moed*. In fact, the significance of the *Moedim*, the feasts, is that they are prophetic, linking the *zemdna*-future with the overarching realities of heaven's time continuum.

Theologian Oscar Cullmann wrote that the early Christians believed that "the entire secular process is determined by divine *kairoi* [the plural of *kairos*]."[6]

THE "FULLNESS OF TIME"

As the linkage of *zemdna-moed* in the Old Testament gives rise to the feasts by which heavenly intervention in space-time is remembered, celebrated, and entered into once more, so there is linkage in the New Testament between *kairos* and *kronos*. This junction of the two qualities of time is expressed in the New Testament by the phrase "the fullness of time."[7] In the Old Testament, the arrival in the chronological calendar of the *Moedim* constituted the fullness of time. In the New Testament, the arrival in chronological time of the material reality to which the Feasts of Israel pointed is the "fullness of time."

Fullness is from the Greek word *pleroma*, which is seen graphically in the filling of a cup to the rim. Chronological time drips in seconds, minutes, hours, days, weeks, months, and years, until the cup of history reaches fullness.

Every event celebrated in the Old Testament looked forward to one thing—the coming of the Messiah. Therefore, Paul wrote in Galatians 4:4 that "when the fullness of the time came, God sent forth His Son, born of a woman, born under the Law." The Son exists eternally with the Father and is thus a remarkable *kairos*-person who becomes incarnate in *kronos*-sequence.

He is literally a Being from another dimension.

When He appears in chronological order, He fulfills all creation history to that point. When He comes again, He will fulfill all of history from the time of the resurrection and ascension to the point of His second coming.

One of the keys, therefore, that helps unlock the understanding of the Revelation visions is the awareness that John was seeing and, through the Holy Spirit, conveying to us the *moed-kairos* actualities within *zemdna-kronos*. If we view them only on the flat plane of the finite time dimension, they make no sense.

CIVIL LEADERS AND THE "PROPRIETY" OF TIME

As it relates to Nebuchadnezzar, Donald Trump, and other leaders, the issue here is *propriety* of time, and the *propitious* coming of people and events, their fifteen minutes of fame, or their "time" on the stage of history—from the least to the greatest.

Take, for example, Nebuchadnezzar's nemesis, Cyrus the Persian. This ancient ruler would have been a footnote in history except for the fact that he allowed the Jews to be liberated from Babylon and return to Jerusalem to launch the restoration that would ultimately lead to the rebuilding of the temple and the advance of God's kingdom proclamation in the world.

If God could use a Persian potentate like Cyrus at the "propitious" moment to restore Jerusalem, He can certainly use a Manhattan billionaire whose moral behavior has been questionable and his knowledge of the Bible limited.

That goes for other politicians as well, including Hillary Clinton. At one point longtime Clinton friend and adviser Dick Morris said Hillary Clinton believed the presidency was her "destiny," and that, in Morris's description, "God put her on earth" to be the American president. What held her back, according to the report, was that the "timing" of her entering the race might be "bad."[8]

And again, had the presidency in 2016 gone to Hillary Clinton or any of Trump's Republican rivals, we would be writing of their "propriety" because it is God who establishes the "seasons" and raises up and puts down rulers, as we have seen in Daniel 2:21–22.

Considering the way time works as revealed in the Bible, the timing of a political candidacy has much more to do with God's purposes than polls, money, or the weakness of others running for the office. Timing is a component of providential history, for the sake of His purposes.

KAIROS IN A BIRMINGHAM ELECTION

I lived through such a remarkable *kairos* in 1979. The place was Birmingham, Alabama. It involved a man who became one of the best friends I ever had.

Frank Parsons and I had met in the White House in 1970. I was then serving on President Nixon's staff as part of a team tasked to plan and oversee safe and peaceful school openings in eleven southern states that fall, when the broadest court-ordered desegregation in history would occur.

Nixon believed that local leaders should play the key role in advising Washington and working for racial harmony in their respective states. The teams were multiracial, drawing together people of widely differing opinions and backgrounds. Frank Parsons was a major leader of the Alabama team, as was Chris McNair, an African American man whose young daughter had been killed in a Sunday school classroom along with three other children when their church building was bombed by racists in 1963.

Our staff brought all eleven state teams to Washington, one by one, to meet personally with the president in the Oval Office. On that summer morning as I walked into the White House West Wing, I was especially glad to see my fellow Alabamians. I did not know when I was introduced to Frank Parsons that we were living through a *kairos* moment that almost a decade later would lead to an even greater *kairos*.

I left Washington and the White House in 1973, and ultimately took up the calling I had first received in 1957 to be a minister of the gospel. In 1979, through a series of events that no one could engineer, I became pastor of McElwain Baptist Church in Birmingham, where Frank and Nona Parsons and their children were active members. Eventually, Frank became chairman of the deacons.

In July 2013, and again in January 2014, Irene and I traveled from our home in Houston to Birmingham for me to conduct funerals for both Frank and Nona, who died within six months of each other.

But in 1979, Frank and I, with others, were headed for an "opportune time" that would change the face of Birmingham.

A mayoral election was scheduled for that year. Tensions were building in the city. The well-intentioned white mayor had allowed actions that reopened some of Birmingham's old wounds. Memories of Bull Connor's police dogs attacking civil rights demonstrators, along with violence like that which had killed McNair's daughter, were beginning to haunt the city once more.

Frank Parsons had sought to build harmonious relationships across all groups. He had earned credibility with many through his work to support the city's schools during the massive desegregation that had occurred in the fall of 1970. He was a committed Christian; a young, dynamic, and proven leader; a dedicated family man; and a successful business owner. Many were excited when Frank decided to challenge the incumbent.

Because of my experience in the political arena, Frank asked me to organize his campaign. Uncertain about whether I should take on the effort, since I was a pastor, I asked my deacon board for guidance. They instructed me to take on the task, and I plunged in. There was no black candidate in the race at that point, and we sought the African American vote, which was substantial in Birmingham.

There were several white candidates, but Frank quickly emerged as the front-runner. Then something happened that horrified me.

Dr. Richard Arrington, a greatly respected educator, entered the race for mayor. He was an African American. Birmingham's demographic had changed through the 1960s and 1970s, and many believed, including myself, that it was time for a black mayor. But none had come forward except Dr. Arrington, late in the campaign.

I was not horrified at the thought of a black mayor, but at the thought of helping lead a campaign in which there would be a standoff between black and white. Frank and I wanted to be part of the city's healing, not a point of focus for racists who might try to link with Frank's campaign.

That's exactly what happened. I found myself turning away people, their money intended for our campaign coffers, and their influence with white voting blocs. I even had to pressure Birmingham newspapers to remove ads supporting Frank that had been placed by racist organizations and individuals without our permission.

It was a nightmare.

To further complicate the matter, our campaign planning committee had determined weeks before we knew of Dr. Arrington's entry that if the final vote showed us losing by a thousand votes that we would challenge the outcome. That decision had been made when all Frank's opponents were white.

On election night Frank and I watched returns in the hotel adjacent to Birmingham's convention center, where our team was preparing what we anticipated would be a victory celebration.

Toward midnight, the final precincts were tallied, and Dr. Arrington had won by about a thousand votes. Across the street in the convention hall Frank's supporters were already contemplating a court challenge.

Suddenly the TV reports shifted to another Birmingham hotel where Dr. Arrington's celebration was held. The rejoicing poured out into the halls and across the city.

I looked at Frank. "What are we going to do?" Frank and I fell to our knees and cried out to God for direction.

As we stood up and watched the Arrington victory party, we realized that if we challenged the outcome, we would bring months of indecision to the city. The old wounds would open wider than ever. Birmingham's streets would again flow with blood.

Though the demands were already rising for us to take the election outcome to the courts, Frank told me, after we prayed, "We won't challenge."

Frank and I walked across the street and entered the hall where a mass of people had gathered, many shouting at us to challenge the vote.

Frank took the podium and spoke some of the finest words I've ever heard from a politician. "I got into this race to witness for my Lord," he said. "I have done that, and now I am throwing my support to Dr. Arrington and asking you to do the same."

It was a *kairos* moment for Frank Parsons and the city of Birmingham. No human planning could have conjured such a situation or its outcome.

Rather than plunging back into a dark night of violence and hatred, there was a new sense of healing and peace. Frank had his "entrance," and, by God's guidance, he knew when it was time for his "exit."

Time under God's control works in mysterious ways. While we cannot see all its mysteries, the Bible has raised the curtain—the meaning of "apocalypse"—for us to get sightings.

Those glimpses of the intersections of *kairos* and *kronos* show us where we are in time . . . even if it is the age of Nebuchadnezzar or Donald Trump.

FIVE

WHERE WE ARE IN TIME

You know how to interpret the weather signs in the sky, but
you don't know how to interpret the signs of the times!
—Jesus Christ, Matthew 16:3 nlt

We know that it is the last hour.
—1 John 2:18

Where are we? When will we get there?

Probably we have all asked those questions. There are two perspectives inherent in them: space (*Where?*) and time (*When?*). Only in the conjunction of the two is reality made manifest in human experience. That means it is every bit as important to know where you are in time as in space.

That was the truth Jesus spoke to the religious leaders when He noted the irony of their ability to perceive signs of spatial phenomena like the coming of a storm or clearing in the skies, but not signs indicating the approach or arrival of *kairos*-time.

Jesus' statement is like telling someone they can see the track but are unable to see the train on the track.

Centuries earlier, the Jewish exiles in Babylon asked the same questions.

They had little need to ask where they were in space. That they knew too well: they were in Nebuchadnezzar's Babylon. But they also knew the prophecy God had given prior to their captivity, and that prophetic word raised the issue of *time*. Jehoiakim had been on the throne of Judah only four years, and, in Babylon, Nebuchadnezzar II was in his first year as ruler when God spoke through Jeremiah:

> "This whole land will be a desolation and a horror, and these nations will serve the king of Babylon seventy years. Then it will be when seventy years are completed I will punish the king of Babylon and that nation," declares the LORD, "for their iniquity, and the land of the Chaldeans; and I will make it an everlasting desolation. I will bring upon that land all My words which I have pronounced against it, all that is written in this book which Jeremiah has prophesied against all the nations." (Jeremiah 25:11–13)

Decades later there was still a remnant among the captives who had not forgotten God's word that had come through Jeremiah. They would have thought about the time question often: Where are we in time relative to those seventy years, and the coming of God's judgment on Babylon and our return to Jerusalem?

Remnant people living in the fallen world of the present ask the same question: Where are we in time relative to the second coming of our Lord, and our return to Him and the New Jerusalem?

TALLADEGA JOURNEYS

On the finite level, the destination questions are mundane, especially when we are very young. All this thinking about space and time takes me back to my childhood. In 1948, when I was six-turning-seven years old, I asked those questions often, especially on what seemed, when we started out at least, interminable auto trips from Birmingham to my grandmother's house in Talladega, Alabama.

Yes, it was the same town that would become famous decades later for its huge racetrack (which did not exist in 1948) and "Talladega Nights" (which did exist in 1948, literally).

My memory of those road trips in the pre-interstate age was that of lumbering our way over two-lane highways that snaked along and around the ridges that marked the edge of the Appalachian chain in northeast Alabama. Years later, after Interstate 20 was carved into those foothills, I would marvel that the distance to Talladega from Birmingham had shrunk by at least twenty-five miles—or so it seemed to me.

But not so in 1948. Back then I would sit crunched in the rear seat, stretching my short frame to get a look at the landscape as it rolled by. Then one of my parents would start marking the towns, villages, hamlets, and special places that gave some indication of where we were in relation to our destination: "Leeds!" . . . "Moody!" . . . "Cook Springs!" . . . "Pell City!" . . . "Lincoln!" . . . "Shocco Springs!"

Those announcements told us where we were in both time and space. Expectations rose as we got closer in space and the remaining time shrunk. The place names were not only signs of physical locations, but signs of the "times." Knowing them meant knowing how much longer it would take to get to Grandmother's house, and what we should do to get ready for arrival.

The final run along Highway 77 would be promising. Pulling myself up on the back of the front seat, I could see out ahead the hills cradling the valley where Talladega sits. And I knew when we reached the outskirts of the town because my mother pulled out her hairbrush, rouge, and lipstick. After primping herself, she reached to the backseat to straighten my shirt, wipe my nose, and comb my hair.

Momma knew where we were, and that dictated her behavior. It was time to prepare to look our best when we arrived at Grandmother's little cottage perched on the rim of a ridge. She had borne nine children, and many of them would be there, ready for a reunion. We would cram into her tiny bungalow, and we children would soon be chasing each other all over those craggy slopes.

History, too, is a long journey on the road of time (or "track" as we have described it). There's an important destination for our personal lives and our nations. Judgment awaits, with its searing light, and the encounter with the Lord of History. If we are in Christ, the enormity of grace is there to throttle judgment, which will be based on our relationship to Him, and the use of the gifts He entrusted to us to bless others and point them to the Lord.

Through the Holy Spirit, Simon Peter had this in mind when he wrote, "What sort of people ought you to be in holy conduct and godliness, looking for and hastening the coming of the day of God" (2 Peter 3:11–12).

So, as soon as mother saw where we were on the road to Talladega, she got us ready, and I could feel Daddy pressing the accelerator, "hastening" our arrival.

Back in 1948, my question as to where we were relative to our destination could have been answered quickly if we could have been swept up in a helicopter and gotten a bird's-eye view. Yet there's a perspective even better than that of a bird—it's the transcendent view, seeing time and history from God's lofty position!

From that higher angle we can better understand the "two men from Babylon," others like them, and the span of history we inhabit.

"COME UP HERE"

Toward the end of the first century AD, an elderly man on the craggy Greek isle of Patmos received from God visions about human time and history. The apostle John had been exiled to the lonely place because of his unrelenting determination to continue preaching the gospel despite commands from authorities not to do so. After all, in his youth, John had actually been with Jesus Christ. He had seen Jesus heal blind people, get the lame walking, and even raise the dead. John could still remember how he had leaned on his beloved Friend's shoulder the night of the Passover meal. The scene at the cross when he had escorted Jesus' mother to the place of her son's execution had never stopped burning in his soul.

There was simply no way John, now an elderly man, would stop at this section of his life journey, no matter what the threats!

However, God had other purposes for John and his incarceration on Patmos with its slave-worked salt mines. The risen Lord would give John God's own perspective of history. The Lord of History would lift the curtain (the literal meaning of *apocalypse*) so that John could see what was really going on in the world in his time, how it fit into the past, and what would happen in the future.

Similarly, the Hebrew exiles in Babylon could comprehend their captivity best in light of God's prophecies, through Jeremiah especially. So, we can only make sense of our lives in the present "age"—be it that of Trump or any other president who has become the icon of a particular period—if we get the higher and broader view.

In Revelation, to see historical events as God does, John would have to look down from God's position above finite time. Therefore, after introductory visions that set the stage for the full view, John saw another amazing scene. He described it like this: "After these things I looked, and behold, a door standing open in heaven, and the first voice which I had heard, like the sound of a trumpet speaking with me, said, *Come up here,* and I will show you what must take place after these things'" (Revelation 4:1, emphasis added).

Decades before, John had been with Jesus and His other disciples when the Lord revealed the whole purpose of finite history as the advance of the good news of His kingdom of righteousness, justice, peace, and Spirit-given joy in the world.[1] Now, in the Revelation visions, John was about to get an eyeful.

THE LION, THE LAMB, AND THE SCROLL

At a certain point in his visions, John heard a voice like "a trumpet," inviting him to the lofty perspective of heaven itself. The aged man was told that from that position, "I will show you what must take place after these things."[2]

"Immediately," wrote John, "I was in the Spirit; and behold, a throne was standing in heaven, and One sitting on the throne" (Revelation 4:2). The spectacular scene included a rainbow enveloping the great throne, which was occupied by a Being glimmering like fine jewels, and, in a sweeping circle around the central throne, twenty-four more, on which white-robed and golden-crowned elders sat. The thrilling visuals were punctuated with powerful sounds and more incomprehensible sights: "living creatures full of eyes in front and behind" who were singing,

"HOLY, HOLY, HOLY is the LORD GOD, the ALMIGHTY, WHO WAS, AND WHO IS, AND WHO IS TO COME." (v. 8)

John watched as the twenty-four elders fell before the Great Being seated on the throne, removed their golden crowns, and cast them at His feet as they cried, "Worthy are You, our Lord and our God, to receive glory and honor and power, for You created all things, and because of Your will they existed, and were created" (v. 11).

Suddenly, John's focus was drawn to a massive scroll in the right hand of God, sealed up tightly with seven seals. An angel swooped into the scene, saying loudly, "Who is worthy to open the book and to break its seals?" (Revelation 5:2).

John was devastated as he experienced the critical moment in this vision and began to weep because "no one in heaven or on the earth or under the earth was able to open the book or look into it" (v. 3).

At last one of the elders John had seen sitting around God's throne came toward him. "Stop weeping," said the man. Then the elder told John, "Behold, the Lion that is from the tribe of Judah, the Root of David, has overcome so as to open the book and its seven seals" (v. 5).

The form of a slain lamb with seven horns and seven eyes emerged in John's vision. In the intuition of the Holy Spirit, John knew the Lamb was the Christ. Suddenly heaven overflowed with "a new song" whose words revealed that Jesus Christ Himself is the Lord of History:

> You are worthy to take the scroll,
> And to open its seals;
> For You were slain,
> And have redeemed us to God by Your blood
> Out of every tribe and tongue and people and nation,
> And have made us kings and priests to our God;
> And we shall reign on the earth. (vv. 9–10 NKJV)

John watched as the Lord began to break the seven seals, one by one, and unfurl the scroll section by section, age by age.

John was an old man when he experienced this vision of time and history. However, perhaps his mind went back to that day decades earlier when Jesus sat with him and the other disciples on the slope of the Mount of Olives and gave them a preview of the future before them and the world.

A GLIMPSE BEHIND THE "CURTAIN"

On that day, Jesus began with the immediate future the disciples and their contemporaries would experience. As we discussed earlier, Jesus and His followers had just crossed the great temple structures on their walk toward the Mount of Olives. Several of the disciples commented on the impressive magnitude of the huge stones constituting the temple and its compound. Jesus shocked them with His response. "Do you see all these buildings? I tell you the truth, they will be completely demolished. Not one stone will be left on top of another!" (Matthew 24:2 NLT).

"Tell us, when will all this happen?" they asked.

And that is another version of the question, Where are we in time?

The Lord of History gave them an apocalyptic glimpse of what lies beyond the veil of time.

As previously noted, *apocalypse* is a word referring to the lifting of a curtain. The book of Revelation is *The* Apocalypse because in those visions the "curtain" is lifted so that the whole stage of history is in view. However, on the slope of the Mount of Olives that day, Jesus gave His followers a slight peek. He began by prophesying the destruction of the temple that would occur some forty years in the future of the disciples' generation. And then Jesus lifted the veil a little higher, disclosing a quick summative view of the distant future.

In looking at what Jesus revealed that day we can also get some sense of the present: *where we are* relative to where we are destined to *go.*

Remember, we said previously that the *telos*—the end-goal, destination, purpose—of finite time and the history of the nations is the proclamation and manifestation of the kingdom of God within the whole world. Now, in a limited way, as John watched, Jesus was revealing some of what will be happening in the world's coming ages.

In Matthew 24:8, after telling of the clash of nations and the prolifer-ation of wars on a scale the disciples sitting around Him that day on the Mount of Olives could not imagine, Jesus said, "These things are merely the beginning of birth pangs."

There is the question again: "*Where are we in time?*" It was on the lips of the disciples as they scanned Jerusalem and the temple from the mount, and it is the question asked across history. The nihilists don't believe the question has any meaning at all, because history is just a series of random events bumping into one another. Henry Ford was nihilistic when he said that history is "bunk." The existentialist doesn't bother with the question, because only the present moment matters.

But everyone has a sense of the "end"—either as a termination or as a destination. Therefore, any person who thinks at all wonders when the "end" will come for them and what they care about.

LEADERS AND THE TONES OF THE TIMES

When we humans try to contemplate the passages of history in time on a strictly immanent, or horizontal, level, we often pinpoint where we have been and presently are by speaking of the "ages" of various leaders and the national (and even international) characteristics that prevail during their periods in power. National leaders set the tone and perspectives of the "ages" of their ascendancy. This is their "legacy," or mark upon history.

The Hebrew exiles who made it back to Judah would tell their descendants about the age of Nebuchadnezzar. In modern times we might say we are living in the "age of Trump."

Frequently, leaders set the tone of their age in their inaugural messages. Nebuchadnezzar said this in his initial speech: "O merciful Marduk, may the house that I have built endure forever, may I be satiated with its splendor, attain old age therein, with abundant offspring, and receive therein tribute of the kings of all regions, from all mankind."[3]

Not surprisingly the "age of Nebuchadnezzar" was all about Nebuchadnezzar, an age of servitude, conquest, and extravagance for the sake of Nebuchadnezzar.

At the very beginning of the American republic, George Washington sought to set the tone of the era, and the very nature of the nation that was being established, when, in 1789, he spoke these inaugural words, in what he called his "first official Act" as president:

My fervent supplications to that Almighty Being who rules over the Universe, who presides in the Councils of Nations, and whose providential aids can supply every human defect, that his benediction may consecrate to the liberties and happiness of the People of the United States, a Government instituted by themselves for these essential purposes: and may enable every instrument employed in its administration to execute with success, the functions allotted to his charge. In tendering this homage

TWO MEN FROM BABYLON

to the Great Author of every public and private good I assure myself that it expresses your sentiments not less than my own; nor those of my fellow-citizens at large, less than either. No People can be bound to acknowledge and adore the invisible hand, which conducts the Affairs of men more than the People of the United States.[4]

By the measure of these thoughts, Washington wanted his "age" to be one recognizing God as the source of the new nation's blessings, and the weakness of human leadership without the Lord of History. In Washington's mind, his "age" would be one of humility, confident faith, and the laying of foundations that would endure.

Donald Trump tried to define the nature of his period in power in words he spoke at his 2017 inauguration: "We, the citizens of America, are now joined in a great national effort to rebuild our country and to restore its promise for all our people . . . Together, We Will Make America Strong Again . . . Wealthy Again . . . Proud Again Safe Again . . . Great Again."[5]

In the president's mind, at least, the "age of Trump" would be one of exuberant recovery and a united effort to get back the qualities he and those who elected him believed America had lost.

The age of Trump also shows that a leader's opponents can try to define the age, and a president's historical legacy. The opposition will work passionately to characterize Trump's time in the presidency as an "age of division," or an "age of hatred." They will attempt to hang his historical legacy on his tweets and what they regard as his boorish style rather than his positive accomplishments.

THE MOST IMPORTANT "INAUGURAL"

There is one "inaugural address" and tone that stands above all others. That message characterizes the "age" of the reign of the Lord of History. Jesus Christ spoke it to a gathering of His neighbors in a synagogue in Nazareth on a certain Sabbath two thousand years ago. On that day, the Lord opened the Isaiah scroll and read:

> The Spirit of the LORD is upon Me,
> Because He has anointed Me
> To preach the gospel to the poor;
> He has sent Me to heal the brokenhearted,
> To proclaim liberty to the captives
> And recovery of sight to the blind,
> To set at liberty those who are oppressed;
> To proclaim the acceptable year of the LORD.
>
> (LUKE 4:18–19 NKJV)

Everyone looked intently and expectantly, as Jesus completed His reading and remarks, and handed back the scroll to an attendant. Jesus' commentary on that passage stunned His listeners, and quickly turned them to indignation: "Today this Scripture is fulfilled in your hearing" (v. 21 NKJV).

Jesus' pronouncements that day at Nazareth gave an indication of what the "age" of the Lord of History will look like. No rabbi had spoken like this, describing himself and the impact he would have on time and history.

The message Jesus gave revealed that the Jubilee age of the Lord of History will be one of restoration and recovery made eternal. Rather than the Old Testament Jubilee being observed only once every fifty years, the everlasting reign of the King of kings and Lord of lords will be the Jubilee continuum—the constant and endless state of things!

So, we yearn to know the answer to the big question: *Where are we in the time of the twenty-first century relative to the universal manifestation of the qualities of the coming kingdom and the eternal Jubilee described by Jesus, contained in the arrival in time and history of the New Jerusalem?*

The Jubilee age is measured on the scale of the transcendent. No human-centered "age" is in view here, whether that of a king like Nebuchadnezzar, an emperor like the caesars of Rome, a prime minister like Churchill, or a president of the United States like Trump and all the others.

The Jubilee is the "age" of the Lord of History, Jesus Christ, "Wonderful Counselor, Mighty God, Eternal Father, Prince of Peace" (Isaiah 9:6). What will the "age" look like when the "government is on His shoulders"?[6] He told us in His inaugural message. But, like His disciples more than twenty centuries ago, we are still little children on the back seat of this ride through time. Hence, we constantly ask the question the disciples posed to Jesus more than two thousand years ago: "What will be the sign of Your coming, and of the end of the age?" (Matthew 24:3).

Jesus answered them by citing certain characteristics that are markers on the journey in time to the coming into the world of the King and His kingdom. It seems the characteristics of the future the Lord described to His disciples that day on the Mount of Olives have intensified exponentially in contemporary times.

Time is pregnant with something. It is as if history is readying to open its womb and give birth.

SIX

BIRTH PANGS!

The present of the Church already lies in the new age, and yet it is still before the Parousia, and so before the actual end time. . . . It is the final time before the end.

—OSCAR CULLMANN

Imagination is a big, wide road, stretching just about everywhere.

It crosses the boundaries of time. We can travel on our imagination back into the past through memory. We can even surge into the future through imaginary speculation, though the windshield gets fogged up and we can only see "darkly," as Paul wrote in 1 Corinthians 13:12 (KJV).

The older I get, the more my mind treks back to my early teen years when I began to think about the future, and how it would look. Perhaps you've taken this journey in imagination as well. I would try envisioning what my wife would be like, along with our children, grandchildren, and great-grandchildren. I would seek a mental picture of where we would live and what I would do as a career. I have to say now that the reality has been far better than I ever could have imagined.

Then one day the happy anticipations of the future turned to dread.

It must have been around November 22, 1955. On that date Russia exploded its first hydrogen bomb. The *Birmingham News*, our local news-paper for which, years later, I would work, carried a dramatic above-the-fold photograph of a nuclear blast's mushroom cloud stretched over all eight columns.

I began to wonder—along with many other people in the Cold War age that was getting hotter—if we would have any future at all.

Looking back from the lofty perspective of sixty-four years, I am happy I did not give up. The Soviet Union imploded, there was no nuclear war, and I have traveled and spoken throughout the very land I had so feared in my late childhood and early teens. The future I tried to imagine when I was fourteen or fifteen was and continues to be more wonderful than the very best of my dreams in those days.

Nevertheless, I can understand the angst of Jesus' disciples. As we saw earlier, He had just dropped on them a banner headline in sixty-point bold type:

NOT ONE OF THESE STONES WILL BE LEFT UPON ANOTHER!

Jesus was speaking in the context of the first century, prophesying what would happen in AD 70 when the Romans ransacked Jerusalem and burned down the temple. However, as we have seen, time is linear-cyclical, with *kairos* events in one period of *kronos*-time serving as harbingers and types of happenings to occur all along the track of history. This is the meaning of the Old Testament, as its types and shadows are fulfilled in the New Testament.

Therefore, the things prophesied in Jesus' Olivet Discourse will occur again, not in exactness, but in broad similarity further down history's ride through time. Thus, the "coming of the Son of Man will be just like the days of Noah," said Jesus. Prior to the flood, people "were eating and drinking, marrying and giving in marriage, until the day that Noah entered the ark" (Matthew 24:37, 38).

Further, wars and tribulations and famines and earthquakes and spiritual delusion will spin repeatedly on the track of time, repeating and building up in intensity and speed as history approaches its goal . . . its planned destination.

In His conversation with His disciples that day about the "end times," Jesus gave more details that they—and we—can expect in the movement across time. These particulars are literal events that would appear in the lifetime of most of His apostles, but also the types of occurrences we will experience in our own age.

A big takeaway that comes from Jesus' words that day on the Mount of Olives is that all history, and the civilizations and nations that "ride the rails" of time, must be understood in the context of Christ's kingdom, and the advance in the world of its proclamation and application. From our perspective, planted at a point of observation along the track of time, the civilizations and nations seem to come and go. However, from God's transcendent perspective, He sees them as a constant no matter where they are on the "rails."

When I think of this, I remember Christmas at eighty-thousand-member Second Baptist Church of Houston, where I served for almost two decades. Every year model train enthusiasts would set up elaborate displays. Their trains would circulate around toy towns, mountains, and forests. The displays were on elevated platforms, and small children could see only that portion of the tracks level with their eyes. So, the people who constructed the model train displays built small enclosed platforms to which the little guys could climb. From that lofty view they could see the whole of the display, not just the section of the train that happened to be passing their position on the floor at a given moment.

In other words, when a child stood on the raised platform, she could see what the "big people" tall enough to see the whole were seeing.

We saw in the previous chapter the invitation of Jesus to John in the Revelation, to "come up here" so John could see time and history from God's viewpoint. *What do we see about nations and civilizations and their places in time and space when we look from that higher angle?*

NATIONS ARE CRUCIBLES

The answer begins to come in Paul's address to a group of intellectuals on Athens's Mars Hill, or Areopagus, recorded in Acts 17. We must link Paul's remarks that day to what Jesus prophesied on another mount, Olivet, years earlier, recorded in Matthew 24. Jesus had told His followers the "end," or purpose-goal-destination of time, would not come until the gospel of the kingdom had been proclaimed in the whole world to every people group on the planet. Now Paul was saying that the crucibles into which that proclamation would be poured will be made up of civilizations and the nations within them. Thus, he told the Athenian philosophers that God "made from one man every nation of mankind to live on all the face of the earth, having determined their appointed times and the boundaries of their habitation, that they would seek God" (Acts 17:26–27).

As we drill down into that Spirit-given revelation, we discover many treasures of truth. The purpose of "nations" is to provide crucibles for the proclamation and application of Christ's kingdom. The ministry of the kingdom is facilitated in shared culture and language. In this sense, a nation, with its unique styles and common language, is a region or zone where the gospel of the kingdom can be concentrated. In a sense, nations—especially in the sense of shared language—constitute a reversal of Babel, where language was confounded.

Therefore, said Paul, God has predetermined the place of civilizations both in their special eras of time (*kairos*) and spatial position. The whole purpose is that, within those places in time and space, people sharing a common experience expressed in a common language will seek God together.

Further, a nation is blessed or brings judgment on itself based on what it does with the kingdom opportunity within its *kairos*, or season of special opportunity. An axiom of history, therefore, is this: *Civilizations and the nations within them are blessed in direct ratio to the freedom they give in allowing the proclamation of the gospel of the kingdom within their borders.*

WHY SO GREATLY BLESSED?

The United States has been a greatly blessed nation because of its role during its special *kairos*-season as a base for the proclamation of the gospel of the kingdom in all the world, and also because of the remarkable freedoms its constitutional system has provided for freedom of worship, thought, and speech.

In contrast, nations that have restricted those freedoms and imposed and/or persecuted churches and others seeking to proclaim and minister the gospel of the kingdom within their borders have not enjoyed the same levels of liberty and prosperity. All nations under such restrictive policies have suffered, whether from the Right, as in the case of Fascism, or Left, in the context of extreme socialism, or Communism. Further, nations that are under regimes promoting state atheism are demonstrably more disadvantaged than those with freedom of belief and practice.

Something remarkable happened in Babylon when Nebuchadnezzar emerged from his period of insanity and withdrawal to the wilderness. The man who had ordered the Chaldeans to infuse Daniel and his friends with the pagan Babylonian worldview, and who had compelled worship of a golden idol, encountered the living God and declared that the Lord of Daniel and the Hebrews is the true God. When that leader turned his heart to God, the nation itself was blessed. Nebuchadnezzar himself described what happened:

> Now at the same time my reason returned to me; and for the glory of my kingdom, my majesty and splendor were returned to me, and my counselors and my nobles began seeking me out; so I was re-established in my kingdom, and still more greatness [than before] was added to me. Now I, Nebuchadnezzar, praise and exalt and honor the King of heaven, for all His works are true and faithful and His ways are just, and He is able to humiliate and humble those who walk in [self-centered, self-righteous] pride. (Daniel 4:36–37 AMP)

A transformed leader came out of that wilderness of humiliation. Babylon got a new king in the same body and bearing the same name, but one would bring blessing rather than terror.

In our time, the secular Left does not grasp why evangelicals and other conservative Christians have given Donald Trump strong support. They don't understand that despite his own personal moral issues, and sometimes unchristian speech and behavior, Trump nevertheless recognizes the importance of religious freedom. Intuitively, perhaps, he is conscious of the correlation between a high quality of life and a nation's granting of religious freedom through its official policies.

"We must cherish our spiritual foundation and uphold our legacy of faith," said Trump in a proclamation designating May 3, 2018, as a National Day of Prayer. But other presidents have made such statements. Was it a formality, or did Trump sincerely believe in the urgency of cherishing and upholding the spiritual values of our society?

Gary Bauer declared in 2019 that the Trump administration "has reached new levels of commitment on the fundamental right of freedom of religion that's unprecedented historically." Trump's critics say that's only because he's trying to placate and hold on to the evangelical base that helped him win the presidency.

However, the Trump administration's concern went beyond just the United States, as noted by former US senator Sam Brownback, Trump's ambassador-at-large for international religious freedom. That liberty is a "foundational right" for all humanity, said Brownback. As a senator, in 1998, Brownback sponsored the International Religious Freedom Act. Subsequent presidential administrations had neglected the bill and the issue it sought to address. "Nobody would really tend it. Then this administration comes along," said Brownback in a *Politico* interview.

So, whether, as many believe, Trump is sincere in his support for religious liberty in the United States and abroad, or merely trying to keep evangelical Christians happy, the way Donald Trump sees it, religious freedom is crucial to making America "great again."[1]

STANDARD OF MEASUREMENT

Whether Donald Trump understands it or not, the standard for measuring American "transformation" or "rebuilding" the nation, leading to making it "great again," is the nation's kingdom mission discussed in chapter 3. Donald Trump is no theologian and perhaps could not elaborate on the doctrine of Christ's kingdom. However, in his 2017 inaugural speech, the new president did emphasize the importance of the nation's spiritual DNA. "We do not seek to impose our way of life on anyone," said Trump, "but rather shine as an example for everyone to follow." In that last phrase, Trump brought to mind the "city on a hill" vision articulated first by Governor John Winthrop in 1630 and quoted by other presidents, including John F. Kennedy and Ronald Reagan.

There is an important caution here regarding using the "city on a hill" phrase too casually. If it is spoken merely in a materialistic context (e.g., referring to the nation's enviable wealth), then the term is misused. Winthrop's life and writings reveal that he was taking the statement directly from the Scripture (Matthew 5:14) and was speaking in the context of God's kingdom, and the blessings inherent in any system that applies the principles of the kingdom as foundational and takes the kingdom mission seriously.

How shall we describe our era? We must return to the Olivet Discourse, and the descriptions Jesus Himself gave. "All these things" happening in the era of the first century were merely "the *beginning* of birth pangs," Jesus told His disciples (emphasis added). This means that the age we inhabit is the "age of birth pangs." What, then, can we expect? Jesus prophetically laid it out for us even as He instructed His disciples on that day more than twenty centuries ago.

THE AGE OF BIRTH PANGS IS AN AGE OF FALSE "CHRISTS" (MATTHEW 24:4–5)

In the world of Jesus' first disciples, there were several noted pretenders to the Messiah role. There was Theudas, sometimes identified as Barabbas, mentioned both in Acts and the history of Flavius Josephus.[2] Theudas died, and failed to rise again, but up popped Judas of Galilee with the claim of messiahship (Acts 5:37). One of the big celebrities vying to be Lord of History in the period of the twelve apostles was Simon the Sorcerer. Another, Elymas, tried to face down Jesus' men, and turn them away from Him to himself. The apostles, however, were still radiant with the resurrection, and could not be turned (Acts 13:6–10).

It seems that in the history of spiritual "Babylon," false messiahs spring forth all along the track of time. That should not surprise us. The literal Babylon, founded by Nimrod and brought to its apex by Nebuchadnezzar, was the empire of human messianism. Nebuchadnezzar himself was the embodiment of the period. He would be the new messiah who would build the world's greatest and most dominant kingdom. The spirit of his ancestors, the Babel-builders, bubbled in his bosom. They wanted to raise a structure that would reach God Himself and in doing so show their own greatness.

In the process, of course, Nebuchadnezzar became a drooling crazy man, but in that insanity he found the true God and his own personal identity in relation to that God.

May it be so in the age of Trump—and Clinton, and Biden, and Sanders, and Warren, and all the rest from all the parties!

America in the age of Trump could fall into the "false Christ" trap if the president's aim to "Make America Great Again" is founded upon humans and their capacities and forgets God, as we discuss in more detail in another chapter. And the secular socialist paradises offered up by his opponents have already proven to be failed states.

"Christs" proliferate in contemporary society. There are many who have a "messiah complex." They offer new kingdoms in the place of that of the real Christ. Messianic utopianism surges on the left and right.

The twentieth century saw the rise of Karl Marx and Communism on the left, and Hitler, Mussolini, Nazism, and Fascism on the right. The twenty-first century in the West has been fertile ground for the emergence of secular progressivist socialism, which has produced *dystopia* more than utopia. According to a 2010 Gallup Poll, 68 percent of people eighteen to twenty-nine years old favored socialism.

Populist politicians on both ends of the political spectrum present themselves as the leaders who will bring in the "kingdom"—from Andrew Jackson to Theodore Roosevelt to Huey Long in Louisiana and George Wallace in Alabama, to name a few.

Trump must be especially careful here. People who think about political philosophy would more likely characterize him as a populist rather than a classical conservative. With God, Trump's MAGA vision can be a great blessing to the world, but without God, MAGA, as we discuss in chapter 12, will be just one more populist tower of Babel leading to greater statist control and politicians who think they are the incarnation of Babylon-building Nebuchadnezzar, if not God Himself.

However, the primary "false Christ" of the twenty-first century is perhaps more ominous than any of the others. Human beings are "hardwired" by their Creator for transcendence. If we don't acknowledge and embrace true transcendence that is God's alone, then we begin worshipping the objects of our own making. In ancient times these objects of worship were the idols crafted by humans. In the twenty-first century, the "gods" are also of human manufacture: *artificial intelligence*.

Today's "secular deities" are "degraded" substitutes for God, said Jakub Bozydar Wisniewski. Sadly, these inadequate idols are "acceptable enough for so-called modern man," whose "spiritual appetite seems satisfied with what is apparently greater than himself, but is also fully reducible to his petty limitations." The idols produced in the human "god factories" provide "the kind of spiritual satisfaction that in no way interferes with (the person's) pursuit of other, more unreflectively appealing, quintessentially earthly kinds of satisfaction, such as that afforded by sensuous entertainment and technological comfort," wrote Wisniewski.[3]

Former Google and Uber engineer Anthony Levandowski predicts that at some point, an artificial intelligence machine will have and be able to process so much data that people will call it "god." Levandowski believes this so passionately he has formed an AI "church" called "The Way of the Future." Its mission "is about creating a peaceful and respectful transition of who is in charge of the planet from people to people + machines."

The AI church's founder has no doubt about the inevitability of artificial intelligence being "in charge." It's only a matter of time. Thus, humanity "should think about how 'machines' will integrate into society (and even have a path to being in charge as they become smarter and smarter) so that this whole process can be amicable and not confrontational."

"The rise of the authoritarian machine seems 'not too distant,'" said Chris Matyszczyk in writing about Levandowski's vision.[4]

There is an ominous element in Levandowski's thought. "We believe it may be important for machines to see who is friendly to their cause and who is not," he said. This will necessitate an Orwellian monitoring system. Levandowski's plan includes "keeping track of who has done what (and for how long) to help the peaceful and respectful transition" from human dominion to AI being "in charge."

Such predictions highlight the foreboding nature of the age of birth pangs.

THE AGE OF BIRTH PANGS IS AN AGE OF WARS AND RUMORS OF WARS (MATTHEW 24:6)

The twentieth century was the bloodiest in history. Jonathan Glover, a moral philosopher who is director of the Center of Medical Law and Ethics at London's King's College, has chronicled the carnage. Some 86 million perished in conflicts ranging from 1900 to 1989, or 2,500 per day, or 100 per hour.[5]

The twenty-first century portends to be an era of war and its carnage. Here's a sampling as I write in late 2019:[6]

- Syria—Between 30,000 and 52,000 have died since its intensification in 2011.

- Afghanistan—Almost 150,000 have perished since 1978 in this apparently never-ending conflict.
- Iraq—Nearly a half million humans have lost their lives since 2003 in what was once Nebuchadnezzar's empire.
- Pakistan—A state of permawar seems to prevail in this nation because of conflict between the government and insurgencies, resulting in more than 20,000 deaths since 2007.
- Sudan—More than 50,000 people have died in the ongoing civil war since 1983.
- Somalia—Struggles for national power since 1982 have resulted in more than 26,000 deaths.

The list of current wars grows rapidly—at times, exponentially. Each conflict is like a spark in a dry California forest, igniting more blazes. For example, according to *The Black Book of Communism*, more than ninety million have died under that system from the twentieth century into the twenty-first. Despite the contemporary support for Marxist socialism in the West, especially among millennials, Communism remains a deadly philosophy.

Jesus' next statement in Matthew 24 describes an important distinct characteristic of the contemporary world.

THE AGE OF BIRTH PANGS IS AN AGE OF "PEOPLE GROUP" AGAINST "PEOPLE GROUP" (MATTHEW 24:7)

In Matthew 24:7, Jesus prophesied that "nation will rise against nation," as well as "kingdom against kingdom." The Greek original reads "*ethnos* against *ethnos*," and "*basileia* against *basileia*." *Ethnos* literally means a "people group."[7] *Basileia* refers to a territory under a king or national leader.[8]

Therefore, Jesus was saying that in future ages wars would be fought primarily by ethnic groups residing in a particular jurisdictional territory against other people groups who live in another jurisdictional territory.

This is a stunning revelation considering the nature of war in the contemporary world.

In 1993, Harvard professor Samuel Huntington published an article in *Foreign Affairs* magazine that predicted what conflicts would look like in the twenty-first century. Huntington's article went on to become an important book, shedding new light on the developing nature of warfare. Huntington wrote:

> It is my hypothesis that the fundamental source of conflict in this new [post-Cold-War] world will not be primarily ideological or primarily economic. The great divisions among humankind and the dominating source of conflict will be cultural. Nation states will remain the most powerful actors in world affairs, but the principal conflicts of global politics will occur between nations and groups of different civilizations. The clash of civilizations will dominate global politics. The fault lines between civilizations will be the battle lines of the future.[9]

Traditional wars have been fought between geopolitical units known as "nations," but the conflicts Huntington predicted for the twenty-first century are between people groups holding to a particular type of worldview and culture. Religion is at the core of worldview formation; hence, it should be no surprise that the world's most threatening conflict as I write is between Islamic civilization and that of the Judeo-Christian West.

THE AGE OF BIRTH PANGS IS AN AGE OF TRIBULATION, PERSECUTION, AND HATRED OF CHRIST'S PEOPLE (MATTHEW 24:9)

In AD 70, the vast fist of Rome struck back at Jerusalem and the Jews for their attempt at rebellion against the empire.

Nebuchadnezzar's dream centuries before, interpreted by Daniel, had revealed the sequence of imperial powers that would ride on the track of time: Babylon would be overwhelmed by Persia, the Persian Empire would give way to Greece, and Greece would be displaced by Rome.

These were not only literal empires historically but the four basic types of imperial domination that would rise sequentially in history:

- Babylon, empire of human messianic dominance
- Persia, empire of military dominance
- Greece, empire of cultural dominance
- Rome, empire of elitist dominance

In AD 66, as Jesus had prophesied three decades earlier, Judah was fed up with Rome's elitist control of its society and became the firebrand of revolution seeking Rome's defeat and expulsion. After all, Judah was the "lion," set apart to bear the "scepter" (Genesis 49:10). Little skirmishes here and there linked like an oil-driven fire racing through a dry forest, until the rebellion became widespread. The Romans were driven out of Jerusalem. A revolutionary government was established in the place of Roman rule.

The emperor Vespasian had to do something, so he dispatched his warrior-son, Titus, to crush the rebellion. He did so with the fury Jesus had predicted on the Mount of Olives that day years before. Jerusalem went down on August 29—the ninth of Av on the Jewish calendar—in AD 70. Bodies were scattered everywhere as the slaughter by Titus's Roman soldiers spread through the city.

Flavius Josephus, a Jewish historian who initially had been a leader of the rebellion before coming over to Rome's side, was an eyewitness to the carnage. He wrote:

Most of the slain were peaceful citizens, weak and unarmed, and they were butchered where they were caught. The heap of corpses mounted higher and higher above the altar; a stream of blood flowed down the Temple's steps, and the bodies of those slain at the top slipped to the bottom. . . .

While the Temple was ablaze, the attackers plundered it, and countless people who were caught by them were slaughtered. There was no pity for age and no regard was accorded rank; children and old men, laymen and priests, alike were butchered; every class was pursued and crushed in the grip of war, whether they cried out for mercy or offered resistance.[10]

The spirit of Nebuchadnezzar at its worst was manifest that day. In years to come, Simon Peter, remembering the excesses of Rome, would call it "Babylon." As we noted earlier, in Revelation, Babylon becomes the symbol of the world system seeking to organize and impose itself without God and in defiance of the Lord of History.

Nebuchadnezzar is alive and well wherever there is oppression and the attempt to stifle the worship of the Lord of History.

Today, by some accounts, one out of every nine followers of Jesus globally suffers literal persecution in the form of death, imprisonment, or exile from society. That's 245 million people.[11] In China, as I write, that persecution extends to many religious groups. However, Christians are primary targets in the very lands from which their faith developed and spread throughout the world. According to a report from the bishop of Truro regarding persecution of Christians today in the Middle East, there seems to be an attempt at genocide.[12] "Christians constitute by far the most persecuted religion."[13]

In Europe and the United States, the persecution is more ideological than physical. For example, the constitutional free speech provision is under assault. A process is under way especially to cut off the prophetic voice, leading to mounting opposition: from marginalization to caricaturization to vilification to criminalization to elimination.

At present, there is still some restraint in the form of laws that hold back the intensity of persecution. However, as that "restrainer" increasingly is removed, there is a corresponding incremental increase in persecution (see 2 Thessalonians 2).

Michael Brown, a Jewish believer in Christ, broadcaster, and columnist, says the hatred today, among other things, is a result of the culture wars.

"Bible-believing Christians are commonly compared to ISIS, accused of wanting to establish a Taliban-type theocracy, and called bigots and haters and Nazis," Brown said.

But another cause of animosity against conservative Christians is their identification with Donald Trump, since 80 percent of evangelicals, along with slightly more than half of US Catholics, voted for him. So, in the eyes of Christian-haters, it is "as if we are responsible for (or in support of) every statement he makes and every stand he takes . . . as they despise him, they also despise us."[14]

"Only 3 in 10 American adults hold 'positive' perception of evangelicals," said a *Christian Post* headline on a story reporting results of a Barna research project. The political relationship between evangelicals and Trump seems to be the reason for the negative perception of evangelicals. This puts "the future of American evangelicalism in a precarious spot," the Barna report said.[15]

THE AGE OF BIRTH PANGS IS AN AGE OF INTERNAL BETRAYAL AND HATRED (MATTHEW 24:10)

Some of the hatred of biblical Christians comes from inside the church itself. Deep schisms began to open between conservatives and liberals theologically in the 1960s. That period was one of upheaval and redefinition. The cultural divide that is now so deep began ripping with a new intensity in that age.

Roger Kimball wrote one of the most penetrating analyses of the 1960s, a decade he summarized like this: "We owe to the 1960s the ultimate institutionalization of immoralist radicalism: the institutionalization of drugs, pseudo-spirituality, promiscuous sex, virulent anti-Americanism, naïve anti-capitalism, and the precipitous decline of artistic and intellectual standards."[16]

"Pseudo-spirituality" was also manifest in churches as theology separated itself from the moorings of biblical faith. Two interviews I had as a young reporter in 1968 revealed something of the spirit of the age.

The first of those interviews was with Thomas Altizer, the leading proponent in that period for "God Is Dead" theology. What shocked me even more than Altizer's refurbishing of an idea first surfaced by Nietzsche in the nineteenth century was the fact that Altizer was on the faculty of Emory University, a school identifying itself as Methodist Christian. Methodism arose from the ministry of John Wesley, the eighteenth-century evangelist who was one of the most passionate believers of all times, a man solid in the faith.

But Altizer and Emory seemed to have constituted the anti-Wesley. They became in the 1960s a primary example of abandonment of the strong biblical view that Wesley carried and that carried him throughout his life and ministry.

The debate over biblical inspiration and authority would spread into the decades to follow, rocking even the nation's largest evangelical denomination, the Southern Baptist Convention. From the perspective of my childhood and youth, that sturdy ship seemed unsinkable. However, by the 1990s cracks had appeared in the hull, and there were important rifts centered on the debate about the inspiration of the Bible.

The establishment within Emory's denomination was already embracing the theological new waves. The storm would burst in 2018–2019 with the Methodist establishment's embrace of the homosexual agenda, including same-sex marriage. Many who held to a strong view of the Bible realized they would have to leave the denomination.

Altizer's ideas led to a loss of emphasis on God's "high and lifted up" transcendence. In fact, as I understood it, it was the *transcendent* God who had "died." Altizer told me he was not referring to a literal death but a withdrawal to such an extent that it *seemed* God was dead. That theology met the spiritual tastes of many supporters of the newly emerging 1960s theology.

Liberal theologians like New Jersey Episcopal bishop John Spong were buttressed in their attempts to question and deny parts of the Bible, if not the whole. Bishop Spong advanced the notion that Paul and Timothy were in a homosexual relationship. He also argued that the virgin birth didn't happen, and neither did Jesus' miracles or resurrection. In the late twentieth century, a group of liberal scholars calling themselves the Jesus Seminar would meet annually to discuss and try to decide which of Jesus' sayings in the New Testament were authentic and which were not.

Then there were the spiritual adventurers who found new justification for syncretism, blending the Bible with New Age thought and "positive thinking" confessionalism.

Norman Vincent Peale, the Trump family pastor in Donald Trump's youth, was a primary example of the new theologies. In fact, Peale's theology might explain some of Trump's beliefs and practices that worry some evangelicals. In 1984, Peale appeared on *The Phil Donahue Show*. There, Peale seemed to espouse universalism, the belief that all paths lead to God and that eventually everyone will be saved.

Peale's insistence was so strong that it shocked Donahue. "But you're a Christian minister," the stunned TV host said. "You're supposed to tell me that Christ is the way and the truth and the life, aren't you?"

"Christ is one of the ways," Peale replied. "God is everywhere."[17]

Ultimately theological arrogance and factionalism would set in. People on both sides who felt they held the theological high ground would begin to hold their opponents in contempt. Theological wars broke out in denominations, movements, and local churches, as Jesus had prophesied would be characteristic of the "birth pangs" age.

The other eye-opening interview I had in 1968 was with California Episcopal bishop James Pike. Though he is celebrated today by theological liberals and the Left, he was controversial in the latter twentieth century. The Episcopal House of Bishops ultimately censured Pike, declaring, "His writing and speaking on profound realities with which Christian faith and worship are concerned are too often marred by caricatures of treasured symbols and at the worst, by cheap vulgarizations of great expressions of the faith."[18]

I met Pike in Augusta, Georgia, where the House of Bishops had gathered for one of its periodic meetings. Pike and I sat in a small room, eyeball to eyeball. By that time Pike had dived into occultism, spurred on by a desire to communicate through séance with his son, who had died by suicide in 1966.

I can still see the stirring intensity in Pike as he described practices in spiritualism strongly condemned in the Bible, especially in Deuteronomy 18. I was not deep in biblical faith in those days and did not consider that Pike's experiences might have come from the dark side. With his third wife, Diane—a spiritualist—Pike would write a book on the topic, *The Other Side: An Account of My Experience with Psychic Phenomena*.

Pike died in the blistering *wadis* of the Dead Sea wilderness after getting lost while on a trip to Israel in 1969, seeking to explore the area of Christ's temptations.

THE AGE OF BIRTH PANGS IS AN AGE OF FALSE PROPHETS (MATTHEW 24:11)

The false prophet issue was such a problem in the first century that Jesus addressed it in the Sermon on the Mount, telling His followers, "Beware of the false prophets, who come to you in sheep's clothing, but inwardly are ravenous wolves" (Matthew 7:15).

Simon Peter also warned about the false prophets proliferating in the ancient world and said they "will secretly introduce destructive heresies" (2 Peter 2:1). John wrote that there were "many false prophets . . . gone out into the world," driven by "the spirit of the antichrist" (1 John 4:1–3).

John's criteria for recognizing false prophets was belief in the incarnation, the coming of Jesus Christ "in the flesh." In John's time there were false prophets who believed that Jesus was a great teacher or a flashy miracle worker, but not the promised Messiah. This, as C. S. Lewis pointed out, is logically impossible, since Jesus Himself asserted His oneness with the

Father. "There is no half-way house and there is no parallel in other religions," said Lewis. The great British writer was blunt when he wrote:

> I am trying here to prevent anyone saying the really foolish thing that people often say about Him [that is, Christ]: "I'm ready to accept Jesus as a great moral teacher, but I don't accept His claim to be God." That is the one thing we must not say. A man who was merely a man and said the sort of things Jesus said would not be a great moral teacher. He would either be a lunatic—on a level with the man who says he is a poached egg—or else he would be the Devil of Hell. You must make your choice. Either this man was, and is, the Son of God: or else a madman or something worse. . . . You can shut Him up for a fool, you can spit at Him and kill Him as a demon; or you can fall at His feet and call Him Lord and God. But let us not come up with any patronising nonsense about His being a great human teacher. He has not left that open to us. He did not intend to.[19]

Tim Challies, a Canadian writer, said that the history of Christ's church "is inseparable from the history of Satan's attempts to destroy her." Challies lists seven types of destructive false voices in contemporary Christianity:[20]

- **The Heretic:** This is the person who teaches what blatantly contradicts an essential teaching of the Christian faith. He is a gregarious figure, a natural leader teaching just enough truth to mask his deadly error. Yet in denying the faith and celebrating what is false, he leads his followers from the safety of orthodoxy to the peril of heresy.
- **The Charlatan:** This type "uses Christianity as a means of personal enrichment."
- **The Prophet:** Such a man or woman claims to be gifted by God to speak fresh revelation outside of Scripture—"new, authoritative words of prediction, teaching, rebuke, or encouragement" but actually "empowered by Satan."

- **The Abuser:** This individual uses his or her leadership position "to take advantage of other people."
- **The Divider:** This person "uses false doctrine to disrupt or destroy a church."
- **The Tickler:** This false leader "cares nothing for what God wants and everything for what men want. He is the man-pleaser rather than the God-pleaser."
- **The Speculator:** This man or woman is "obsessed with novelty, originality, or speculation."

But the false prophets proliferating today aren't limited to churches. The role of the prophet is to be both a "foreteller" and a "forthteller." The "fore-telling" ability comes as God gives direct revelation as to what will happen in the future, and the prophet gives warning, encouragement and hope, and/or guidance regarding preparation for what's ahead. Prophetic "foretelling" may also come through prophets who have been unusually gifted by the Holy Spirit to discern trends and events and predict outcomes.

The "forthtelling" function of prophetic ministry is proclamation. The prophet will declare God's message emerging from and related to historical events. Prophetic people will not give merely messages of comfort, but they will also call for repentance, helping individuals and societies connect the dots between causes and consequences.

There is a correlation between the darkness of a nation and the rising of the prophets within it. The principle is given throughout the history of Israel, especially in Isaiah 9:2. While the prophetic pronouncement applies to the Jewish nation in its immediate and mid-range future, the principle holds across time:

> The people who walk in darkness
> Will see a great light;
> Those who live in a dark land,
> The light will shine on them.

This especially applies to countries founded on the basis of a covenant with God. Old Testament Israel is the number one example of a covenant nation. But, as we saw in chapter 2, the United States and other countries that arose from a Judeo-Christian worldview sought covenant with God. From John Winthrop in 1630 to 1776 and Thomas Jefferson's Preamble to the Declaration of Independence; to 1789 and George Washington's declarations in his inaugural speech; to 1863 when Abraham Lincoln, with Congress, summoned the nation to repentance before the Lord of History; to June 6, 1944, when President Franklin Delano Roosevelt led the nation in prayer via radio as the Allies stormed Normandy beaches against Hitler; to 1984 and Ronald Reagan's warning that if the United States ever forgets that "we are one nation under God, then we will be a nation gone under," America's heart at its best has throbbed with the sense of a special relationship with the Lord of History.

Certainly, there is danger there. Without proper biblical balance, such a belief could lead to a civil religion—the worship of the nation and its leader, as in the days of Nebuchadnezzar in Babylon—or the warped tendency to claim every action is ordained by God, be it in domestic policy, international relations, or military decisions.

Nevertheless, at America's very beginnings, the Founders looked to the Lord of History and sought to submit the nation to Him. There was a consensus that prevailed up to the 1960s that the United States was founded through the biblically revealed Judeo-Christian worldview. Even skeptics like Ben Franklin recognized it when he spoke of the refreshing atmosphere of the era of the First Great Awakening and, on another critical occasion in Philadelphia, supported a call for prayer when the Constitutional Convention seemed deadlocked.

Though the possibilities of distortion are there, Ronald Reagan was right. We are living in an age when we seem to be "going under." This is the inference behind Donald Trump's vision to "Make America Great Again." But it also drove an early 2019 campaign theme proclaimed by Joe Biden that he wanted to take America back to the way it used to be—before Trump.[21]

The remarkable and *exceptional* blessings on our nation have come from its relationship with God, but that also carries a greater accountability. As the country and its civilization veer away from God and move deeper into darkness spiritually, philosophically, legislatively, God in His goodness sends the prophets to sound a warning and guide the nation back to Him. At the same time powerful people and their movements try to silence the prophetic voice.

TRAIN FROM SKAGWAY

Irene and I once took a fascinating train ride from Skagway, Alaska, into the White Pass and Yukon region that had experienced a massive gold rush in 1898. As the antique train chugged up through the mountains, the guide alerted us that we were going to see a fascinating old cantilever bridge. Going up, we finally spotted its ruins off to the left. Girders still stretched and crossed, and the rails atop the bridge were still there. However, a closer look showed that there were many places where the support structures had fallen. It was a chilling thought to imagine the train we were on making a wrong turn and winding up on that bridge, only to plunge into the gorge below as the bridge collapsed.

Thankfully the route angled away to a newer bridge, sturdy enough to carry the train's weight.

So it is that when the "train" of a nation, riding the tracks of time nears a dangerous passage, God sends prophets to shout: "This route is dangerous! Follow my signals to the safe route!" How foolish would an engineer on the White Pass train journey be to ignore the warnings of the failed bridge ahead. What a blessing to have guides to show the way to the safe and sturdy crossing.

But what if the prophet-guides give mixed warnings and confused directions? One shouts, "Turn right!" Another cries, "Go left immediately!" Yet another says, "Steer straight ahead!"

How do we know which is right? There must be some standard that will help us know which way to go.

In some ways this was the challenge before Joshua as he sought to lead the Hebrews into the promised land, where they would establish a new nation. Many were the voices thundering on his ears to turn this way or that. Joshua appealed to the Lord of History for guidance, and God pointed the way by and through His Word to the young man. And then the Lord instructed Joshua:

> Only be strong and very courageous; be careful to do according to all the law which Moses My servant commanded you; *do not turn from it to the right or to the left,* so that you may have success wherever you go. This book of the law shall not depart from your mouth, but you shall meditate on it day and night, so that you may be careful to do according to all that is written in it; for then you will make your way prosperous, and then you will have success. (Joshua 1:7–8, emphasis added)

No, America is not the new Israel, but the Lord of History laid down principles for Joshua that would bless all countries if they took them seriously. Nor is the "left" or "right" of our times the same in detail as they were in Joshua's, when they referred to the choice of literal paths by which he could have led the Hebrews. Yet "right" and "left" in our day refer to spiritual and philosophical paths, both of which would lead the United States off course.

America has no shortage of soothsayers, would-be prophets, analysts, and prognosticators. There are tens of thousands who, in somber voice or print, try to tell us what is really happening, what we should do, and whether we should go right or left. Their grave countenances stare at us Big Brother–like from TV screens. Attempting to sound like wizened sages, their ponderous tones tell us how to think, what is really happening according to them, and who the good guys and bad guys are. For most of the establishment media nowadays, there is no doubt that Donald Trump is the "baddest" of the bad guys.

The other side has its own oracles, many screeching about falling skies, the end of the world, and certain doom. By their standards of reportage and opinion, if it bleeds it leads, and that includes the body politic.

There is much more we can learn about the age of birth pangs through Jesus' talk with His disciples that day on the Mount of Olives—so much it would require another book on that one theme. So here's a summary of the times in which we live and the future just ahead for us. These synonyms seek to capture Jesus' characterizations and prophecies concerning the birth pangs period:

Age of Anxiety

There is much to fear in "Babylonian" societies that have lost their vision of the kingdom of God and their own route to destiny, while tribulation seems to loom on the horizon.

Age of Antinomianism

Lawlessness abounds where the transcendent absolute is denied and only the law of self sets the boundaries of behavior.

Age of Aggression

In worlds that have spurned the highest love and replaced it with intense desire, violence becomes a treasured instrument for conquest.

Age of Anticipation

People sense there are changes ahead and try to anticipate what impact they will have, but without the promised kingdom, dread more than eager hopefulness rises in national psyches.

Age of Advantage

The many who believe they are the entitled few, the advantaged elite, slide easily from anticipation to expectation.

Age of the Amoral

Classifications based on morality versus immorality are meaningless with the loss of the sense of the kingdom's transcendent truth, and the amorality of "anything goes" becomes the "new morality."

Age of Agony

Brutality is a daily occurrence, not only in back alleys but in churches, schools, and other public places; and the wails of mothers of children who have died in their classrooms is as loud as the weeping of Rachel brought on by Herod's cruelties.

Age of Exponential Acceleration

Change is happening so fast—especially in the information sector—that the new bursts upon us before we can assimilate the old.

Age of Delusionary Apparitions

Sensationalism rocks the foundations of lives that were once anchored in reality . . . UFOs, occultism, and religions that give the delusion that the worshipper is also the object of worship ensnare multitudes.

Age of the Artificial

Artificial intelligence races across the networks, artificial lovers feign what was once passionate romance, and Alexa and Siri are the twin goddesses to whom many bring their petitions.

Age of Coarse Awfulness

From first graders to the president of the United States, coarseness pervades the kingdom-less culture, shocking the small fraction of the population that can still be shocked, but hardly noticed by the indifferent mass.

Age of Irreverent Awelessness

The wonder has gone out of a world in which a CGI dash across a movie-screen galaxy is more a marvel than the actual galaxy itself.

Age of the Asundering

Fragmentation and division intensify between races, genders, classes, and generational groups, leading to a breakdown of unity and a weakened society.

Age of Accusation

The loss of the sense of personal responsibility and the notion of individual sin necessitates the pointing finger transferring blame to someone else.

Age of Antipathy

Hatred is a vogue word in a culture that views any challengers to one's lifestyle choices as evil opponents rather than considering the possibility they might be right.

Age of Apathy

Caring is too costly, robbing one of precious time to focus on the idolatry of self to the exclusion of the irritating other.

THE POSITIVE

Rather than leaving our brief look at the age in which we live here on a list that includes many negatives, let's focus for a moment on a positive feature of the birth pangs age, contained in Jesus' words in Matthew 24:14, which describe the whole goal of time and history: *"This gospel of the kingdom shall be preached in the whole world as a testimony to all the nations, and then the end will come"* (emphasis added).

The best news about the age of birth pangs is that it is a period of the proclamation of the gospel of the kingdom—the lordship of Jesus Christ for individuals, their nations, civilizations, and the whole world—on an exponential scale.

If anyone can speak accurately regarding the exponential expansion of the gospel of Christ, it is evangelist David Stockwell. Now in his seventies, Stockwell began evangelistic preaching at age seventeen. He has a brilliant mind, graduating from Houston's prestigious Rice University—which he attended on a scholarship—with a degree in behavioral science. He is a scholar of the primary biblical languages—Hebrew and Greek. Stockwell has spent his entire career as an evangelist and now focuses on equipping leaders for evangelism across the world.

He reports that what he is experiencing now is unlike anything he has seen in his decades of ministry. "We are living in the most bountiful harvest of souls in all of history," said Stockwell. "More people are coming to Jesus Christ as Lord and Savior than ever before as God is moving in power and glory throughout the nations."

Several mission groups monitor statistics that reflect what Stockwell is observing in his international ministry:[22]

- Campus Crusade (Cru) reports that *The Jesus Film*, which presents the life and ministry of Christ, and leads viewers to a moment of decision, has been translated and shown in about a thousand languages, with 200 million worldwide indicating decisions to receive Christ as Savior.
- According to another global missions organization, Vision 2020, there were 360 non-believers for every committed Christian in AD 100, but now that gap has shrunk to only seven to every believer.
- Vision 2020 also reports that in Africa 20,000 people accept Christ daily. Further, in 1900 only 3 percent of Africans were Christian, but in the twenty-first century the number is now 50 percent.
- The Open Doors ministry notes that there are 60 to 80 million followers of Christ in China, despite intense efforts by the Communist government and its official policy of state atheism to stamp out Christianity there.

- There was no Protestant church in South Korea in 1900, but now the country is 30 percent Christian, and there are 7,000 churches in Seoul alone, among them some of the largest in the world, according to Vision 2020.
- Asia Access has found that daily in the countries they serve 50,000 Asians turn to Christ.

Jesus' prophecy about the "gospel of the kingdom" being preached globally probably stretched the disciples' faith that day on the Mount of Olives. They could not image the extent of the world and how it would be possible that a movement that had begun in a small country in backward places, among what the Roman oppressors regarded as nobodies, could reach into the whole world.

The good news in our time is that the *good news* is spreading globally, just as Jesus said it would.

SOMETHING WONDERFUL IS COMING

The bad news about the age of birth pangs is tribulation and suffering. The good news is that it is the precursor of the birth of something new and wonderful. As any human mother will attest, the more intense the "pangs," the closer is the birth.

We have used several metaphors for "time," but here we see a beautiful image: time as the "mother" in whose womb lies the future. Conception occurred when the literal seed of the infinite Messiah was sown into the womb of a finite woman living in a particular spatial location that fulfilled the prophecy of Micah 5:1–2 and in a temporal location that aligned with "the fullness of time" (Galatians 4:4).

The big question people ask when a woman is pregnant is this: "How far along is the pregnancy?" This is the hottest query regarding time in the birth pangs era. *If time is pregnant, how far along is the pregnancy?*

Two Bible texts answer the question.

Acts 2 tells of the day of pentecost when Jesus' followers, gathered in an "upper room," were suddenly ignited by the Holy Spirit. In that moment, Christ's church came into being.

Striking things happened in that pentecost event, and a crowd came to see. Simon Peter told them that "this is what was spoken of through the prophet Joel." The Old Testament prophet had declared that "in the last days" God would pour out His Holy Spirit "on all mankind." A representative group of "all humanity" was in that room when the Holy Spirit came down. This is why flaming tongues rested on the disciples' heads, and "each one" of the people who spoke languages foreign to that spoken in Israel "was hearing them speak in his own language."

What is crucial here regarding our location in time are the words written down by Joel as much as nine hundred years before the pentecost event: *"In the last days . . ."* Therefore, the "last days" have begun, as indicated by the fulfillment of the Joel prophecy in the Upper Room on the day of pentecost nine centuries later.

The other scripture that indicates where we are relative to the "birth" to which the "pangs" lead is found in 1 Corinthians 10. There, under the inspiration of the Holy Spirit, the apostle Paul wrote of the experience of Moses and Hebrews during the exodus in the wastes of Sinai. Paul said to the Corinthian church (and to all the church across time): "Now these things happened to them as an example, and they were written for our instruction, upon whom *the ends of the ages have come*" (vv. 10–11, emphasis added).

Therefore, if the Corinthians two thousand years ago were living in the "ends of the ages," that means that stage of the "pregnancy" of time had started at some previous point. In his penetrating study *Christ and Time*, Oscar Cullmann said the "Christ event" (His first coming, incarnational ministry, atonement, resurrection, and ascension) is the "mid-point" of time and history. What follows that is the latter period, whose starting point is marked on the day of pentecost.

The age of birth pangs is therefore the latter part of the "pregnancy."

Counting the birth of our two children, six grandchildren, and four great-grandchildren, my wife and I have observed twelve pregnancies in our family. We know the markers of the various stages. We have experienced the excitement when it was obvious that we were in the last stage of those pregnancies and began to anticipate the birth that would soon come.

At the climax of the pregnancy of time, here's what is coming into the world:

- The New King
- The New Cosmos
- The New Heavens
- The New Earth
- The New Kingdom
- The New Person

In other words, what is coming is the fulfillment of the plan of the ages the Creator-God had in mind originally when He brought it all into being!

Nations play a big role in that plan. They are crucial, in fact. Therefore, God raises up through His permissive or intentional will the leadership of those nations, according to His plan for the manifestation of His kingdom in the world. The principle, as we have seen, is revealed in Exodus 9:16 and repeated by Paul in Romans 9:17, when the apostle reminded his readers of God's word to Pharaoh through Moses: "For this very purpose I have raised you up, to demonstrate My power in you, and that My name might be proclaimed throughout the whole earth."

And so, centuries later, Ronald Reagan, along with Pope John Paul II, believed that "the Divine Plan applied to nations, and not just individuals."[23] Since the nations are so crucial in the birth pangs era, what kind of national leadership does God either directly place in power, or permit to lead in His sovereignty over history? These national leaders, like Nebuchadnezzar, Trump, and all the others, become the faces of their periods in power. They embody their "age" in time.

The Bible is clear about the kind of leaders God prefers. Throughout history He has used the unlikely, complex, and unexpectedly powerful.

The great danger of the age of birth pangs and the leaders of nations in that period, especially in the latter stages, where we now seem to be, is that the spirit of abortion is on the land. Considering our position in history, this should not surprise us. Further, the spirit of abortion seems to be upon time itself. This dark power wants to abort the very purpose of the "pregnancy" of *kairos*-time before the treasure in its womb comes forth. Failing that, Apollyon, the destroyer, stands at the very birth canal of *kronos*-time, to catch and kill the newborn.

Perhaps nothing is so symbolic of this deep spiritual issue in the age of birth pangs than the extremes of the literal abortion movement gaining official sanction. And perhaps nothing shows that as much as the belief and pronouncement of Virginia governor Ralph Northam in January 2019. He was speaking in support of proposed legislation in his state regarding babies who survived abortion attempts.

"If a mother is in labor, I can tell you exactly what will happen," said Northam, who is also a physician. "The infant would be delivered . . . kept comfortable . . . resuscitated if that's what the mother and family desired, and then a discussion would ensue between physicians and the mother."[24]

Depending on the outcome of that discussion, the physician who is the "deliverer" of the child from the womb might become a "destroyer."

SEVEN

DESTROYERS AND DELIVERERS

They have as king over them, the angel of the abyss; his name in Hebrew is Abaddon, and in the Greek he has the name Apollyon.

—REVELATION 9:11

Jews watching Nebuchadnezzar demolish Jerusalem and the temple would have viewed him as a destroyer of their civilization. Seventy years later, Jews languishing in the Babylonian captivity would see Cyrus the Persian as their deliverer.

But in between, the Hebrews in Babylon were preserved from genocide because of the presence of one of their countrymen, Daniel. Early in his captivity, Daniel had had the Spirit-given courage to refuse the command of Nebuchadnezzar himself that Daniel and his friends be pulled into the teachings of the Chaldeans. This class of powerful people constituted the preservers, protectors, and propagators of Babylonian political correctness. In his refusal, Daniel conserved the Hebrew civilization of which he was a vital part and that would someday be the foundation of the world's freest, most prosperous societies.

Even Nebuchadnezzar, the vicious ruler who sought destruction of the civilization that had been a blessing to Daniel and his fellow Hebrews, will ultimately bow in worship to the true Lord of History, the God of Daniel, Shadrach, Meshach, Abednego, and their fellow Jews.

The conflict between Daniel and Nebuchadnezzar and his Chaldeans is a type of the struggle going on throughout history. Ancient mystics wrote of the *musica universalis*, the "music of the spheres." They saw harmonious relationships between the celestial spheres and their movements in space in relation to one another, like notes in a musical composition. "There is geometry in the humming of the strings. There is music in the spacing of the spheres," said Pythagoras, the Greek mathematical genius who lived some five hundred years before the coming of Christ.

In the seventeenth century AD, scientist-philosopher Johann Kepler wrote *Harmonices*, a five-part exploration into the harmonics of the universe. Kepler said these tones could be perceived by the soul but that they are not audible to the ears.

In modern times, the more we know about the cosmos, the more some are inspired to try to make the tones audible.

THE MOTIF IN THE OPUS OF TIME

Whatever the case, a close study of history shows that as there are motifs in a great musical composition, so there is a motif running across the opus of time: the recurring Destroyer-Deliverer manifestations. In every generation there arises the destroyer spirit whose aim is the obliteration of the City of God, which is the expression of His kingdom and the highest form of civilization. Wherever there is righteousness and justice, peace, and God-given joy, the destroyers will try to assault and, in words given through Isaiah, cause the earth to "tremble," kingdoms to shake, the world to become a "wilderness," and will "overthrow its cities" (Isaiah 14).

The Destroyer-Deliverer theme repeats in our day. The subconscious question whenever any new leader arises is whether he or she is a destroyer or a deliverer. So, we ask the question now: *Is Donald Trump a destroyer or a deliverer?*

"Joe Biden Is Worried Donald Trump Might Destroy Western Civilization . . . But It's Nothing Personal," heralded a *Vanity Fair* headline in 2017. Writer Abigail Tracy reported on a speech that year made by former vice president Joe Biden to the World Economic Forum in Davos, Switzerland. Biden told the group he was concerned that the then-new Trump administration would "accelerate Russia's plot to 'collapse the liberal international order.'"[1]

However, far from Davos and its lofty Swiss peaks, a reader of a Wisconsin newspaper saw it otherwise: "Western civilization will perhaps be saved by Donald Trump."[2]

Trump's opponents accuse him of trashing everything from Christianity to the Constitution. Yet on some future day young adults whose lives might have been snuffed out in an abortion chamber might awaken to the fact that Trump, through his opposition to abortion, was their deliverer.

Trump's supporters do see him as a great deliverer, recovering the nation from the leftist ideologies of the Democrats and the socialists who, in the eyes of Trump's fans, would themselves destroy America. They remember too well the announced intention of Trump's predecessor, Barack Obama, who said on October 30, 2008, just days from his election: "We are five days away from fundamentally transforming the United States of America."

In today's political and philosophical jungle and its entanglements, it's hard to figure out who may be destructive of civilization and who would bring down everything we care about.

Many would say it's a matter of perspective. Faithful Muslims would say that Muhammad was a deliverer, establishing a civilization that now occupies a large swath of the planet. Charles Martel, leader of the Christian forces at the Battle of Tours in AD 732, would consider the founder of Islam a destroyer of the Christendom, which, for Martel, was the best of civilizations.

And what about those who define civilization in economic terms? Many socialists would exalt Marx and Lenin as civilizational deliverers, while capitalists and free market proponents would see them as destroyers of the most successful economic order.

WHY SUPPORT FOR SOCIALISM?

Cultural commentator Alexander Zubatov cited factors contributing to the growth of support for socialism among young people in the West. At the top of Zubatov's list is "ignorance of history." When youths today "think socialism, they don't think Stalin; they think Scandinavia," he said. A major factor in this ignorance is the "ideological monoculture" in many of today's institutions of higher learning. "The supporters of socialism are not simply the young, but they're disproportionately young people who are college educated," wrote Zubatov.[3]

Clearly, there is a need for a standard by which we can discern between movements that pretend to elevate society and those that actually sustain and strengthen true civilization. Discovering that standard means knowing the worldview and values of those who lead movements and institutions, including political parties and government.

Is there a perfect standard by which we can sort out who's a destroyer and who's a deliverer?

The originators of the word *civilization* sought to do exactly that in their choice of a term that would label the ideal social and cultural system. *Civilization* was used first by Frenchman Anne-Robert-Jacques Turgot in 1752. The word appeared in print in 1756, in the work of another Frenchman, Victor de Riqueti. *Civility* was the word preferred by Samuel Johnson. There was yet another opinion stated by Felipe Fernández-Armesto: "All definitions of civilization . . . belong to a conjugation which goes: 'I am civilized, you belong to a culture, he is a barbarian.'"[4]

But such a view still does not establish an absolute standard for determining destroyers and deliverers.

In an address in Poland that *Wall Street Journal* columnist Peggy

Noonan described as "a grown-up speech that said serious things,"[5] Donald Trump showed awareness of the importance of sustaining civilization:

Each generation must rise up and play their part in [their culture's] defense. Every foot of ground and every last inch of civilization is worth defending with your life. . . . I declare today for the world to hear that the West will never, ever, be broken. Our values will prevail. Our people will thrive. And our civilization will triumph.

Trump then described some of the values and contributions of Western civilization:

We write symphonies. We pursue innovation. We celebrate our ancient heroes, embrace our timeless traditions and customs, and always seek to explore and discover brand-new frontiers.

We reward brilliance. We strive for excellence and cherish inspiring works of art that honor God. We treasure the rule of law and protect the right to free speech and free expression.

We empower women as pillars of our society and of our success. We put faith and family, not government and bureaucracy, at the center of our lives. And we debate everything. We challenge everything. We seek to know everything so that we can better know ourselves.

And above all, we value the dignity of every human life, protect the rights of every person, and share the hope of every soul to live in freedom. That is who we are. Those are the priceless ties that bind us together as nations, as allies, and as a civilization.

In those remarks, Trump was echoing Winston Churchill, who many decades earlier had also spoken of the Judeo-Christian civilization he and his allies spent so much blood rescuing from the claws of Fascism-Nazism. In that civilization, said Churchill, there "resides all that makes existence precious to man, and all that confers honour and health upon the state."[6]

Civilizations do need saving, because, as Christopher Dawson reminds us, civilization is a fragile thing. Dawson's fellow British writer Malcolm Muggeridge understood well the delicate nature of a civilized society, and concluded that civilizations "wax and wane" and that "the world is full of the debris of past civilizations." In every generation "from the Garden of Eden onwards such dreams of lasting felicity have cropped up and no doubt always will." Fallen human nature is the culprit. "It's in the nature of man and all that he constructs to perish, and it must ever be so."[7]

Arnold Toynbee traced the development and decay of nineteen historic civilizations that have come and gone. The stages he discovered through which they all passed were genesis, growth, time of troubles, universal state, and, finally, disintegration.[8] Alexander Tytler, another student of civilization, saw the pattern of collapse like this: bondage, faith, great courage, liberty, abundance, selfishness, complacency, apathy, moral decay, dependency.[9]

THUNDERING TYRANTS

Destroyers thunder through civilizations like the proverbial bull in a china closet, shattering, scattering, demolishing everything in sight. Deliverers, the best civil leaders, grasp the deeper implications and importance of civilization, and become strengtheners of the positive values and principles. They govern with a sense of stewardship.

That stewardship was given humanity in the garden of Eden, when God authorized Adam and Eve to be "fruitful and multiply. Fill the earth and govern it" (Genesis 1:28 NLT). They were to be custodians of civilization. This command was given to the human beings prior to their fall into sin and the corruption of human nature. *Dominate* for a person without sin meant loving oversight and concern, not stern mastery and greed-driven misuse of nature.

Cain, the son of Adam and Eve, and his line, reveal the anti-civilizational corruption that enters humanity and, by extension, the whole world, including the universe (Romans 8), after the fall. Cain was the first human destroyer to appear in history. Genesis 4 tells how Cain and Abel, direct sons of Adam and Eve, brought offerings to God. Cain, a farmer, brought an offering "of the fruit of the ground" (v. 3), but Abel, "a keeper of flocks," brought an animal sacrifice. "The LORD had regard for Abel and for his offering; but for Cain and for his offering He had no regard," says verses 4–5. The reason is that Abel's offering involved the shedding of the animal's blood, which pointed to the sacrifice of the Lamb of God for the world's salvation to come millennia in the future through Jesus Christ.

Infuriated, Cain killed his brother. In doing so, he was unwittingly seeking to destroy the bearers of God's kingdom and the civilization it produced that were in the loins of Abel. Further, Cain's murderous act was sheer anarchy, foreshadowing the "man of lawlessness" (2 Thessalonians 2:3) and the antinomian mentality and behavior at the root of the destruction of all civilizations.

Adam and Eve had another son, Seth, who would replace Abel in God's plan for history. Ultimately, there are two lines that emerge from Eden. Seth's line would produce many deliverers, while that of Cain would raise up destroyers, like the evil Lamech (there is a "good" Lamech in the line of Seth). The evil Lamech was a killer who boasted of his viciousness (Genesis 4:23–24). Nimrod was a pride-consumed "mighty hunter," defying God (Genesis 10:8). He would lay in history the foundations of Babylon, a literal city and empire that would someday become the primary type of nations seeking to organize themselves without God and in defiance of God—the city of man as opposed to the City of God. It is this spiritually corrupt lineage that would lead to the consummate statement in Genesis 6:5–6: "Then the LORD saw that the wickedness of man was great on the earth, and that every intent of the thoughts of his heart was only evil continually. The LORD was sorry that He had made man on the earth, and He was grieved in His heart."

But there was one human being who still reflected—however tenuously—the positive character of the line of Seth. "Noah found favor in the eyes of the

LORD" (Genesis 6:8). Noah was a remnant man, foreshadowing the "called out" who would ultimately be fulfilled in the church, the body of Christ. Noah would be a foreshadowing of the remnant that preserves civilization during periods of destructive upheaval.

Noah, weak as he would prove to be, was a deliverer. He was called "a righteous man, blameless in his time," a person who "walked with God" when the rest of humanity was turning away from the Lord (Genesis 6:9).

A DELIVERER FOR EVERY DESTROYER

So, throughout history, just when the destroyer is about to "overthrow the cities" and "make the world a wilderness" by crushing civilization, God brings a deliverer on the scene. Many are unexpected types who may not be God-followers, yet in His sovereignty they are brought to the fore at just the right time and put into just the right place. Thus, for every

- Cain there is a Seth
- Lamech there is a Noah
- Nimrod there is an Abraham
- Pharaoh there is a Moses
- Nebuchadnezzar there is a Daniel
- Goliath there is a David
- Antiochus there is a John the Baptist
- Nero there is a Constantine
- slaveholder there is a Lincoln
- Hitler there is a Churchill
- Stalin there is a Solzhenitsyn

. . . and so on, across history, until the consummation of all epochs of finite time.

Above all, standing against Apollyon is Jesus Christ, the Messiah,

Redeemer, and Lord of History, who brings the New Jerusalem and its sparkling civilization (Revelation 21:10–21), of which dark Babylon is the antithesis.

Thus, again, the vital question: Is boisterous Donald Trump a "bull in the civilizational china closet" or a deliverer? Before we can seek an answer to that question, we must think about what civilization is, and its importance.

The Bible and other literature from the ancient world—especially that of the Greeks—saw civilization in terms of the "city," or, in Greek, *polis*. Niall Ferguson, a scholar of civilizations, wrote: "A civilization, as the etymology of the word suggests, revolves around its cities."[10] Before the Golden Age of Greece, the prophet Jeremiah understood the significance of the city when the Lord revealed through him that "in its welfare you will have welfare" (Jeremiah 29:7). But this *polis* of security, progress, liberty, and prosperity demands continual maintenance. Hence, the Jeremiah passage also has an exhortation: "Seek the welfare of the city where I have sent you into exile, and pray to the LORD on its behalf."

The people who enjoy the benefits of the "city" must take care of its welfare, even if it is not the city of their choosing, as in the case of the Jews in Nebuchadnezzar's Babylon. They are nevertheless there by God's choice, and for His purposes. That includes the Babylonian world system we inhabit today.

The highest expression of civilizational order is the kingdom of God. The gospel not only advances best in the crucibles of civilizations, but true civilizations thrive under the functional characteristics of the kingdom: righteousness, justice, peace, and transcendent joy (Romans 14:17).

For this reason, Apollyon, as we saw above from Isaiah 14, always seeks the destruction of the "city." In the fallen world there is continual conflict between cosmos and chaos, light and dark, good and evil. The attack is centered on the human *polis*, whose God-given purpose is to extend the qualities of the heavenly city—the "New Jerusalem"—into the realm of a people's everyday living. Isaiah wrote that, because of the attempt made by Lucifer-Apollyon to seize God's throne, the throne of the kingdom of heaven, and therefore of the whole cosmos, the destroyer is "cut down to the earth." As we noted previously, John saw this in the Apocalypse:

> And there was war in heaven, Michael and his angels waging war with the dragon. The dragon and his angels waged war, and they were not strong enough, and there was no longer a place found for them in heaven. And the great dragon was thrown down, the serpent of old who is called the devil and Satan, who deceives the whole world; he was thrown down to the earth, and his angels were thrown down with him. (Revelation 12:7–9)

In that context, let's look again at Isaiah's Spirit-given description of the aim of Lucifer-Apollyon to destroy civilization, represented in the "city" established on transcendent foundations:

> Those who see you will gaze at you,
> They will ponder over you, saying,
> "Is this the man who made the earth tremble,
> Who shook kingdoms,
> Who made the world like a wilderness,
> And *overthrew is cities,*
> Who did not allow his prisoners to go home?"
> (ISAIAH 14:16–17, EMPHASIS ADDED)

It was the *polis* in the civilizational sense about which Augustine wrote in his classic *The City of God*. What Augustine said there is strikingly relevant for our times. Kingdoms without justice are "great robberies," he said.[11] Augustine issued a warning that the president of the United States and all other civil officials must heed: "He that becomes protector of [sin] shall surely become its prisoner."[12]

How can civilization be sustained amid intense assaults from both the spiritual and material domains? Any civil leader who does not focus on that question is not worthy of the people's trust. Sadly, the destroyers seek the exploitation of ordered society, while deliverers give themselves, often sacrificially, for its endurance and enhancement.

MOST IMPORTANT FACTOR

The most important factor in sustaining high civilization is recognition and acknowledgment of God's majestic transcendence. "Blessed is the nation whose God is the LORD," wrote the psalmist (Psalm 33:12). This is not a principle for Old Testament Israel alone, but for societies in general. Zhuo Xinping, a Chinese intellectual, believed the secret of Western civilization was in the "Christian understanding of transcendence." This doctrine, he said, "played a very decisive role in people's acceptance of pluralism in society, and politics in the contemporary West." Zhuo Xinping said that it is only in the context of transcendence that people can understand such concepts in Western civilization as "freedom, human rights, tolerance, equality, justice, democracy, the rule of law, universality, and environmental protection."[13]

God's transcendence was in view when Augustine wrote: "The bodies of irrational animals are bent toward the ground, whereas man was made to walk erect with his eyes on heaven, as though to remind him to keep his thoughts in things above."[14] In that statement, Augustine was echoing the apostle Paul, who wrote, "Therefore if you have been raised up with Christ, keep seeking the things above, where Christ is, seated at the right hand of God. Set your mind on the things above, not on the things that are on earth" (Colossians 3:1–2).

The only way to handle earthly affairs is from the heavenly perspective. That goes for paupers and presidents, and everyone in between. Only from that lofty perspective can leaders get the strength to resist the constant pull downward exerted by the destroyers.

Because of the human fall into sin, the universe is trapped in slavery to "corruption" (Romans 8:21), meaning dissipation of energy, decline, decay, deterioration, death. As an orbiting spacecraft, so with people and their nations and institutions: there must be a "lift," a boost upward against the gravitational pull downward.

Among the most important questions we can ask of those who would lead us is: *What gives you your lift?* "Winning a hard-fought election," Lyndon Johnson might respond. "Sexual conquest," John F. Kennedy and Bill Clinton might reply. "A hole-in-one," Dwight Eisenhower might say. "Killing an elephant," Teddy Roosevelt might reply. "Closing a profitable deal," Donald Trump might answer.

Yet it is the transcendent focus that gives the greatest lift to the human—spirit, soul, and body. The higher a man or woman goes in earthly leadership, the more he or she must reach heavenward. Psalm 96 says:

> Say among the nations, "The LORD reigns";
> Indeed, the world is firmly established, it will not be moved;
> He will judge the peoples with equity.
> Let the heavens be glad, and let the earth rejoice;
> Let the sea roar, and all it contains;
> Let the field exult, and all that is in it.
> Then all the trees of the forest will sing for joy
> Before the LORD, for He is coming,
> For He is coming to judge the earth.
> He will judge the world with righteousness
> And the peoples in His faithfulness. (vv. 10–13)

COMMITTING TO THE VALUES

Sustaining civilization also requires committing to the values that arise from the transcendent worldview. Dennis Prager, an Orthodox Jewish rabbi and scholar, asked: "Why is the Left hostile to Western civilization?" Prager said that "after decades of considering this question, the answer, I have concluded, is: Standards." The Left hates standards, continued Prager, "because when there are standards, there is judgment. And Leftists don't want to be judged."

That attitude, however, demolishes the contributions a good civilization can make to humanity. So, said Prager, religions based on the Bible "affirm a morally judging God," something that the Left sees as "anathema. . . . For the Left, the only judging allowed is Leftist judging of others. No one judges the Left. Neither man nor God."[15]

Yet the values the Left rejects are the very standards of healthy civilization expressed in the Ten Commandments. In the light of these foundational values of Judeo-Christian civilization, the contrasts between the City of God (the New Jerusalem) and the City of Man (the new Babylon) are starkly revealed:

COMMANDMENT	DESTROYER'S OBJECTIVE
You shall have no other gods before Me.	Nothing is transcendent, but the human authoritarians are supreme.
You shall not make idols.	You must worship the supreme leaders and superior people.
You shall not take the name of the LORD your God in vain.	You shall revere only the great and mighty who are your masters.
Remember the Sabbath day, to keep it holy.	There is no sanctity of time, but all must celebrate special days as determined and commanded by the supreme leaders.
Honor your father and your mother.	Father and mother are suspect since they may belong to reactionary periods .
You shall not murder.	Murder is permitted in the case of the unwanted and those who may be drags on the state.
You shall not commit adultery.	There are no restrictions on sexual activity since the greatest good in sex is pleasure.
You shall not steal.	There is no private property; everything belongs to the collective, and controlled by the leaders who may take whatever they want.
You shall not bear false witness against your neighbor.	You are commanded to report any criticism of the supreme leaders, their philosophy, and the state arising from it.
You shall not covet.	However, the supreme leaders and the state can covet, and are authorized to confiscate from you whatever they wish.

This brings us back to the critical question: Is Donald Trump a deliverer or destroyer of civilization? Many of the historic deliverers have been surprising, enigmatic people, like Lincoln and Churchill. But the best way to answer the question about any of the deliverers is in the context of the civilizational destroyers in their periods.

Who would that be in Trump's moment on the stage?

The most obvious candidate in the eyes of many would be Left Secular Progressivist Socialism, the "LSPS Church." This belief system is striking hard at the Judeo-Christian foundations of America and Western civilization.

Charles Taylor, in his epic work *A Secular Age*, said that the joining of spirituality and self-discipline both in Catholic and Protestant (including evangelical and pentecostal) thinking and practice "was seen as positively, and as linked firmly to the sense of civilizational order." Taylor then quoted the Duke of Devonshire, speaking in support of the South London Church Fund:

> Can you imagine for one moment what England would have been like today without those churches and all that those churches mean? . . . Certainly, it would not have been safe to walk the streets. All respect, decency, all those things which tend to make modern civilization what it is would not have been in existence. You can imagine what we should have had to pay for our police, for our lunatic asylums, for criminal asylums. . . . The charges would have been increased hundredfold if it had not been for the work the church has done and is doing today.[16]

"America is dying from an idea she only dimly understands," said James Ostrowski, in his study of progressivism.[17] It is vital that we comprehend the nature of this beast. Some have even referred to it as America's new "state religion" since it is embraced by so many in the establishments who set the national consensus and shape the culture. Meanwhile, generations are being propagandized in educational institutions to see the progressivist worldview and its many doctrines as the great hope for the future—almost messianic.

In fact, in 1961, US Supreme Court Justice Hugo Black categorized "secular humanism" as a "religion" among those that "do not teach . . . a belief in the existence of God."

I have expanded the title for this system to "Left Secular Progressivist Socialism" to attempt to capture all the theory implies. To grasp the ideas inherent in the system, we must look briefly at the four words:

Left

This term refers to the *position* of Left Secular Progressivist Socialism on the philosophical spectrum. In political philosophy there is a continuum. On one end is the extreme Left; on the other, the extreme Right. Those who fall into the center of the spectrum are considered "centrists." There are variations, with some philosophies falling on the center-left side and others on center-right.

As to the origin of these terms, one theory is based on the seating in the French Assembly during the fiery age of the eighteenth-century French Revolution. "Conservatives" were those groups (or "estates") that supported the status quo of the monarchy and sat to the right of the podium. Members of the assembly who favored revolution and the overthrow of the monarchy and the classes supporting it sat to the left. Whatever the origin, the classifications have come down to our time.

There is often confusion. For example, Communist socialism is regarded as falling on the left, while Fascist socialism (the Nazis) falls to the right. The German Hitler regime showed the ugliness of Fascism to the extent that most people reject it outright. Strangely, Communist atrocities under various left-wing dictators like Stalin, Pol Pot, the North Korean Kim family, and many others have seemed not to have repulsed some contemporary proponents of socialism.

Secular

This word applies to the *theological/spiritual* aspect of Left Secular Progressivist Socialism—again, the "church" of "LSPS." Secularism is the outright rejection of God, His transcendence, and His kingdom order of righteousness, justice, peace, and Spirit-given joy as the foundation and character of true civilization. Nimrod, and his defiance of God, is its spiritual father as he was Babylon's. Humanist Manifesto II (1973) described it this way: "No deity will save us; we must save ourselves."[18]

The danger is that no matter how much people try to reject the transcendent Lord, the more they need transcendence. This is among the great truths articulated by Augustine in his *Confessions*. The rejection of transcendence and the embrace of secularism mean that human beings and their institutions, in the spirit of the antichrist, are placed in the transcendent role.

Jordan Peterson faces this frankly, if not intentionally, in his book *12 Rules for Life: An Antidote to Chaos.* In his introduction to the book, Dr. Norman Doidge, an MD, said it all when he observed that without the belief in a transcendent ideal, we are "unchaperoned" and "left to our own untutored judgment, we are quick to aim low and worship qualities that are beneath us." Dr. Doidge also pointed to the "hunger among many younger people for rules, or at least guidelines," and said there is "good reason." They are the first generation to have been educated in a system that holds that morality is relative, but also the contradictory idea that "one group's morality is *nothing but* its attempt to exercise power over another group."

The outcome, according to Dr. Doidge, is that "many people cannot tolerate the vacuum—the chaos—which is inherent in life, but made worse by this moral relativism; they cannot live without a moral compass, without an ideal at which to aim in their lives."[19]

Progressivist

This word refers to the *policy context* of Left Secular Progressivist Socialism. United States government policymaking has been under the influence of progressivism since at least 1912, when all three of the major candidates for the presidency—William Howard Taft, Woodrow Wilson, and Theodore Roosevelt—identified as progressivists, as Ostrowski noted.[20]

This policy philosophy appeared in a period when important parts of the church were caught up in early-twentieth-century idealism. Prior to the First World War, the Victorian age was viewed by its inhabitants as having reached a new summit of civilization. Theologians and notable pastors began to embrace postmillennialism, the idea that human effort would achieve the qualities of Christ's kingdom and at the zenith of human accomplishment Christ would come (or might not even be needed, according to some extreme liberal theologians of that period).

Smatterings of secularist influence were also embedded in this philosophical brew. At the heart of Left Secular Progressivist Socialism is the faith that the state can produce the ideal society of the movement's dreams. "Government has been growing steadily and rapidly since the dawn of the Progressive Era," wrote Ostrowski. "It is inevitable," he said, that "under progressivism, the state will grow until it controls everything and absolutely . . . a totalitarian state."[21]

Socialism

This term expresses the aim of Left Secular Progressivist Socialism. Though he was writing not long after the assassination of Abraham Lincoln, historian Orestes Brownson almost prophetically summed up socialism and where it would lead. "Humanitarian democracy [or the 'social democrats,' as he called it],

> . . . which scorns all geographical lines, effaced all individualities, and professes to plant itself on humanity alone, has acquired by the [Civil] war new strength, and is not without menace to your future. . . . The humanitarian [i.e., socialist] presently will attack distinctions between the sexes; he will assail private property, as unequally distributed. . . . There is [in "humanitarian" socialism] inequality, therefore injustice, which can be remedied only by the abolition of all individualities, and the reduction of all individuals to the race, or humanity, or man in general. He can find no limit to his agitation this side of vague generality, which is no reality, but a

pure nullity, for he respects no territorial or individual circumscriptions, and must regard creation itself as a blunder.[22]

Having rejected "the supernatural order, and the possibility of a Justice more than human, the [social democrat] . . . tends to erect Envy into a pseudo-moral principle." This leads to "a dreary tableland of featureless social equality . . . from which not only God seems to have disappeared, but even old-fashioned individual man is lacking."[23]

"TAP-ROOT" OF AMERICAN ORDER

"The tap-root of American order began to grow some thirteen centuries before the birth of Jesus of Nazareth," wrote Russell Kirk. "Through Moses, prophet and lawgiver, the moral principles that move the civilization of Europe and America and much more of the world first obtained clear expression."[24]

If Trump fully grasps the importance of this Judeo-Christian foundation for America, and proves himself through his policies and actions, he will be remembered by history as a civilizational deliverer.

But, considering the ways of God, that should be no surprise. The Lord of History seems to delight in surprising us by elevating those the world writes off as inconsequential, unelectable, unworthy, unlikely, unfathomable, and utterly enigmatic.

However, there is a huge danger. There are demonic forces who want to influence and control Trump, as they did Nebuchadnezzar and other arrogant, dominating figures in history. Wherever there is a concentration of power, there is a clustering of demons whose goal is to destroy civilization by destroying its leaders.

Christlike humility is the best weapon against this demonic horde because it takes away the pride through which they gain entry into a human soul. "God resists the proud, but gives grace to the humble" (James 4:6 NKJV).

God had to humble Nebuchadnezzar radically. One day as he strutted on the roof of his spectacular palace, looking with pride upon his city, Nebuchadnezzar fell into a state of extreme hubris. He said to himself: "Is this not Babylon the great, which I myself have built as a royal residence by the might of my power and for the glory of my majesty?" (Daniel 4:28–30).

While the king was in the middle of his self-congratulatory speech, there was a thundering interruption:

> King Nebuchadnezzar, to you it is declared: sovereignty has been removed from you, and you will be driven away from mankind, and your dwelling place will be with the beasts of the field. You will be given grass to eat like cattle, and seven periods of time will pass over you until you recognize that the Most High is ruler over the realm of mankind and bestows it on whomever He wishes. (vv. 31–32)

Then came the shocking result: *"Immediately the word concerning Nebuchadnezzar was fulfilled"* (v. 33). The great king, the man from Babylon who had made Babylon great, fell into delusionary madness. The number seven in the Bible signals the completion of some purpose. God had a purpose for withdrawing His hand from Nebuchadnezzar and allowing him to become an exile in the wilderness. Nebuchadnezzar would not come out until God's goal was reached. Thus, the king who built the golden statue and demanded its worship came to look like a wild man—eating grass like a lumbering, foraging bull; his body sweating from the blistering heat of the day and covered with the grimy dampness of the morning; his hair long, stringy, and thick as an eagle's wings; and his fingernails as long and foreboding as a predator-bird's claws (vv. 32–33).

So, while praying that Donald Trump will have wisdom for leadership, those who take seriously the biblical admonition to pray for leaders should intercede for God to give this imposing man true Christlike humility (1 Timothy 2:2). Otherwise Trump's continual preening might become more than comic self-caricaturing and he could find himself in the wilderness, insane with self-delusion until his "seven periods of time" have come.

God's purpose for Nebuchadnezzar's exile in the wilderness was fulfilled one day when he woke up to God's transcendence over him, Babylon, and the world's history. Nebuchadnezzar himself reported on what happened:

But at the end of that period, I, Nebuchadnezzar, raised my eyes toward heaven and my reason returned to me, and I blessed the Most High and praised and honored Him who lives forever;

> For His dominion is an everlasting dominion,
> And His kingdom endures from generation to generation.
> All the inhabitants of the earth are accounted as nothing,
> But He does according to His will in the host of heaven
> And among the inhabitants of earth;
> And no one can ward off His hand
> Or say to Him, "What have You done?"
> (DANIEL 4:34–35)

"At that time my reason returned to me," said Nebuchadnezzar in verse 36, and he found himself king again.

No leader who makes the confession of Nebuchadnezzar will succumb to the clusters of demons who try to close in on people in power.

In the light of Donald Trump's accomplishments in his first term, fair and objective historians in the future might see him as one of America's great presidents. However, if he does not lift his eyes to heaven in recognition of the Source of his abilities and contributions, he will be seized by extreme hubris, and remembered as a man who succumbed to the powers of darkness circling him like a pride of lions looking at their next meal (1 Peter 5:8).

If Trump fully grasps the importance of what Russell Kirk described as the "tap-root" of the Judeo-Christian foundation core for America, and proves himself through his policies and actions, he will be remembered by history as a civilizational deliverer. In that case, Donald Trump will also be a hall-of-fame member of the enigmatic, unexpected heroes of civilization.

However, the higher the office, the greater the spiritual assaults. There are demonic forces who want to take their stand in Trump's soul on the immense ground of pride, as they once did in Nebuchadnezzar and other arrogant, dominating figures in history. For wherever there is a concentration of power, there is a clustering of demons, whose goal is to destroy civilization by destroying its leaders.

Christlike humility is the best weapon against this demonic horde because it takes away the self-glorying pride whereby they gain entry into a human soul. Donald Trump needs much grace, and so does the nation he seeks to lead.

EIGHT

POWER AND THE CLUSTERING OF DEMONS

Demons are found to look after their own ends only, that they may be regarded and worshipped as gods, and that men may be induced to offer them a worship which associates them with their crimes, and involves them in one common wickedness and judgment of God.
—SAINT AUGUSTINE, *THE CITY OF GOD*

E very time I enter the White House, I feel a dark presence there."
The man who spoke those words to me during a phone call was a spiritual giant of his generation, and a consultant to President Richard Nixon. He confirmed something I had also felt while working in the White House but lacked the spiritual discernment to understand.

I had left Washington in 1973 and was serving as a pastor in a quiet community in south Alabama. Yet the memory of the madness that had brought down a president of the United States burned in my thoughts.

According to some theories, Nixon, in struggling with Cold War opponents and working intensely to end the Vietnam War, had decided to embrace a Machiavellian tactic: make your enemies think you're crazy and ready to unleash horrible weapons upon them, and you will get them to the negotiating table.

"I call it the Madman Theory," Nixon told his chief of staff, Bob Haldeman. According to Haldeman, Nixon wanted people who were negotiating with the North Vietnamese to give the enemy the impression that Nixon was so uncontrollable that he might push the nuclear button to force North Vietnam's surrender.[1]

However, Henry Kissinger thought that as the implications of the Watergate scandal and Nixon's role in the cover-up began to crush the president, Nixon really did begin to go mad.

My office was in the Eisenhower Executive Office Building (EEOB), the ornate nineteenth-century structure within the White House compound. Occasionally I would watch as the president, surrounded even inside those barriers by Secret Service agents, would cross over to a private office within the EEOB. It was a den to which he could retreat when working on complex policy issues . . . or on the verge perhaps of losing his mind.

One night as Nixon's resignation loomed, he summoned Kissinger to the EEOB hideaway. According to Kissinger, Nixon was almost drunk, sitting in the dark room. At one point the president wept, and at another asked Kissinger to kneel with him and pray. When the prayer was done, Kissinger, uncomfortable, arose from his knees, but Nixon stayed in the prayer position. The immensity of the scandals loomed before him, and, said Kissinger, Nixon cried out, "What have I done? What happened?"

Richard Nixon was not the only president to be plunged into torment while occupying that office. Hatred and scorn of Lyndon Johnson in 1968 was not unlike what Donald Trump has experienced in his presidency. A big difference is that there are those who are passionate in their support for Trump, while most of the passion regarding Johnson was directed against him.

"The assaults" on Johnson and his presidency in 1968 intensified and were "unprecedented in their extent," wrote Eric F. Goldman. There was severe "personal venom" and a wide "variety of people engaging in them." A 1968 Gallup Poll showed LBJ with only a 36 percent support level. As Johnson became increasingly aware of the vitriol, his mind grew distorted. "Increasingly he was seeing himself as the lonely, traduced figure limned against history, resolutely doing right, grimly awaiting the verdict of the future," wrote Goldman.[2]

Johnson, in Goldman's view, was "seriously flawed" in his "personal characteristics." Further, LBJ was "the wrong man from the wrong place at the wrong time under the wrong circumstances."[3]

Such is the crushing confluence that can plunge a human being into insanity or open him or her to the demonic that cluster around them, or both.

THE KENNEDY EXAMPLE

John F. Kennedy, Johnson's predecessor, may be the most graphic example of a spiritually assaulted national leader. The problem was so obvious that Seymour M. Hersh wrote a book titled *The Dark Side of Camelot*.

Soon after Kennedy's assassination, his brother Robert had locks placed on JFK's White House files. According to Hersh, Robert Kennedy "understood that public revelation of the material in his brother's White House files would forever destroy Jack Kennedy's reputation, and his own as attorney general."[4]

Joseph Kennedy set the pattern for his sons. The father seemed to be amoral. He courted Hollywood starlets and had affairs with them that sometimes took place in his own house. The elder Kennedy seemed to have taught his sons by example that Kennedys were above the moral conventions that governed the lives of lesser breeds of humans, and that Kennedys could do whatever they wanted.

John F. Kennedy, like his father, saw no wrong in bringing women for liaisons into his "house," which happened to be the White House.

Joseph Kennedy's amoralism stretched all the way to global affairs. The

elder Kennedy was a major fundraiser for Franklin D. Roosevelt's cam-
paign—a "bundler," as he might be called today. In gratitude, FDR named
Joe Kennedy as United States ambassador to the Court of Saint James (Great
Britain) in the critical buildup period to the Second World War. There, Joe
Kennedy was noted for his tacit support for Hitler and the Nazis prior to the
war's breakout. Roosevelt had to bring him home.

Aside from the issues of the day, what drove the Kennedys to walk on
the "dark side of Camelot"? And once in the White House, what influenced
JFK to continue in patterns that could destroy him and his presidency—and
perhaps even the nation, since some of his relationships could have made
him vulnerable to blackmail or led to the spilling of national secrets?

There was a certain similarity between John F. Kennedy, Nimrod, and
Nebuchadnezzar. In fact, there is a link between all leaders of nations and
civilizations, including Nebuchadnezzar and Donald Trump. That link is
what we might call "the Mighty Ones syndrome."

Ultimately, the Mighty Ones syndrome draws its energy from the spirit
of the antichrist. We noted earlier that this is the spirit of Nimrod-like defiance of God, opposition to the Christ, the true Lord of History. It is also the
spirit of *imposition*, in that the antichrist seeks to impose himself on the very
throne of Christ, who alone is King of kings and Lord of lords.

The Kennedys reveal the dizzying hubris that is the practical outcome
of the embrace of this spirit. Robert Kennedy voiced it in his own campaign
for the presidency when he said: "At stake is not simply the leadership of our
party and even our country. *It is the right to the moral leadership of the planet.*"[5]

Henry Fairlie noted that this was no mere claim to "*opportunity* to exercise the moral leadership of the planet . . . but a *right* to it." Fairlie described
this as "messianic rhetoric," which came to characterize the Kennedy style.
They believed they could rule the world's arts, science, letters, fashion, and
taste, "all to create in the society an elevated sense of national purpose."[6]

It is important to understand what we are dealing with here, because the
same spirit that drove the Kennedys can drive Donald Trump and any other
occupant of the White House, no matter the political party.

RESIST THE SPIRIT OF THE WORLD

Nancy Pearcey emphasized the urgency of spiritual discernment when she wrote that "Christians are called to resist the spirit of the world, yet that spirit changes constantly (in its forms, styles, and strategies)." So, "to resist the spirit of the world, we must recognize the form it takes in our own day," she said. "Otherwise, we will fail to resist it, and indeed may even unconsciously absorb it ourselves."[7]

It is frightening to think of haughty, hubristic, spiritually naïve people occupying the Oval Office. Yet, with rare exceptions, like Abraham Lincoln and Calvin Coolidge, those are the types who run for the presidency, especially in the hype of the contemporary media age with its celebrity worship and fascination with the modern version of the *giborim*—the "mighty ones."

Such a personality type is especially vulnerable to the demons that cluster around them. The problem is *power*, which is to the "principalities" and "powers" (Ephesians 6:12–18 NKJV) what a rotting roadkill carcass is to vermin on a hot day.

This is because *power is the fundamental temptation.*

To understand this, we must go all the way back to Eden and the primordial period when God created human beings. The Bible tells us three major realities that help us understand how good and evil and spiritual warfare work in our world.

First, it tells us that "God is love." The apostle John wrote that "the one who does not love has not become acquainted with God [does not and never did know Him], for God is love. [He is the originator of love, and it is an enduring attribute of His nature]" (1 John 4:8 AMP).

That summary statement appeared eons after creation, but God's loving character is evident throughout the Scriptures. Love is the essence of God's Being, and, therefore, all He does is love-motivated, love-centered.

Second, the Bible reveals that humans are made in His image. To be made in the image of God means that we have freedom as God is free. God is infinite but sets His own boundary: love is the context God chooses for all His relationships with His creation, including the human being. That immense heart of love allows us freedom to choose to operate within the boundary of love as well.

From our freedom we have made the tragic choice of evil, which is based on a distortion of true love. New Testament Greek has several words for love, an advantage not available in English. *Eros* is love expressed on the physical level. *Philostorgos* is the affection of soul for family and friends.[8] *Agape* is love as God loves. It is unconditional, no strings attached, and sacrificial.

We are seized by erotic temptation, but also healthily loving friends and family, but *agape* is spiritual love, straight from the heart of God. It is the core of John 3:16, that "God so loved the world, that He gave His only begotten Son" for its salvation. It is the love Jesus had in mind when He said, "Greater love has no one than this, that one lay down his life for his friends" (John 15:13). And then Jesus did exactly that.

Third, the Scriptures show that our choice to personally reject His unconditional love and activate it in our relationships with others brings grief to His mighty heart. Yet He loves us enough to continue granting us liberty. We have the power to choose the Lord or Lucifer; we can select the fruit of the forbidden tree or the Tree of Life.

PARENTS UNDERSTAND

Every good parent should be able to understand this. As a father there were times when I wanted to lock my children in a room to protect them. I wanted to secure them from the world that wanted to exploit and abuse them. But imprisoning them, even in a comfortable chamber, would not be loving. Love takes huge risks because we allow our offspring to make their own choices, within reasonable limits. This parental practice comes straight from the heart of God the Father.

All this means that we have mighty power. This will be the point of Lucifer's attack on Adam and Eve. Genesis 3 reveals what happened:

> Now the serpent was more crafty (subtle, skilled in deceit) than any living creature of the field which the LORD God had made. And the serpent (Satan) said to the woman, "Can it really be that God has said, 'You shall not eat from any tree of the garden'?" And the woman said to the serpent, "We may eat fruit from the trees of the garden, except the fruit from the tree which is in the middle of the garden. God said, 'You shall not eat from it nor touch it, otherwise you will die.'" But the serpent said to the woman, "You certainly will not die! For God knows that on the day you eat from it your eyes will be opened [that is, you will have greater awareness], and you will be like God, knowing [the difference between] good and evil." And when the woman saw that the tree was good for food, and that it was delightful to look at, and a tree to be desired in order to make one wise and insightful, she took some of its fruit and ate it; and she also gave some to her husband with her, and he ate. (vv. 1–6 AMP)

"Take the power over your own lives!" That was the essence of Lucifer's temptation, and the heart of the rebellion in Eden. The human beings surrendered themselves and their progeny to everything that sin is—the lusts of the flesh, the lust of the eyes, and the boastful pride of life (1 John 2:16).

Therefore, power is the fundamental temptation, and just as Lucifer attacked at that point in the garden of Eden, so his demons assault us personally and institutionally.

What does all this have to do with Nebuchadnezzar and Donald Trump, palaces and White Houses, and all forms of rulership since the fall? Just this: *wherever there is a concentration of power, there will be a clustering of demons, and the greater the concentration of power, the greater the clustering of demons.*

THE OVAL OFFICE: THE GREATEST HUMAN POWER

The Oval Office is the greatest place of human power on earth.

Power can function properly only when it is under proper authority. Therefore, the American Founders, coming from an age that had been touched by the Great Awakening and the thundering voices of prophetic preachers, placed healthy restraints in the founding documents. God's transcendent authority was above all, as made clear in the Preamble to the Declaration of Independence:

> We hold these truths to be self-evident, that all men are created equal, that they are endowed by their Creator with certain unalienable Rights, that among these are Life, Liberty and the pursuit of Happiness.—That to secure these rights, Governments are instituted among Men, deriving their just powers from the consent of the governed,—That whenever any form of Government becomes destructive of these ends, it is the Right of the People to alter or abolish it, and to institute new Government, laying its foundations on such principles and organizing its powers in such form, as to them shall seem most likely to effect their Safety and Happiness.

Therefore, "powers" can be exercised only under proper authority, flowing from God to the people, and through them to the government they choose, all "under God." This is a major shift in governing style that had dominated six thousand years of recorded history, as we saw in chapter 3.

It's important, then, to understand crucial differences between power and authority:

- Authority is granted from the higher to the lower; power is seized by the strongest.
- Authority is accountable to its transcendent source; power is accountable only to itself.

- Authority is sustained through loving relationship and service; power is sustained by raw strength.
- Authority leads through example and the free choice of those who are led; power controls through manipulation, intimidation, condemnation, domination.[9]

Where mighty people like Nebuchadnezzar, Trump, or any other leaders try to use power without authority, there is opportunity for the demons to surge in. All they are waiting for is for someone to open the door so the powers of evil can find a "stronghold" from which they can accomplish their evil purposes.

The biblically revealed "principle of place" involves all the elements we have discussed above. *Freedom*, given to humans from the *love* of God, means that the powers of darkness may not trespass. Godly human freedom is a boundary wall to those who would "steal and kill and destroy" (John 10:10). God is so serious about this that, compelled by His own choice of *agape*, not even the Lord of all will intervene in a human being without an invitation—a function of intercessory prayer.

THE PRINCIPLE OF "PLACE"

Therefore, a demonic power must be given "place" in a person's life through the free choice of that man or woman. Paul illustrated this in Ephesians 4:26–27, where he wrote, "'Be angry, and do not sin': do not let the sun go down on your wrath, nor give place to the devil" (NKJV). There is an anger that is right—righteous indignation over evil and injustice (Psalm 4:4). However, the wrong kind of anger results in the bitterness and hostility that gives permission for the powers of darkness to enter our souls and find places to occupy within us.

There is a more extensive list of wrong thoughts, behaviors, and relationships that give ground to the powers of darkness in a man or woman given in

Paul's letter to the Galatian Christians. The apostle called them "the deeds of the flesh." They include "immorality, impurity, sensuality, idolatry, sorcery, enmities, strife, jealousy, outbursts of anger, disputes, dissensions, factions, envying, drunkenness, carousing, and things like these" (Galatians 5:19–21).

People "who practice such things will not inherit the kingdom of God," Paul warned.

By these standards it is easy to see how vulnerable to demonic influence—and even control—Nebuchadnezzar was in his day and Donald Trump and all the others were and are in their times.

One of the most promising things that happened to Donald Trump on the day of his inauguration occurred before he reached the Capitol steps where he would be sworn in.

Trump asked straight-spoken evangelist James Robison to be the speaker at his preinaugural worship service at St. John's Episcopal Church, across Lafayette Park from the White House. James called on Trump to stand before the congregation. James then declared to Trump and the listening crowd that the first time they met, James, who is not timid or intimated by power, spoke to Trump "about humility and meekness." James reminded Trump on that inauguration day that meekness is "not weakness" but "taking great power and submitting it with the kind of biblical direction that enables it to fulfill what its strength enables it to do . . . like taking the power of a thoroughbred like Secretariat and yielding it to the wisdom and guidance of a 100-pound jockey."

James, in words that might seem surprising, told Trump, who was standing before the audience,

> Sir, the meekness that God has given you is as great as any I have ever witnessed. . . . If you yield to the gifts of God and the strength that He put in you, not for your purposes but for His Kingdom's purpose, you'll win a triple crown . . . I think you have been designed and gifted by God for this moment, if you, too, together will submit to the wisdom God freely offers, it's going to be an amazing journey.[10]

Christlike humility seems to come hard for the Nebuchadnezzars and Trumps of the world—and that encompasses most national leaders—but it is the only means of destroying the ground of pride that demons seek to occupy in the human soul. If Trump wants to escape the clustering of demons, he must come back in his mind and heart to that day in the little church across from the White House.

REAGAN AND HUMILITY

Ronald Reagan was not a perfect man—a fact he would readily acknowledge— but he was exemplary in his humility. Bill Clarke was both Reagan's most trusted assistant, and a spiritual ally. "There was no pride there at all," Clarke said of Reagan. The president believed that "we can accomplish anything if we don't concern ourselves with who gets the credit." Reagan, said Clarke, "had total confidence in the Divine will," and believed he was in the presidency "as an instrument of God." Reagan's view of his instrumental role was healthy. He didn't think he was *the* instrument, but "one of many." Reagan, Clarke continued, "was an amazingly humble person. True humility."[11]

The demonization of a culture begins in the heart of the leaders. Those who sit in the gates of nations open those great doors to the powers of darkness when they open their own souls to the destroyers. Therefore, says the Bible, "When there is moral rot within a nation, its government topples easily. But wise and knowledgeable leaders bring stability" (Proverbs 28:2 NLT).

Good governance begins in the heart of the leader. Governing a nation, then, is a spiritual matter even more than it is a political and legislative issue. Ideal government is in a partnership between a healthy church and a healthy civil administration.

This becomes clear in a strange vision experienced by the prophet Zechariah centuries ago, as we see in the next chapter.

NINE

THE Z-4 ALLIANCE

The world of secular culture [in the eighteenth and nineteenth centuries] was at once creative and destructive, but essentially transitional and impermanent, and this instability was due to no other cause than to that very separation and dislocation of the inner and outer worlds of human experience.

—CHRISTOPHER DAWSON

State and Church both belong in the Kingdom of Christ, and yet not in the same way.

—OSCAR CULLMANN

Ronald Reagan, president of the United States, and Pope John Paul II, the Polish pope, came to believe they were destined to work together on what some historians would consider the greatest achievement of the twentieth century: the end of the Cold War, through the defeat of Communism and the collapse of the Soviet Union, the major nation promoting and trying to force Communism globally.

History proved them right.

In 1917, the powers of darkness that cluster around centers of power crushed Russia. Though Communism claimed to focus on the material, nevertheless it was a spiritual movement in the worst sense of the word, determined to push the Lord Jesus Christ off the throne of nations and history and impose their own version of godless utopia through raw power rather than true authority.

In the view of Communist theoreticians, radical socialism would displace and replace the kingdom of God as the highest form of civilization. This despite the historical examples that had tragically revealed the destructive nature of socialist systems, like North Korea. However, one of the most revealing examples occurred in the colonies established in New England.

Initially, all property was held in common, and individuals could get food from a community supply to which everyone was to contribute. But eventually takers outnumbered givers. Thus, according to Professor Lawrence W. Reed,

> The disincentives of the socialist scheme bred impoverishment and conflict until, facing starvation and extinction, [Governor William] Bradford altered the system. He divided common property into private plots, and the new owners could produce what they wanted and then keep or trade it freely. . . . Over the centuries, socialism has crash-landed into lamentable bits and pieces too many times to keep count—no matter what shade of it you pick: central planning, welfare statism, or government ownership of the means of production. Then some measure of free markets and private property turned the wreckage into progress. *I know of no instance in history when the reverse was true*—that is, when free markets and private property produced a disaster that was cured by socialism. None.[1]

In the 1980s, both President Reagan and Pope John Paul II recognized the spiritual implications of radical socialism. This compelled Reagan to call the Soviet Union the "evil empire" and the pope to speak of its "atheistic ideologies" that constituted "the evil of our times," resulting in a "degradation, indeed a pulverization, of the fundamental uniqueness of each human person."[2]

MATERIALIST SYSTEM, SPIRITUAL MYSTIQUE

Ironically, the atheistic Communist revolution in Russia even had its own spiritual mystique regarding history, based on the philosophy of G. W. F. Hegel. He advocated the theory that the rational, natural, materialistic forces in the hearts of humans, linked with the passage of time, would lead to an inevitable advance toward pure Communism, creating the "Workers' Paradise."

In seeking to implement Hegel's theory, mingled in their own thought, Vladimir Lenin, Joseph Stalin, Leon Trotsky, and their cohorts would try to rip history from the hands of the Lord of History, even though they believed He did not exist. The leaders of Russia's Bolshevik Revolution of 1917, like all who would follow them down through history, would not concern themselves with authority but do all possible to accumulate and use raw power.

One of the people observing the revolution, and deeply affected by it, was Nicolai Berdyaev. As we note later, eventually he would turn against Marxism and become a Christian. Part of what propelled Berdyaev to this decision was what he learned about the philosophy of history through the rigors of the Communist revolution that he suffered along with his nation.

A reviewer of Berdyaev's book *The Meaning of History* wrote that Berdyaev recognized that "The history of man and the world is rooted in 'celestial history,' in the deepest interior spiritual life, which can be equated with heavenly life, the life of eternity, the life of God. The source of history lies in this experience of the human spirit which is in direct communion with the divine spirit."[3]

As Winston Churchill recognized, the materialism of the Marxists would imprison whole nations behind the "Iron Curtain" they were bringing down.

There could be no freedom of worship of the transcendent God, for the Communist masters would tolerate no recognition of any power higher than themselves. State atheism became the official policy of all nations living behind that seemingly impenetrable drapery of iron.

After the collapse of Communism in 1989–90, I traveled throughout the former Soviet bloc helping conduct leadership workshops mainly in churches. Communism had depleted leadership infrastructures in churches, families, education, governance, and commerce. Anyone who rose to prominence without the sanction of and absolute obedience to the leaders would have been seen as a threat and cut down quickly. The Marxists said they were building "peoples' republics," but there was nothing in these grim states that was truly about the people. It was centered on the leaders and their enrichments.

MEMORIES OF EVIL DISASTER

And so, my memories even now illustrate the evil disaster of Communist rule. I can see in my mind's eye an elderly couple at a subway station, standing at the top of the stairs, frying a piece of rancid-looking sausage in a scarred iron skillet, hoping someone would buy the meat . . . a young woman, in what was then Czechoslovakia at midnight pushing away the ice in a small lake where she was being baptized, hoping the constantly probing eyes of the state would not see her . . . pastors in a conference in Bulgaria, suddenly troubled as they spotted a man who had been a "red pastor," passing himself off as a genuine church leader but actually an agent of the secret police . . . the scattered litter of old airplanes cannibalized for their parts rusting alongside the taxiways of major airports . . . a translator in the Ukraine, who suddenly pulled away from us while on a street-walk because he saw a peddler trying to sell a rotten banana, which our translator looked upon with amazement . . . elevators without light bulbs because they would be so quickly stolen by those who spent most of their evenings in dimness or outright darkness . . . grocery store lines leading to nothing because the shelves at the end of the queue were depleted . . . but more than anything else, the sadness, weariness, and despair that was in the eyes and upon the faces of people whose lifetimes had been scarred under this cruel system.

Then, suddenly and miraculously, it all came crashing down.

The president and the pope provided the spark that ignited the fuse. Powerful Western nations had tried everything possible following the end of the Second World War in 1945 to beat Communism. Monstrous weapons, the most frightening in history, had been developed; wars in places whose names people in the West barely new, like Vietnam and Cambodia, had piled up bodies in the struggle to stop the spread of the cancerous philosophy. Trillions of dollars had been spent, but still the malignancy spread.

And then the two men came on the scene.

President Ronald Reagan and Pope John Paul II both believed that God is the Lord of History. "Christ cannot be left out of the history of man in any part of the globe," said Pope John Paul II.[4] "I've always believed that we were, each of us, put here for a reason, that there is a plan, somehow a divine plan for all of us," said Reagan at the National Prayer Breakfast in 1982.

As the president and the pope examined the crosscurrents of their lives, and the similarities in their experience, they came to believe—and history confirmed—that God had brought them together "for such a time as this," words that describe Queen Esther's crucial moment in history as well as Reagan's and that of John Paul II.

So, as Paul Kengor and Robert Orlando wrote: "A Catholic pope from Poland. A Protestant president from America's heartland. . . . A priest and a philosopher. A Hollywood star and politician. . . . At first glance, Pope John Paul II and President Ronald Reagan seemed to have little in common."[5] Yet *"both John Paul II and Ronald Reagan firmly believed in the Divine Plan and felt sure they had been called to play their roles in it."*[6]

Both men, within a short time span from one another, would survive assassination attempts—the pope from a would-be killer working for Communists who feared the Polish pope's popularity in his homeland especially would ignite an anti-Communist revolution, and Reagan at the hand of a crazed man who wanted to get the attention of a Hollywood starlet.

After his close call with death, Reagan's attention was focused on God. "Whatever time I have left is for Him," said the president.[7]

SPARED BY GOD FOR A PURPOSE

The pope and the president had already developed a friendship. Reagan wanted to make Pope John Paul II an ally in the Cold War. The men found a "philosophical kinship."[8] However, after the assassination attempts, they came to believe that God had spared their lives for what Reagan called "The DP"—the Divine Plan, which was to "defeat Communism."[9]

And that is what happened in their time. The revolutions that brought down Communist rule in Eastern Europe were often centered in the church. In Poland and Hungary, it was the Catholic Church, inspired by the Polish pope. In Romania and Czechoslovakia (now the Czech Republic), evangelicals, pentecostals, and others were involved—as I personally witnessed shortly after those revolts.

Reagan's moral, political, and strategic leadership imparted courage to others across the Communist bloc. When first confronted by the Berlin Wall, Reagan was repulsed at the implications of trying to keep people imprisoned in a land where there was little hope for freedom. When he stood in West Berlin, peering at the grim structure on June 12, 1987, Reagan famously said rhetorically to the leader of the Soviet Union: "Mr. Gorbachev, tear down this wall!"

Strategically, Reagan began to pursue development of a space-based nuclear defense system some tagged as "Star Wars." There was resistance from the American Left, but Reagan knew the Soviets and their economy, weakened by socialist Communism, could not compete. The actions by the Polish pope and American president fueled the fuses of discontent and grew courage across the Communist world. As a result, nations were freed from the cruel system.

Those events are some thirty years in the past as I pen these words. Communism is trying to make a comeback. I am reminded of the beast from the sea described in Revelation 13. In the apocalyptic visions, John saw a beast rising from the sea. In the Bible's prophetic language, the "sea" symbolizes nations and civilizations in upheaval (Revelation 17:15).

The monster John saw had immense power, symbolized by its ten horns and seven heads, with the horns crowned by diadems (Revelation 13:1). The "dragon"—Satan himself—gave the beast his power (v. 2).

As John watched, he reported: "I saw one of his heads as if it had been slain, and his fatal wound was healed. And the whole earth was amazed and followed after the beast" (v. 3).

Thus, there are several issues here amazingly relevant for our times. First, the beast—the Antichrist—rises out of troubled, stormy nations, a major characteristic of the age in which we live. Second, the beast is systemic; that is, it is made up of many parts represented in the horns and heads. We can therefore conclude that John saw what we have called the Babylonian world system, organized without the Lord of History and in defiance of God.

It's possible that Communism is a manifestation in our time of the head that *seems* to have been slain and is now experiencing the healing of this "fatal wound," especially to the amazement of people who remember the Cold War, Reagan, and Pope John Paul II. The wonder is from the fact that the "resurrection" of the decapitated beast seems to be happening in the *West*. In the United States, for example, there is a troubling rise of interest in and favor for socialism.

"TELL THE REST OF THE STORY"

Tragically and ironically, those rejoicing in the "revival" of the beast are largely young people living in the prosperous, free West that the beast aims to destroy. Marc Thiessen, former speechwriter for President George W. Bush, was concerned that a Gallup Poll showed 58 percent of young Americans favoring socialism. Seven in ten millennials indicated support for a socialist presidential candidate.[10] Thiessen cited Richard A. Grenell, a former US ambassador to Germany, in underscoring the importance of teaching young people about socialism. "I think we have a responsibility to tell the rest of the story," Grenell said. He thinks it important "to show the end of socialism . . . what we need to be able to do is tell the rest of the story."[11]

The point here is not necessarily that Communism is *the* severed head of the beast that returns to life shown in Revelation 13 but that it is a historical type that appears throughout the cycles of time in various forms, as discussed in chapter 4.

The "beast" draws its power from Satan himself; therefore, the present battle is that of the light of Jesus Christ and His kingdom against the latest manifestation of the dark satanic system. This is a spiritual conflict, and we urgently need the same kind of partnership now as was characterized by Ronald Reagan and Pope John Paul II.

It doesn't have to be a president and a pope. Donald Trump and Pope Francis are more antagonists than allies. But what is needed is the type of alliance described in Zechariah 4, and thus I call it a "Z-4 Alliance." It is also modeled practically in Daniel's interactions with rulers of Babylon, beginning with Nebuchadnezzar and including Belshazzar (a regent under Nabonidus), Darius, and Cyrus.

During the reign of Darius over Babylon, Zechariah, a prophet among the Hebrew captives, received a powerful—and revealing—vision from the Lord. Zechariah 4 gives the detail and shows how God sees the completeness of the authority needed to resist and overcome the destroyer. This type of alliance is what it takes for a nation to stand against the clustering of demons that affects all areas of the concentration of power.

It is the kind of alliance that existed between President Reagan and Pope John Paul II.

ZECHARIAH 4:1–7: THE LAMPSTAND AND THE "TWO TREES"

Zerubbabel led more than forty thousand of his fellow Hebrews home to the promised land after their liberation from Babylon through the decree of Cyrus. Back in Jerusalem, Zerubbabel became the civil leader, the governor, of Judah, then a Persian province.

Zerubbabel and his people faced an enormous task in Jerusalem. As they rounded the hills toward the end of their long journey, perhaps they saw what appeared to be yet another mountain in their path. As they got closer, they could see it was the rubble from Solomon's great temple, destroyed by the Babylonian invaders seventy years earlier.

Most of the returnees had been born in Babylon but all their lives had heard of Jerusalem and the longing to return there from older generations. Many may have wondered, *Is this ruin what the old-timers were dreaming of?*

Zerubbabel and Joshua, the high priest, knew they must mobilize the people to restore the temple, the city, and its walls—but especially the temple, the very center of their nation. The task, however, was beyond their capacities. Ultimately, they would succeed, and in doing so provide important principles and truths that would span history. Among them is a biblical methodology for the relationship of church and state, and their partnership in establishing and maintaining civilization.

It was imperative that Zerubbabel and Joshua not collapse in a heap of despair themselves. They occupied the two God-ordained offices of authority that together could lead the nation. If they allowed the immensity of the job to cause them to shrink back, there was no one else among the people recognized as being in an office of authority from which to lead.

Zechariah 4:1–7 describes the scenario vital for our own times:

> Then the angel who was speaking with me returned and roused me, as a man who is awakened from his sleep. He said to me, "What do you see?" And I said, "I see, and behold, a lampstand all of gold with its bowl on the top of it, and its seven lamps on it with seven spouts belonging to each

of the lamps which are on the top of it; also two olive trees by it, one on the right side of the bowl and the other on its left side." Then I said to the angel who was speaking with me saying, "What are these, my lord?" So the angel who was speaking with me answered and said to me, "Do you not know what these are?" And I said, "No, my lord." Then he said to me, "This is the word of the LORD to Zerubbabel saying, 'Not by might nor by power, but by My Spirit,' says the LORD of hosts. 'What are you, O great mountain? Before Zerubbabel you will become a plain; and he will bring forth the top stone with shouts of "Grace, grace to it!"'"

The Lord's message to Zerubbabel was that the Spirit of God Himself would be the power that would overcome the mountain of rubble.

In the twenty-first century, we stare at the moral, spiritual, and philosophical rubble that was once the best of Western civilization. Many are overwhelmed at the extent of destruction, while others, in hapless delusion, dance over and through the ruins. Those who understand the tragedy in the mountain of debris are overwhelmed and wonder if greatness can be recovered.

Donald Trump's mantra may seem impossible: "Make America Great Again." The challenge is daunting. Many, perhaps Trump included, have forgotten, or, considering the state of historical studies and teaching in many schools today, never knew what the true greatness looked like, what it was built upon, and what held it together. However, those who, like the men of Issachar, understand the times and what needs to be done feel faint at the enormity of the crisis.[12]

We must lock our focus on the principle behind the promise God gave to Zerubbabel in antiquity: "'Not by might nor by power, but by My Spirit,' says the LORD of hosts" (Zechariah 4:6).

As we dig down into this revelation from God that came to Zerubbabel in his day, we uncover treasures essential for our understanding of church and state today. These truths are as relevant in the age of Donald Trump—or any other chief of state—as they were in the period when Zerubbabel and Joshua occupied seats of authority.

The great danger in a tight relationship between civil leaders and spiritual leaders is the potential for creating at least an informal theocracy. Church and state are indeed to be separate, and that prevents a theocracy. But church and state must not be rivals, otherwise the nation will be plunged into religious wars like those that characterized Europe in the Middle Ages and Renaissance.

MAINTAIN KINGDOM FOCUS

While alert to the theocratic temptation, the focus on the kingdom of God must not be lost. Even those who do not acknowledge its reality or believe in the blessings of a civilization established on its principles intuitively recognize the need for kingdom qualities. Proverbs 29:2 says, "When the righteous are in authority, the people rejoice; but when a wicked man rules, the people groan" (NKJV).

General Omar Bradley served directly under Dwight Eisenhower in the Second World War and later in the Joint Chiefs of Staff. He was concerned about the growing civilizational crisis he observed in his later years as the arms race and Cold War threatened the world. "We have grasped the mystery of the atom and rejected the Sermon on the Mount," he said. "Ours is a world of nuclear giants and ethical infants."[13]

We need the vision of the kingdom today and the understanding of the importance of the core institutions that preserve and protect its values, as the temple did for the ancient Hebrews. Even if the temple of cedar and stone no longer stands in Jerusalem, the temple manifestation and ministry have continued across the ages.

Jesus Christ was, in the period of His incarnation, the living manifestation of the temple. John, for example, inspired by the same Holy Spirit who revealed truth to Zechariah and energized Zerubbabel, wrote that the Word Incarnate, Jesus the Christ, "tabernacled," or "pitched His tent" among us (John 1:14). In view is the "tent of meeting," the predecessor to the temple, that was set up wherever the Hebrews wandered in the wilderness. In its deepest interior was the ark of the covenant with its mercy seat, where God was manifest in His glory.

After Jesus' ascension, His body, the church, took on the temple role. The apostle Paul wrote that our bodies individually are the "temple of the Holy Spirit" (1 Corinthians 6:19–20). The apostle Peter said that Christ's people are also the "living stones" that "are being built up as a spiritual house for a holy priesthood, to offer up spiritual sacrifices acceptable to God through Jesus Christ" (1 Peter 2:4–5).

Therefore, in the present age, the biblical church bears the primary role of proclaiming and ministering God's kingdom in the world, in accord with the grand goal Jesus gave in Matthew 24:14. In that sense, the New Testament church is in the "Joshua position" in Zechariah's vision.

But there are "two trees," and Zerubbabel represents civil governance, the state. Therefore, for the effective ministry of the kingdom in the world, it takes church and state working together. This does not mean they merge and become one, but that each has a distinctive role in the great overarching mission. What establishes the boundaries between church and state is the lampstand, placed at the center, representing the presence of God amid the two "trees."

Briefly, here are crucial takeaways that emerge in Zechariah's vision, coupled with the revelation that has come in Jesus Christ and the New Testament:

- Civilizations, and the nations within them, exist to make possible the proclamation and ministry of Christ's kingdom in the world.
- The church within a nation is to have the freedom to proclaim the gospel of the kingdom, and the material resources through a prospering society to minister the kingdom and its truth globally. (In such a situation, everyone benefits, not only those who share the spiritual beliefs.)
- The state is to protect these rights and freedoms and establish policies that make the nation prosperous.

- Both church and state are to recognize that God Himself defines their limits, and they must not try to cross over and usurp the role of the other.

This means *the church must not try to become the state*. This is what happens in theocracies. Theocratic systems inevitably become oppressive because those in civil leadership are claiming God as the source of their power, therefore asserting that they have divine and thus absolute sanction for their policies and actions.

On the other hand, *the state must not seek to become the church*. When this occurs, the state assumes it has power not only at the immanent level but at the transcendent itself. The state becomes the object of worship and must be obeyed. This is seen especially in those countries that embrace state atheism. It's not that their leaders believe there is no god, but that they and their institutions *are* god. Such governing styles are driven by the spirit of antichrist. In New Testament Greek, *anti-* means not only "against" but "in the place of." As we have said, the spirit of antichrist is both opposition and imposition, which is clearly recognized when the distinctive roles of church and state are confused and they try to usurp one another's positions as determined by God.

THE ZECHARIAH VISION AND THE "TWO WITNESSES" (REVELATION II:I–I6)

Many centuries after Zechariah's vision, the aged apostle John saw what appeared to be a continuation of that shown to and through Zechariah. John was shown "two witnesses" who had an important role with respect to the temple. God gave the pair authority to speak "prophetically" for a specified period.

In case there was any doubt that Zechariah's vision was linked here, an angel (messenger of God) told John, "These are the two olive trees and the two lampstands that stand before the Lord of the earth"[14] (Revelation 11:4).

The two witnesses will prophesy throughout the world, and upon completion of their mission, the "beast that comes up out of the abyss will make war with them, and overcome them and kill them" (v. 7). Their bodies will lie in "the street of the great city which mystically is called Sodom and Egypt, where also the Lord was crucified" (v. 8). Jerusalem was the site of the crucifixion of Jesus Christ, but its joining to the other "mystical" cities indicates that the holy city has become part of the world system in opposition to God, which is presented in Revelation as Babylon.

In the broadest sense, then, the two witnesses have both proclaimed and been destroyed within and by the Babylonian world system.

Who are the two witnesses? If, as we have seen, they are a continuation of Zechariah's vision, they are not two individuals but representative of two institutions that have collaborated in the proclamation and ministry of the gospel of the kingdom, the same as in Zechariah's vision: the ecclesiastical and civil authorities.

FORETASTE OF THE KINGDOM

We see confirmation that the harmonious functional relationship (not the union) is essential for the advance of the gospel of the kingdom in the world.

Where there is healthy society that blesses those in it and the world around it with goodness, justice, peace, and transcendent joy, there is a foretaste of the kingdom of God (Romans 14:17). It takes the partnership between heaven and earth and the partnership between church and state to have such a healthy society.

Prophetically we see that God ordains special *kairotic*, or "opportune," seasons, when this healthy relationship flourishes and blesses its society. Then, because of sin, the temptations of power, and the rise of lawlessness, this relationship is fragmented, and chaos comes to the society.

The Antichrist, whom John saw in his vision as a "beast," is also "the man of lawlessness" Paul described in 2 Thessalonians. Again, the Antichrist is the spirit of opposition against Christ and imposition, in the sense he tries to push Christ off the throne and impose himself there.

At some point, therefore, the cooperation of the church in its kingdom role and the state in its kingdom function will be destroyed. A period of "deadness" will ensue. There will be people who grieve over this "death" of the functional relationship between the "two witnesses," and others who will rejoice. Rather than the healthy partnership, the state will be a major instrument of the antichrist spirit and the primary opponent of the church. New restrictions and persecutions will fall upon Christ's body, in the pattern of the worst of Rome.

In modern times we have seen this in various parts of the world, especially in nations under tyrannies of the Left (primarily socialist Communism) and of the Right (Fascism). As I write, there are new outbreaks of violence against churches in Africa and Asia, and especially in China. The death of the two witnesses of Revelation is on another scale altogether. The shattering of their partnership in proclaiming and ministering the gospel of the kingdom will have worldwide effect.

Then, in the *kairos*-cycle God will bring the witnesses back into their kingdom-oriented functional relationship for one last glorious period (perhaps the Millennium). Finally, the seventh trumpet will sound, heralding the completion of the mission to fill the world with the kingdom proclamation. The earth will be transformed. Christ and His kingdom of righteousness, justice, peace, and Spirit-given transcendent joy will be the nature of the whole world.

This is why there is a continual "collusion" between heaven and earth until the greatest interaction—the coming of Jesus Christ and the "New Jerusalem," which is the symbol of God's kingdom in the world.

WHERE TRUMP ET AL., FIT

How does the Trump presidency, or any, for that matter, fit into this scheme?

God sovereignly raises up—directly (intentionally) or indirectly (permissively) unlikely, complex, and powerful leaders in accord with His sovereign purpose and objectives for history and nations.

The American Left, driven by the secular social progressivism that has consumed it, sees conservative churches that take the Bible as authoritative as the prime resistance to their cultural agendas. They do all possible through the courts, streets, media, and schools to make sure the prophetic voice of the church is shut down.

Meanwhile extremists on the right dream of new theocratic regimes using their muscle to impose Old Testament statutes on the society.

Sometimes the leaders surprise us. As I write, Donald Trump, a man from "Babylon," is president of the United States. Few would have predicted that a previously philandering casino king would have become a major defender of the church and the gospel she proclaims.

Such a society would be a blessing to all inhabiting it. Yet if civil government tries to impose Christianity on the nation, there will be no blessing, because it will be institutional, requiring control by expansive government, law, and regulation rather than a living faith. There must be a healthy alliance between the spiritual and civil leadership of the nation, but, as I stressed above, this alliance cannot be human-contrived, or it will deteriorate into a disastrous rivalry.

History has been there before.

Human beings cannot organize or otherwise construct a true "Z-4 Alliance." "Not by might nor by power, but by My spirit" applied to the building of the temple, but the principle applies here. There should be attempts to build bridges between presidents and spiritual leaders. But the partnership between Daniel and Nebuchadnezzar in the king's post-wilderness period could be brought about only by the sovereign Lord of History. The same is true of the partnership between Zerubbabel and Joshua, and, in more recent times, Reagan and Pope John Paul II.

While the true Z-4 Alliance can come only from God, humans do have a role in this: intercession. John recorded a fascinating dynamic, when he wrote, in Revelation 8:3–5 (AMP):

Another angel came and stood at the altar. He had a golden censer, and much incense was given to him, so that he might add it to the prayers of all the saints (God's people) on the golden altar in front of the throne. And the smoke and fragrant aroma of the incense, with the prayers of the saints (God's people), ascended before God from the angel's hand. So the angel took the censer and filled it with fire from the altar, and hurled it to the earth; and there were peals of thunder and loud rumblings and sounds and flashes of lightning and an earthquake.

There are people within the earth to whom God gives authority to "stand in the gap" before Him on behalf of the world and all its inhabitants (Ezekiel 22:30). They are called the "saints." Politicians have power, but the saints have something greater—God-given authority. Their petitions to the Lord of all go directly to His throne. Then, in the perfect *kairotic* moment as determined by His plan for history, their prayers for the world that align with His will are poured back upon the world.

IDENTIFYING THE SAINTS

Who are the saints? Their title in New Testament Greek is *hagios*—literally, the people who are "sanctified" or "set apart" and "consecrated" regarding their relationship with God and their purpose in earth. They are elected as a member of a legislative body is elected to represent the interests of their people before the highest authority, the only One with the authority to elect them.

It is these men and women who, in the style of Jesus of Nazareth, and through the empowerment of the Holy Spirit, have the authority to represent the world before the throne of the Lord of History. They alone have the "vote" for creation that God Himself recognizes. Jesus Christ, as Lord of History, gave them this authorization when He gave their spiritual ancestors the "keys of the kingdom."

The "saints" are set apart by their identification with Jesus Christ and His lordship over all and by their anointing by the Holy Spirit. They "elected" the Lord, and He "elected" them. It is through that identification with Jesus Christ as Lord that the "saints" are able to come to the throne, not with arrogance but with "boldness and confident access" through their faith in Christ (Ephesians 3:12). And when there, they discover that is the throne, not of law and judgment but of mercy and grace (Hebrews 4:16).

Such "saints" constitute the *strategic remnant* within the world.

TEN

THE STRATEGIC REMNANT

Time is short. The world is at the brink of eternity. Right now we have the greatest opportunity to rise up and take the victory of the cross to the last corners of this earth. The Lord Jesus is graciously calling a remnant to the joys of simple obedience. For those who respond, I believe there is an opportunity right now to share in the last great move of God before Christ returns.

—K. P. YOHANNAN, FOUNDER AND
PRESIDENT, GOSPEL FOR ASIA

One day a true remnant man walked into my office at the White House, and I did not know it.

A friend we'll call "Ernie," himself a remnant person and leader of a group whose mission was to take Christ's ministry into Washington's government agencies, had phoned earlier. As he did from time to time, he asked if he could bring a visitor to my office for fellowship, encouragement, and prayer.

Ernie told me the man worked in the foreign ministry of Romania. I tried to cloak my surprise. Romania, in those intense Cold War days, was governed by one of the most oppressive Communist regimes in Eastern Europe.

President Nixon was pursuing détente with the Soviet Union and Communist world. In line with that policy objective, Nixon himself would be the first president since 1949 to visit the People's Republic of China and Chairman Mao. Thus, I felt comfortable in allowing the man from the Communist nation to come to my office.

Yet I was still concerned about how to interact with this individual who was part of the government of a nation imposing state atheism on its people.

"Ernie, should I treat him as usual, including praying for him?" I asked during the phone call.

"Yes," Ernie replied. "He's a brother in Christ." *How could that be?* I wondered.

I went through the steps to get the two men on the White House visitors' list, and a half hour later Ernie and the guest, whom I'll call Yuri, were sitting across from me. I wanted to bless and encourage Yuri, but it was I who was on the receiving end of blessing and encouragement that day.

After the visit, later that afternoon, I phoned Ernie. "What was that all about?" I asked. "How did Yuri become a follower of Christ in Romania?"

Ernie explained that on his travels he looked for followers of Christ—remnant people—wherever he visited. At some point during a conversation, he would give a new acquaintance a small metal cross as a gift. Based on the recipient's response to the cross, Ernie would know if the individual was a believer, or at least open to the gospel. Ernie told me that on the day in Bucharest when he presented Yuri with that cross, Yuri had received it gladly.

However, Yuri quickly signaled Ernie to be quiet and to follow him. Yuri led Ernie to a park with a large lake. That was the only way to escape listening devices planted everywhere by Communist Romania's secret police.

When they had rowed out to the middle of the lake, Ernie felt secure in speaking directly. "Yuri, the Lord is searching for His man inside the foreign ministry of Romania," said Ernie, his piercing eyes looking deep into Yuri's heart.

"I am that man!" Yuri declared immediately.

I never heard what ultimately happened with Yuri, but almost a half century later I remember him. I can even see his face and where he was sitting that afternoon in my small White House office.

Romania's then-ruler, Nicolae Ceaușescu, was a hardcore Marxist. His reign was so oppressive that his own people executed Ceaușescu and his wife during the 1989 uprising that overthrew Communism there.

I think of Yuri and wonder if he survived and was able to continue his role as a remnant man inside the Romanian government.

REMNANT PROFILES

I have had the blessing of meeting many other remnant people through the years: a young Iranian pastor in Singapore for a leadership conference at the very time American diplomats were being held as hostages in Tehran . . . an elderly pastor in the Czech Republic, whose hands and fingers were distorted from beatings received during the Communist era . . . a group of uniformed Soviet soldiers relishing in their new freedom, worshipping in a church in Kiev not long after the collapse of Communism . . . business leaders who openly identified with Christ in the People's Republic of China and even formed an organization called the Chinese Christian Business Association . . . a band of Indonesian believers lifting up praise and worship in a park bordering the Amsterdam boulevard where a hellish festival was thrusting obscenities into the air.

And, of course, I remember the remnant people within Nixon's White House who ministered to me and others. I rejoice when I realize there are also remnant men and women in Trump's White House.

Also, for me, the face of the remnant is an African diplomat posted to several nations during his career as an ambassador for his country, but also, in his own heart, as an ambassador for Christ's kingdom. He planted not only the flag of his African homeland in foreign soil but also the church of the Lord Jesus Christ.

My beloved friend was assigned to a European country that had severed itself from the Judeo-Christian worldview that had brought it blessings of freedom and prosperity, and the diplomat planted a church in the heart of its capital city. His congregation met in an elaborate stone church edifice that once housed a thriving congregation in the era when the country still considered itself Christian.

Pass that building on a Sunday, and you might still hear sounds of thriving spiritual life once more as a group of African and Asian immigrants, Gypsies, and a few Europeans lift their voices in enthusiastic worship. Then comes the diplomat with a powerful message from God's Word.

I think of all these remnant people and am reminded also of those remarkable individuals Paul referred to in his letter to the Philippians. Paul, himself a remnant man, was in Rome as he wrote, guarded twenty-four hours a day by a Roman soldier. It's hard not to smile when we read this line in Paul's closing words to the Philippian believers: "All the saints greet you, *especially those of Caesar's household.*"[1]

"Caesar" was the despicable Nero whose persecutions of Christians— and others—was inhuman. Yet somewhere in Nero's vast establishment were gardeners, cooks, nannies, watchmen, sundial custodians, equestrians, food tasters, entertainers, animal keepers, messenger boys, librarians, stenographers, physicians, and shoemakers (to name a few) who were followers of the Jewish Messiah, who, they discovered, was also the Messiah for all the nations.

THE JOKE IS ON NEBUCHADNEZZAR

Daniel was such a remnant man in Nebuchadnezzar's house. In bringing in the Hebrews, the Babylonian ruler had unwittingly brought remnant people into his own land.

You might say the joke was on Nebuchadnezzar.

But it was no joke. The end of the matter was that Nebuchadnezzar became a believer in and follower of the God of Daniel and his people, and Daniel himself rose to a position of high influence not only in Nebuchadnezzar's court but in that of several later Babylonian rulers, all for the sake of the penetration of the kingdom of God into the world's most powerful nation at that time.

One prays there are Daniels and Danielles in Trump's house—or whoever may be president, prime minister, premiere, or whatever the potentate in the time and place you inhabit while reading these words.

When I think of the penetration of the kingdom into nations and their institutions, I think of the remnant in the context of Jesus' parable in Matthew 13:33: "The Kingdom of Heaven is like the yeast a woman used in making bread. Even though she put only a little yeast in three measures of flour, it permeated every part of the dough" (NLT).

There are four dynamics in the process of transformation Jesus described here, all of them showing the mission and goal of the remnant.

Preparation

The preparation of the yeast, or leaven, is through separation to undergo the process of fermentation. A piece of dough is pulled out from the original mass and set in a place where it can be transformed before it is placed back into the lump.

The best environment for fermentation is one that would be uncomfortable for many human beings—high humidity and warmth—but the chunk of dough undergoing fermentation eats it up, literally.

A dying of sorts is also involved in this process. Wastes build up within the dough going through the rigors of transformation. Those wastes help create the flavor that will enrich the bread, which is the end goal.

No wonder Jesus used leaven—or yeast—as a parable of the kingdom. Remnant people are kingdom people. That is, they have a radical commitment to the lordship of Jesus Christ. Separation from the world and dying to the flesh are crucial in the process of transforming a man or woman into a remnant person who will penetrate their worlds with the gospel of the kingdom and ministry of Jesus.

Peter wrote to the remnant church in Rome and to all remnant people across all times and places: "Beloved, do not be surprised at the fiery ordeal which is taking place to test you [that is, to test the quality of your faith], as though something strange *or* unusual were happening to you" (1 Peter 4:12 AMP).

So if you are committed to the Lord of History, and you feel the heat, loneliness, pain of separation, rejection, and isolation, take hope from the fact that your testimony is being formed and you are undergoing preparation to be put back in the "lump" as a transformed person, an agent of Christ's transformation.

Penetration

When the period of preparation is complete, and the piece of dough has been transformed through its "season" of separation, it is placed back in the dough-lump from which it had been taken.

Simon Peter understood this well. Inspired by the Holy Spirit, Peter began his letter to Jesus' followers scattered throughout many places like this: "Peter, an apostle of Jesus Christ, to those who reside as aliens, scattered throughout Pontus, Galatia, Cappadocia, Asia, and Bithynia, who are chosen according to the foreknowledge of God the Father, by the sanctifying work of the Spirit, to obey Jesus Christ and be sprinkled with His blood . . ." (1 Peter 1:1–2).

When Peter labeled himself an "apostle," he was not bestowing an honorific title upon himself. Rather, he knew the meaning of *apostolos*. The Greek word itself brings to mind the remnant calling: "a messenger, envoy, delegate, one commissioned by another to represent him in some way."[2]

Perhaps there echoed in Peter's spirit and soul the words of Jesus decades before when, as He faced His time on the cross, the Lord prayed for His disciples, including this petition: "I am no longer in the world; and yet they themselves are in the world. . . . I do not ask You to take them out of the world, but to keep them from the evil one. . . . As You sent Me into the world, I also have sent them into the world" (John 17:11, 15, 18).

For Jesus' followers, now the "world" is not only geographical but also institutional. He sends us into homes, schools, governing institutions, the workplace . . . wherever our daily journey takes us.

This is clear in the Great Commission, when the Lord tells His followers, literally, "As you are going, make disciples . . ." (Matthew 28:19). Some versions translate the verb *go* in the imperative. However, it is a participle, carrying the idea of "going." The imperatives are making disciples, baptizing them, and teaching them to observe everything Jesus taught the original disciples. Therefore, Jesus is saying that *as we are going* into the world in our daily routines, we should see ourselves as "sent" wherever we are, for the purpose of making disciples—learners—of Him and His kingdom.

When all was well for Daniel in Judah prior to Nebuchadnezzar's raid and the Hebrews' captivity, Daniel did not think of going on a mission trip to Babylon. But in "going" into Babylon as an exile, Daniel fulfilled his mission. It took separation from his homeland, persecution in Babylon, and deprivation by refusing the king's invitation to dine at his table for Daniel and his associates to be prepared for ministry in Nebuchadnezzar's court and country.

God's permissive will allowed the Hebrews to be taken captive, but God's intentional will put Daniel in Nebuchadnezzar's palace as an ambassador of the greater kingdom of God.

Permeation

In the dynamics of dough making, the leaven, now inserted back into a particular part of the dough ball, begins to work its way for that small point of beginning into the whole. It does not stop, noted Jesus, until it is *all leavened* (Matthew 13:33).

As Nebuchadnezzar would discover, the Jews and their spiritual influence affect whole civilizations positively. Babylon in Nebuchadnezzar's day would be permeated with the teachings of the Jewish exiles living there. It seemed nothing could stop their growing influence in Babylonian society. Ultimately one of their number—Daniel—became a leading official in the land where he had been brought decades earlier as a captive.

The thriving of the Jews under their God eventually turned even the heart of the king himself to the Lord of Daniel and his fellow Jews.

Another powerful ruler, centuries later, reflected, too, on the survival and spread of the Jews globally. Frederick the Great asked his physician this question: "Zimmerman, can you name me a single proof of the existence of God?" Zimmerman answered quickly. "Your majesty, the Jews."[3]

Earlier in this book we met Nicolai Berdyaev, a Russian Jew who became a committed follower of Christ, though he had been a dedicated Marxist. In Russia, a land of dread pogroms aimed at the extermination of Jews, Berdyaev began contemplating the apparent indestructibility and presence of the Jews everywhere, left Communism, and became a Christian. Berdyaev wrote about the undeniable facts that led him to his decision:

How probable is it that a tiny people, the children of Israel, known today as Jews, numbering less than a fifth of a per cent of the population of the world, would outlive every empire that sought its destruction? Or that a small, persecuted sect known as the Christians would one day become the largest movement of any kind in the world?

Further, wrote Berdyaev in his book *The Meaning of History*:

I remember how the materialist interpretation of history, when I attempted in my youth to verify it by applying it to the destinies of peoples, broke down in the case of the Jews, where destiny seemed absolutely inexplicable from the materialistic standpoint. . . . Its survival is a mysterious and wonderful phenomenon demonstrating that the life of this people is governed by a special predetermination, transcending the processes of adaptation expounded by the materialistic interpretation of history. The survival of the Jews, their resistance to destruction, their endurance under absolutely peculiar conditions and the fateful role played by them in history: all these point to the particular and mysterious foundations of their destiny.[4]

Nebuchadnezzar had already learned these truths centuries before. And he could not help but note the changes the Jews brought everywhere they went.

Precipitation

The pinch of dough that has now been transformed into leaven and inserted back into the original lump precipitates catalytic action, transforming the rest of the lump with its own characteristics, resulting in bread.

President Woodrow Wilson noted the catalytic effect of the Jews and Judaism, and said: "The Laws of Moses as well as the laws of Rome contributed suggestions and impulse to the men and institutions which were to prepare the modern world; and if we could have but eyes to see . . . we should readily discover how very much besides religion we owe to the Jew."[5]

The nature of the permeation and precipitation of the "leaven" of God's kingdom in the world is illustrated by one of the most dramatic events of the twentieth century: the Allied Normandy invasion on June 6, 1944, "D-Day."

Because I was born two days before the Japanese attack on Pearl Harbor and America's entry into the Second World War, I have a special interest in the cataclysm that impacted so much of the world. The Normandy invasion especially fascinates me, and I was eager to visit those French beaches. Irene and I had that opportunity first in 1995. We have been back several times since then, taking folks with us, including Second World War veterans.

In 1995, vestiges of the fiftieth anniversary observation the year before were still in view. The most moving was the message painted everywhere, on roofs, the sides of barns, and along the roadways that returning veterans of the original invasion traveled on the way to the beaches: "Welcome to our liberators."

Some of the French people who painted those signs had been alive during the invasion that launched the march toward defeat of the Nazis. They still remembered and acknowledged that the huge sacrifice on Utah, Omaha, Gold, Juno, and Sword beachheads had set them free from Hitler.

They had been the first to feel the impact of the invasions. But the Allied military forces had to move on and permeate all the places in Europe held by the Nazis. And everywhere they went, the liberating forces precipitated transformation from enslavement to freedom.

In present times there is much preoccupation in churches regarding the Second Coming. There is a distortion when we become "Dunkirk-minded" rather than "Normandy-minded." The primary focus of the British troops and their allies at France's Dunkirk coastline was escape. This is not to disparage them, because many would come back in 1944 and give their lives at Normandy. Nevertheless, getting out of Dunkirk in 1940 was the top priority.

The Normandy mentality was to invade, advance, and not stop until the mission was complete—victory, total victory, as Churchill put it many times.

So, with respect to the end of the world and the coming of Christ, we must set the focus on remaining until the gospel of the kingdom has been proclaimed throughout the world and every *ethne*—every people group— has had opportunity to hear and respond to it.

Only God knows when that happens, and only He knows when the *telos*—the kingdom purpose of history—has been reached.

The moment the first Allied soldier put his boot on one of those beaches, it was over for Hitler. It would take many months to take the victory to Berlin, his capital, but nevertheless, he was done for when the Allies landed more than six hundred miles away.

Thus, the moment the Lord Jesus Christ was conceived in Mary's womb and entered human time and history, it was over for Apollyon and his demonic armies. Yet the victory won by the Son of God's invasion into the devil-occupied world must advance incrementally, like leaven permeating and precipitating transformation in a lump of dough . . . or the invasion of Europe that drove out Hitler and the Nazis.

It happened that way in Babylon in the age of Nebuchadnezzar, and so it is happening in the age of that other man from "Babylon," Donald Trump.

One of a baker's major concerns is preserving freshness. This calls for another type of "remnant" mixed into the loaf. In our day there are artificial preservatives, but two thousand years ago bakers had to rely on natural items like garlic, cloves, and honey.

God's remnant people play a preservative role in a deteriorating society and culture. A small remnant would have saved Sodom. In His teaching on the Mount of Olives recorded in Matthew 24, Jesus described the horrors of the great tribulation that is to come. "Unless those days had been cut short, no life would have been saved," said the Lord of History. However, "*for the sake of the elect* those days will be cut short" (Matthew 24:22, emphasis added).

The same theme is found in 2 Thessalonians 2, where Paul wrote about the coming of the "lawless one." The apostle said that the "mystery of lawlessness is already at work." However, there is restraint on lawlessness and its chaos that will have to be removed before the lawless one is fully manifest (v. 7).

CHARLES COLSON: AN EXAMPLE

The late Charles Colson, my dear friend and colleague in the Nixon White House, came to understand the remnant and leavening principles firsthand. He and his work show how the strategic remnant works.

One of the most surprising phone calls I ever received occurred one day in 1974. I was pastor of a small church in south Alabama, across the bay from Mobile. The caller was an old friend from Washington. I don't remember all he said that day, but I remember one line: *Chuck Colson has accepted Christ.*

I was tempted to reply, "Sure, and I'll buy the Brooklyn Bridge!"

But I didn't. I just sat there for a moment, stunned. I knew God was powerful, and the conversion of Colson proved just how mighty is the Lord of History.

I had known Colson at a distance "BC" (before Christ), and though I did not know it at that moment, I would soon get to know him closely "AD" (the year of the Lord's coming into Chuck's life).

No one who knew Chuck both before and after his encounter with the

Lord of History could remain an atheist or agnostic. He had been tagged by critics as the "evil genius" in Nixon's inner circle. Nothing could explain Chuck's transformation apart from the Holy Spirit's catalytic impact in his personal life.

But Chuck would not stop there. The Lord had "invaded" his life, and Chuck wanted everyone to have opportunity to experience Christ's liberation.

I visited Chuck three times while he was imprisoned for Watergate-related convictions just three hours from my home in south Alabama. He told me about how other inmates were seeking his advice in legal matters. But Chuck was developing a passion that would go beyond that. He was hungry to read and learn from the Bible, then to help other prisoners know and grow in the Lord.

Some months later, after his release, Chuck called me. He asked if I would fly to Washington and meet with him and a few other friends. So, on a brittle winter day, I found myself in a circle of a dozen or so men to whom Chuck poured out the vision that would become Prison Fellowship (PF). The group's only partisanship was the kingdom of God. It didn't include just Republicans, but prominent Democrats, like Senator Harold Hughes of Iowa, whom Christ had freed from alcoholism. PF would be leaven in hundreds of prisons internationally. It would pervade and precipitate other related ministries. What was born of Charles Colson's travails would become some of the most impactful ministries of all time. On top of that, Chuck would be regarded by many as among the greatest apologists, or defenders of the Christian faith, on the level of C. S. Lewis.

But the leavening effect of Chuck's life and ministry organizations passed through the same process we saw above: He was "prepared" by being "separated" from society in prison. Chuck's soul and spirit were "penetrated" by the witness of people who were devoted to Christ. The "permeation" of the kingdom and the role he was to have in it began when Chuck was himself an inmate. God used Chuck to "precipitate," to be a catalyst of change and redemption for tens of thousands of people and hundreds of institutions.

In God's wonderful kindness I had a phone conversation with Chuck just days before he died. He was about to leave for a speaking engagement. He told me that he didn't feel well physically, but he was going to honor the commitment. Chuck didn't return to his earthly home from that journey. Instead, he went home to heaven.

That was Chuck Colson—remnant man.

On those first long nights in his prison bunk bed, Chuck, like Elijah at his lowest, could have concluded that he was the only Christian there—but that was not Chuck's way of seeing things. God was building a strong faith in Chuck's soul, and there was no need for God to remind him that He had in "reserve" seven thousand who had not bowed before the idols of the age (1 Kings 19:18). After leaving his own imprisonment, Chuck would spend the rest of his life discovering and edifying the remnant inside penal institutions around the world.

IDENTIFYING THE STRATEGIC REMNANT

How then do we identify a remnant man or woman?

First, it's important to know that every person who is born again in Christ is incorporated into the church that is the body of Christ. It is the remnant community. However, not all Christians *function* in their remnant role. Nevertheless, the potential to live and minister as a remnant person is there for every person truly in Christ and indwelt by His Holy Spirit. Growing into the remnant role comes with the process of sanctification, through which we move gradually to spiritual maturity.

We hear Paul's passionate desire for Christ's followers to develop in their remnant role when he wrote in Galatians 4:19, "My children, with whom I am again in labor until Christ is formed in you . . ."

Therefore, God gifts the church with leaders who are to focus on "equipping of the saints for the work of service, to the building up of the body of Christ; until we all attain to the unity of the faith and of the knowledge of the Son of God, to a mature man, to the measure of the stature which belongs to the fullness of Christ" (Ephesians 4:12–13).

This highlights the fact that the Lord of History, Jesus Christ, God incarnate, the Messiah, is *the* remnant person. As such, He is the remnant of fallen humanity and therefore qualifies to atone for the sins of us all. To grow in Christ through the sanctifying work of the Holy Spirit is to grow in the remnant function.

Jesus Himself, again in His great prayer for His disciples recorded in John 17, indirectly reveals characteristics of remnant people:

- Jesus has manifested the name of the Father to remnant men and women so they don't know Him merely in a generic sense but in personal relationship.
- They are people to whom He entrusts the Word that the Father entrusted to Him.
- Remnant people are hated by the world because of their identification with Christ and His message.
- Remnant individuals are not "of" this world in the sense of their identification, nor do they belong to the world that wants their allegiance.
- The remnant is not taken out of the world because that's the place for their ministry.
- They are, however, pulled out of the "lump" that is the world to undergo transformation so they can be put back into the world to be catalysts of Christ's transforming work.
- Remnant men and women are commissioned by Christ to work under His authority in making disciples, baptizing people, and teaching them everything Christ teaches them as they are going into the world.
- Therefore, remnant people are set apart, dedicated for the continuation of the ministry of Jesus wherever they go in the world.

Since the remnant identity is one of functionality, and not merely designation or title, it's important to review crucial functions of remnant people.

Ministering before the throne of God on behalf of civilizations, nations, institutions, and individuals is a major task of remnant people. I will never forget the first time I walked on the floor of the United States House of Representatives as acting chief of staff for a member of Congress. As I watched him vote on an issue impacting his district, I gained a new understanding of intercessory prayer.

Second Chronicles 7:14 reveals the representative function of remnant people: "And My people who are called by My name humble themselves and pray and seek My face and turn from their wicked ways, then I will hear from heaven, will forgive their sin and will heal their land."

Intercessory prayer is the "vote" of the representatives of humanity before the throne of God. And if the remnant people are "members" of the "legislature," then Christ's church is the "House of Representatives."[6] So, in 2 Chronicles 7:15, God said of the temple—of which the biblical church is the successor—"Now My eyes will be open and My ears attentive to the prayer offered in this place."

National repentance is as important as personal repentance. In 1863, President Abraham Lincoln and Congress recognized this and declared a national day of repentance, fasting, and prayer as America was riven by the War Between the States.

I read about this historic event and began to wonder: *But how many of a nation's citizens must repent before God recognizes their contrition and answers their prayer? One hundred percent? That* likely would not happen unless God intervened directly with a powerful manifestation. Even then there would be skeptics who refused to bow the knee.

What God looks for is the repentance of the remnant on behalf of their nation. Again, this is the issue raised in Ezekiel 22:30–31: "I searched for a man among them who would build up the wall and stand in the gap before Me for the land, so that I would not destroy it; but I found no one. Thus I have poured out My indignation on them."

Will God pour out His wrath on America in the age of Trump and his successors? Will God find a remnant to stand in the "gap," to call down blessing on the land? The situation seems grim. Statistics indicate membership and attendance numbers in American churches are shrinking fast. But there is hope, because as church membership and attendance decline, there is also a "quickening" of the "remnant of God's people," according to Sam Rohrer, president of the American Pastors Network.

Rohrer estimates that about 10 percent of people in US churches are remnant men and women in their spiritual maturity and commitment to Christ and His kingdom. While the numbers seem disappointing, "true change in America will happen through the 'Rise of the Remnant,' or those who are left with a passion that still remains for God," Rohrer believes. "I say there's a rising of a remnant at the same time that we see a rising of the unchurched in America. That's positive, but it's also a matter of great urgency to understand what is before us."[7]

THE HOPE

The hope is that the intensifying spiritual, moral, social, cultural, and political sickness in the nation will awaken more followers of Christ to the urgency of functioning as remnant people. If so, their first priority will be building healthy churches crucial for the nation's health.

Meanwhile, the present-day Babylon sickens, and people wonder if the civilization will survive. Those who have written off the church look to politicians as the restorers of health to the nation.

The situation is similar to that of the period of Nebuchadnezzar. Had Babylonians been looking to their king for the restoration of sanity, all they would have found would have been a formerly exalted monarch gone wild in the wilderness. But then something amazing happened. Nebuchadnezzar came out of his mental stupor and declared that the hope of his nation and all others was in the God of Daniel.

Fast-forward to our day, and we encounter the same twist of irony. Donald Trump's opponents—and even some of his allies—believe he is crazy. And yet hardly anyone, friend or foe, could have predicted that the Donald Trump the nation thought it knew would stand one weekend in 2016 in an African American church in Detroit and tell the congregation: "Christian faith is not the past but the present and the future. . . . Now, in these hard times for our country, let us turn again to our Christian heritage to lift up the soul of our nation."[8]

Trump has put the focus for lifting up the soul of the nation where it should be—the church in the nation—as Nebuchadnezzar did centuries ago for his own country.

Is the church healthy enough to lift up the nation's soul? That's one of the most important questions for the demoralized, divided, diseased age in which we live.

ELEVEN

HEALTHY CHURCH, HEALTHY NATION

The manifold wisdom of God might now be made known through the church to the rulers and authorities in the heavenly places.

—THE APOSTLE PAUL, EPHESIANS 3:10

All the aspects of any civilization arise out of a people's religion: its politics, its economics, its arts, its sciences . . . until human beings are tied together by some common faith, and share certain moral principles, they prey upon one another. . . . At the heart of every culture is a body of ethics, of distinctions between good and evil . . . founded upon the authority of revealed religion.

—RUSSELL KIRK

In 1973 I left the White House and Washington with the growing conviction that the most potent and important organism in the world is the truly biblical church. It is the authentic church within a civilization and its nations that sets and sustains the spiritual boundaries that give the society its identity and links it with the kingdom of God.

I refer to the real church as an organism rather than an institution because the genuine church, in its invisible global unity, whatever its designation, is the body of God the Son, infused with the breath of God the Holy Spirit, and pulsing with the heart of God the Father.

Government, I had learned, can force change, but only the Bible-based, Spirit-empowered, Jesus-centered, kingdom-impassioned church can restrain the power holders and bring transformation to people and their institutions.

I had also begun to learn that the health of a nation is in direct proportion to the health of the church within the nation. This realization is even clearer and more intense within me now, after all these decades since the awareness arose in my spirit and soul.

An incident in Central America in the 1970s opened my eyes widely.

Ernie, my friend mentioned previously, had invited me to be part of a small team from Washington to meet with Costa Rican president José Figueres in his home. What transpired that day showed me that ours was a delegation doing the diplomatic business of the kingdom of God.

President Figueres's wife had become a serious believer in Christ, and she hoped we would bear witness to her husband and other political leaders from the Central American region who had also been invited.

We met for breakfast at Figueres's beautiful ranch outside San José, the Costa Rican capital. Figueres was a connoisseur of art, especially that of the ancient Incas and Aztecs. Magnificent and massive carvings and sculptures were positioned throughout the grounds of Figueres's ranch. We strolled among them, admiring the craftsmanship that had produced them, and then went in for breakfast.

About a dozen people sat around a large table in an elegant private dining room. The group included political leaders from other nearby Central American countries. I would discover later that they were followers of Christ.

However, at the heart of President Figueres's concern that day was regional tensions that he feared would erupt in a war. After breakfast he surfaced these issues. He looked across the table at a political leader from one of the neighboring countries. Figueres said his intelligence sources had reported that the neighboring country might be preparing to overthrow him, and that he might have to arm his citizens since his Constitution did not permit him to raise an army. In fact, Figueres himself, in an earlier presidential term in 1948, had disbanded the military so more money could be spent on domestic needs.

After making his worrying statement, the president sat down. An awkward silence descended on the room. I was the only person from the White House present but knew I could say nothing, lest it be implied I was speaking for President Nixon—something I was not authorized to do.

Dr. Richard Halvorson was among the four people from the United States. Dick was pastor of Fourth Presbyterian Church in the Washington, DC, area, and one of Ernie's close associates. He would later become chaplain of the United States Senate. He was a prominent evangelical leader noted for his wisdom, symbolized by the brilliant white hair crowning his head.

After a few moments of quietness, Dick said simply, "*Senor Presidente*, let's pray about your problem." And pray we did, going around the table, including the leader Figueres saw as a potential threat.

I was amazed at the change in the atmosphere of the dining room. It seemed the spirit of war had been driven out by the intercessions of the remnant men around that table. I wished such a dynamic were present in Paris when Henry Kissinger was trying to negotiate peace with North Vietnam's representatives.

A remnant of the "church universal" had assembled in that room that day at President Figueres's ranch, under his gracious hospitality and open heart. The remnant did the business of the kingdom and ministered peace amid a tense situation. There were people present who would not compromise their larger role as ambassadors of Christ's kingdom for the sake of debate or expediency.

They represented God's kingdom as young Daniel had done in Nebuchadnezzar's house.

DANIEL'S MOST IMPORTANT DECISION

In fact, the most important thing Daniel ever did for himself, his own people, and even Nebuchadnezzar and future history was his determination not to eat the "choice food" at Nebuchadnezzar's lavish table (Daniel 1). Many of those tasty morsels would have violated the diet laid down in the law of Moses. Those dietary restrictions had preserved the life and well-being of the Hebrews. The requirements had come from God Himself, protecting His covenant people. In refusing the invitation to dine with Nebuchadnezzar on his fare, Daniel was drawing the proverbial line in the sand. He would not compromise, no matter how tempting the king's allurements were.

He was also prefiguring in type the truth Paul would state centuries later: we cannot dine at the table of demons *and* the table of the Lord (1 Corinthians 10:21).

But Daniel did not refuse as an act of insolence or disrespect. Daniel 1:8 tells us that the young man "*sought permission* from the commander of the officials that he might not defile himself" (emphasis added). Daniel respected authority, and that's among the reasons God could trust him with great power.

Some seventy years in the future, remnants of the Hebrews would be able to start going back to Judah in three waves. In 538 BC one remnant group returned to Jerusalem and began rebuilding the temple under Zerubbabel by the permission of Cyrus the Persian, who had conquered and then controlled Babylon. Had Daniel and his friends compromised decades earlier, the Jews would have been absorbed into Babylonian society and culture. Had Daniel trashed the Mosaic law and fattened himself at Nebuchadnezzar's table, that holy law would have been tossed aside.

Decades after the first wave of the remnant people had returned to

Jerusalem and begun reconstruction—starting with the temple—another remnant of the Jewish exiles, led by Ezra, made the journey to the homeland of their ancestors. The first remnant group had launched the physical restoration of the temple, but Ezra and this second wave of Hebrews would focus on spiritual restoration. Without that, the physical temple would have been meaningless.

In 445 BC, Nehemiah, with the authorization of Artaxerxes, the Persian ruler he served, led the third wave of remnant people back to Jerusalem and started rebuilding the walls and gates.

The sequence here is important. It moves from inward to outward. The first group of the returning remnant centered its energies on the temple, the heart of the Jewish nation. The second wave worked on the spiritual restoration that gave meaning to the physical temple. Finally, Nehemiah and his returnees wrapped it all up in secure outer boundaries.

The destroyers of our souls work from outward to inward. They begin with an attack on the outer structure of our lives, or bodies. Once those walls are penetrated and weakened, the enemy can flood into our souls, gaining control over our psyche. Thus the Bible reports that when Eve "saw that the [forbidden] tree was good for food, and that it was a delight to the eyes, and that the tree was desirable to make one wise, she took from its fruit and ate; and she gave also to her husband with her, and he ate" (Genesis 3:6). There is the sequence of evil's forced takeover and change in our lives and society: "the lust of the flesh and the lust of the eyes and the boastful pride of life" (1 John 2:16).

But the restoration of Jerusalem from the inside out shows how the Holy Spirit works not merely restoration but transformation in our lives from inward to outward. He begins at the deep core of our being, the spirit, where the event of *justification* takes place. Then the Spirit's transformative work in us moves into the soul, the arena within our being where the process of *sanctification* moves forward, gradually transforming our minds, emotions, and wills. Finally, there is another event that transforms our bodies, *glorification*, whereby the mortal body is clothed in the resurrection body of Christ.

THE IMPORTANCE OF THE SPIRIT'S HEALTH

Daniel, in his resistance of Nebuchadnezzar's temptations, had to rely on the health of his spirit. His body might have craved the delicious foods at the king's table. Their succulence might have filled his mind with thoughts of grand feasts. Daniel's emotions might have surged with pride at the thought of dining at Nebuchadnezzar's side, with all the fame and adulation that will bring him. And Daniel's spirit might have caved in and compromised.

But everything rode on Daniel's healthy spirit. If it became unhealthy, all would have been lost. It was Daniel whom God had chosen to be *the* remnant man initially within Babylon. Through identification with him, Shadrach, Meschach, and Abednego also became remnant men, and remained so even as they were cast into the fiery furnace. Then, through the identification of generations of Hebrews with Daniel and his friends, there arose the remnant people who would constitute the waves of returnees that would carry out the restoration of the temple and the city—and blessing to the world.

The Old Testament remnant's impact on global history was huge. That included the contributions of Daniel through his engagement with Nebuchadnezzar and other rulers in Babylon and Persia. The worldview emerging from the old covenant, to which Daniel clung with great tenacity, provided structural coherence that would be the strength of the greatest of human civilizations.

Russell Kirk contemplated the "enemies of the permanent things" and wrote a book of that title. "Spiritual disorder brings on political anarchy," Kirk concluded.[1] Everyone who cherishes liberty should thank God for Daniel and the remnant people who stood firm in Babylon, and their descendants who restored the temple and Jerusalem.

As we discussed earlier, the Lord Jesus Christ is *the* Remnant Man for all humanity. Those who identify with Him become remnant people. Their spiritual health is crucial to their society. Thus, the health of the nation, its society and culture, is dependent on the health of the church within the nation.

Christopher Dawson, the twentieth-century philosopher of history, highlighted the importance of Daniel in his day and the church in ours when he wrote:

> We are only just beginning to understand how intimately and profoundly the vitality of a society is bound up with its religion. It is the religious impulse which supplies the cohesive force which unifies a society and a culture. The great civilizations of the world do not produce the great religions as a kind of cultural by-product; in a very real sense the great religions are the foundations on which the great civilizations rest. A society which has lost its religion becomes sooner or later a society which has lost its culture.[2]

Neither of the "two men from Babylon" understand fully the larger purposes for which they have been raised up or allowed to lead a nation or civilization. Therefore, whether a tyrannical monarch like Nebuchadnezzar or a democratically elected chief of state like a president of the United States, they will inevitably try to use and compromise the Daniels and the churches with the "delicacies" of their table of prerogative and power.

When there is compromise, the remnant becomes unhealthy, and the nation suffers.

Jesus emphasized the importance of His remnant community when He called His people "the salt of the earth" and "the light of the world." Angelo Codevilla showed how the health of this community helps produce a healthy society—especially in relation to civil governance. Western Christianity, he said, "made society and individuals less dependent on government than ever before or since."[3]

Jesus' concern for the health of the remnant community is evident when He asked, rhetorically, "But what good is salt if it has lost its flavor? Can you make it salty again? It will be thrown out and trampled underfoot as worthless. You are the light of the world. . . . No one lights a lamp and then puts it under a basket" (Matthew 5:13–15 NLT).

Unhealthy churches have lost their zest as well as their ability to give light to "the people who walk in darkness . . . who live in a dark land" (Isaiah 9:2). So, again, *the health of a nation is in direct ratio to the health of the church within the nation.*

History is full of examples.

THE "SICKENING" OF THE CHURCH

The earliest church was truly "catholic," meaning "universal" in the sense that it was essentially one in doctrine and practiced throughout the known world of, primarily, the Roman Empire. After Constantine conquered the Western Empire in AD 312, he embraced Christianity. The church evolved into an institution of power rather than the living, simple community that was the first-century church, with its spiritual and moral authority.

It didn't take long for spiritual anarchy to sicken the church. One of the worst outbreaks of the malignancy occurred in the Renaissance era. The church exchanged the keys of the kingdom for the sword of fleshly power. In the 1400s Italy was divided into states that warred against each other in their quest for power. Families like the infamous Borgias were able to buy high church offices, and even the papacy, with their wealth and muscle.

There was no spiritual restraint, no yielding to the control of the Holy Spirit, no submission to God's Word in the written Scripture. In fact, the church leaders of that era—as Martin Luther would later report—rarely even read the Bible. They committed adultery, fornication, incest, murder, and other sinister crimes to buy for themselves and their families the rich offices of the church. For example, in March 1492, Giovanni Lorenzo de Medici was made a cardinal—the highest office next to the pope—at age sixteen. The Medicis were one of the families competing with the Borgias for power. Spiritual anarchy was the style, and fleshly power was the weapon.

A SICK CHURCH AND THE FRENCH REVOLUTION

The eighteenth-century church in prerevolutionary France was rich and fat. It looked good on the outside, with exquisite rituals, lavish accoutrements, and impressive institutions. However, it was a sick church.

Thomas Carlyle, in his extraordinary volumes on the French Revolution, imagined the grand "estates," or dominating establishments in prerevolutionary France, strutting through the boulevards. "The Clergy have got up," wrote Carlyle, "enforcing residence of bishops, better payment of tithes." Carlyle thought of "Abbe Maury," a church leader, as a face of the pride and pomp of the church itself, and said of Maury, "Thou shalt have a Cardinal's Hat, and plush and glory; but alas, also in the long-run—mere oblivion like the rest of us; and six feet of earth!"[4]

Edmund Burke watched all this from his perch in the British Parliament with a wary eye. The church's sickness, and the excesses it brought on, stirred a reaction in France that would add to the nation's unhealthy culture. Destroying their civil government and attacking the church, sick as it was, had upset the authoritative balance that ensured true freedom rather than mob rule. The nation was headed for disaster, Burke prophesied—accurately, as it turned out.[5]

A SICK CHURCH AND AMERICAN SLAVERY

As the French Revolution was boiling in 1789, across the Atlantic in the new United States a crisis was simmering that would come to full fury in 1860. Slavery was spreading, and because of theological confusion in unhealthy churches, the prophetic voice that might have warned of inevitable judgment was mostly silent.

A few people understood that severe consequences were ahead, even among slaveholders like Thomas Jefferson. Having penned the profound words in the Declaration of Independence recognizing the equality of all humans, he was aware of the incongruity of one human being made in the image of God and endowed by their Creator with "certain unalienable rights" treating as chattel another human being made in the image of God and endowed by their Creator with "certain unalienable rights."

In fact, the inconsistency between his ideals and the slavery he regarded as economic necessity produced a storm in Thomas Jefferson's soul. He confessed that, "I tremble for my country when I reflect that God is just: that his justice cannot sleep for ever: that considering numbers, nature and natural means only, a revolution of the wheel of fortune, an exchange of situation, is among possible events: that it may become probable by supernatural interference!"

Jefferson was wrestling with the conviction that slavery was such an evil that it was going to cause God to bring judgment on the new nation—which He did from 1860 to 1865.

But there were sick churches in the Deep South who taught that slavery was not sin that would draw the wrath of God. People with stricken consciences looked to the church for justification for holding slaves, and too often they got what they wanted to hear rather than what they needed to hear. Because of the sickness of the churches, the Confederate States of America was a sick society.

Historian Mark Noll explored the link between church and nation in the Civil War era and titled a section of his book on that topic "Broken Churches, Broken Nation."

Methodist and Baptist denominations split into Southern and Northern fragments, Noll pointed out. This schism "worked an echoing effect on the body politic."[6]

Henry Clay, who represented his state of Kentucky in both the US Senate and House of Representatives (where he was Speaker), realized implications of the schisms in these great churches and said that "this sundering of the religious ties which have hitherto bound our people together, I consider the greatest source of danger for our country."[7]

South Carolina's John C. Calhoun, a staunch defender of slavery, nevertheless recognized the link between the health of the church and the health of society. In an 1850 speech Calhoun told the Senate that as the major denominations broke apart, "nothing will be left to hold the States together except force."[8]

Calhoun indirectly underscored the fact that when recognized authority breaks down, raw power takes over.

And the history of the War Between the States proved it.

A SICK CHURCH AND THE RISE OF NAZISM

Dietrich Bonhoeffer was a remnant man in Nazi Germany, but, as Sir Winston Churchill's great-grandson, Jonathan Sandys, and I wrote in *God and Churchill*, much of the German church was desperately sick.[9] We cited Leon Poliakov, a Russian Jew and French historian. Poliakov wrote that in the buildup to the Nazi takeover, "the search for a new religion became an endemic phenomenon and it is no exaggeration to describe it as a philosophical psychosis."[10] That happened despite the fact that in the nineteenth and early twentieth century Germany was a nation full of theologians. Young seminarians in some schools in the 1920s and early 1930s seeking a doctorate in theology had to learn German because so many of the books they would be required to read would be in that language.

How could a country known in some quarters as a "theological nation" produce Hitler, the Nazis, and rampant anti-Semitism?

A philosophy that had begun to sicken the German theological establishment—with shining exceptions like Bonhoeffer—had arisen in the eighteenth century. J. S. Semler, born in 1725, became a prominent German academic and "the father of the destructive school of German rationalism."[11] That rationalism produced a hermeneutic—or interpretive methodology— that weakened belief in the authority of Scripture. Ultimately, Semler totally rejected the idea of the divine inspiration of the Bible. Rudolf Bultmann in the twentieth century built on Semler's theories and taught that the Bible should be "demythologized," or stripped of its supernatural, or "mythical," writings.

Many German churches fell into this theological sickness because their pastors no longer believed in or preached that the Bible was truly the Word of God, inspired through His Holy Spirit, and thus authoritative for people and their nation. Rather than judging Nazi culture by the standard of God's revealed Word, they allowed Nazi culture to judge the revealed Word of God.

This is an important warning for contemporary churches who are bending scriptural truth to conform to emergent spiritual, moral, and cultural trends.

The demonic spirituality of Nazism was able to fill the void for many people. However, the Confessing Church arose to oppose the effort by the Nazi Party to unify all the churches in Germany to one national denomination that promoted Nazi ideas. Thus, as Jonathan and I concluded in *God and Churchill*, Hitler knew that at some point he would have to do to the remnant church what he was doing to the Jews. Feisty pastors like those in the Confessing Church challenged him and dared to preach against Nazism until they were carried off. Eventually the dictator would need to rid himself of them altogether, but first he would co-opt the official German church and make it a servant of Nazi ideology and a legitimizer of its evils.

HEALTHY CHURCH, HEALTHY NATION

This brief survey of sick churches and societies shows the importance of understanding what healthy churches look like, and the impact they have on their societies. In visiting and working with churches and their leaders in more than twenty nations, I have observed these characteristics that healthy churches everywhere—no matter what the culture—share:

- Healthy churches are Jesus-centered.
    Such churches recognize that they exist incarnationally in their

societies to continue the earthly ministry of Jesus. Therefore, they worship God, intercede for their communities and nations, and proclaim the gospel of the kingdom. Healthy churches make disciples of the people who respond to the proclamation and serve human need in Christ's name.

- Healthy churches are Spirit-energized.

They welcome and receive the manifest presence of the Spirit through the leadership gifts He has placed in the body, and the ministry gifts distributed across all the body. Healthy churches realize that only the Holy Spirit can bring the fruit of the Spirit—the harvest, true repentance, and the fruits of character. The success of the healthy church comes from the realization and operational philosophy that, to paraphrase Zechariah 4:6 again, it is not by (human) might or power, but by the Holy Spirit that transformation comes. The healthy church recognizes that it is the primary agency of the Spirit's ministry in the nation.

- Healthy churches are Word-anchored.

They are not sickened by false doctrine and don't chase spiritual fads, because they measure everything by the revealed Word of God. They are not tossed to and fro by every wind and wave of false doctrine, because the Bible is their anchor.

- Healthy churches are kingdom-envisioning.

They see Jesus Christ as Lord of people's lives, Lord of the church, Lord of the nations, Lord of History, Lord of all. Healthy churches are not isolated cults, believing they are the only true church or ministry, but they see, appreciate, and partner with other ministries who see the kingdom.

- Healthy churches are what I call "0^2 Churches."

They link "orthodoxy" and "orthopraxy." Such churches minister to their societies and the people within them—whoever they are—through two Spirit-energized functions, the *pastoral* and the *prophetic*.

Babylonian-style culture leaves a lot of wounded people in its invasive path, and churches must be ready to help them find healing. Yet the problems individuals face today because of the sick culture are more complex than in the past.

Thom Rainer, a specialist in helping churches be healthy, lists ten areas where pastors need special preparation for ministering in the twenty-first century:

1. They must learn the "new language" of social media.
2. They must learn how to relate and communicate within a non-Christian culture.
3. Pastors in the twenty-first century must recognize that people attending their churches are increasingly "convicted Christians and not Christians in name only" because of the decline of "cultural Christians" within society (in the West primarily).
4. Church ministers in the twenty-first century must adopt a new work/life balance because in the computer age with constant communications, "the world of work and personal life is becoming increasingly blurred."
5. Pastors and other church members must face the reality of unregenerated church members "who may cognitively assert belief in Christ but have really not had a conversion."
6. Ministers must learn to see their local communities as mission fields because many "are changing with an influx of new ethnic groups and people of other religious beliefs."
7. Pastors in the twenty-first century must "earn respect" daily because the title of "pastor" or other church-related nomenclature is no longer respected in the culture.
8. Church leaders must learn to communicate in a more critical world.
9. Leadership training is crucial for church leaders because of the increasing challenges to organizational leaders in the twenty-first century.
10. Church revitalization is an urgent need because some "nine out of ten of our churches are in need of some level of major revitalization."

Despite all this, Rainer says he sees "this new reality and this new mission field as a great opportunity." It requires a "missional mindset" and "total dependence on the One who sends us to the mission field. And that is exactly where God wants us."[12]

The second ministry healthy churches must activate in contemporary culture is the prophetic function. Sometimes it will be in the form of "future-telling." There are leaders in the body of Christ who are able to alert people to specifics of what will happen in days to come. Some leaders speak prophetically because God gives them special illumination. The Lord of History has also given the gift of discernment at high levels to others who have prophetic voices within churches. They are like the "sons of Issachar," who have special insight into the problems and challenges of the times and what spiritual leadership is to do in light of the needs.

The "forth-telling" style of the prophetic is of great importance in the contemporary age. This ministry speaks hard truth into the culture. But it doesn't stop there. The whole point of the prophetic ministry is to give guidance. The prophetic function is so vital that Paul wrote: "Pursue love, yet desire earnestly spiritual gifts, but *especially that you may prophesy*" (1 Corinthians 14:1, emphasis added).

The prophet Hosea wrote of Jacob, whose name was also synonymous with the nation that would arise from his seed: "But by a prophet the LORD brought Israel from Egypt, and by a prophet he was kept" (Hosea 12:13).

Prophets therefore point out the wrong path, lead people to the right path, and keep them on track. With so many unhealthy, even deadly "paths" being carved out in the twenty-first century, the healthy church *must* function in the prophetic.

If she does so, she herself will have to face the fact Thom Rainer mentioned. She will not necessarily be respected or well received by the culture. In fact, the "Chaldeans" of our times—the entertainment, information, academic, political, and corporate establishments—will try to silence the prophetic. The sequence appears across history: marginalization, caricaturization, vilification, criminalization, elimination.

The "two men from Babylon," the Nebuchadnezzars and Trumps, and all men and women who lead nations, have as a major responsibility protecting the principle of freedom of religion. In a free society that will mean all kinds of religious bodies, some beneficial to the nation's well-being and some destructive. Yet the freedom that the Judeo-Christian worldview encourages will also flourish.

C. S. Lewis wrote that receiving Christ and the work of the Holy Spirit into one's life is a "good infection," spreading transformation toward Christlikeness in the person. The same is true for the church.

Churches are sick when a spiritual virus invades, advances, and takes over. Then the sick church infects its society. The antidote is Jesus Christ working in us personally and corporately. The specifics of recovery for churches are prescribed by Jesus Himself in His messages to the churches of Revelation. The Lord addresses seven churches spread across Asia Minor. Seven is the number of completeness; therefore, these are all the types of churches that will appear throughout history.

- To the "Ephesus" church weakened and sickened because it has "left its first love": "Remember from where you are fallen, and repent" (Revelation 2:5–6).
- To the "Smyrna" church, whose health is threatened by persecution and tribulation: Don't be distracted and anxious about hard times ahead, but focus on and develop determination to be faithful no matter what (Revelation 2:8–11).
- To the "Pergamum" church that has been sickened by distorted, enculturated, or extrabiblical teaching: Cast it out and repent by turning back to healthy exposition of the inspired Word of God (Revelation 2:12–17).
- To the "Thyatira" church, whose health has been corrupted by giving a place for false prophets and teachers: Give leadership to the remnant within your midst who didn't fall for the doctrinal virus, and hold tight only to that which is taught and consistent with the inspired Word of God (Revelation 2:18–29).

- To the "Sardis" church that is spiritually dead: Wake up, shape up, and build up the good things that you haven't lost, and look up to the remnant people in your midst who have not been sickened spiritually, doctrinally, or functionally (Revelation 3:1–6).
- To the "Philadelphia" church that has much opportunity ahead (and could get sickened by pride, egoism, and the temptation to enlarge popularity and appeal): Recognize that harder times are ahead, don't relax in your apparently favorable environment, and get ready to persevere in testings that loom in your future (Revelation 3:7–13).
- To the "Laodicea" church that is lukewarm, self-satisfied, but blind to the seriousness of its sickness: Get real! Understand how bad off you are and what can bring healing. Put on some clothes, because you are naked and don't know it. Clothe yourself in Christ!

LIMITS OF THE "TWO MEN FROM BABYLON"

While civil governments, led by the "two men from Babylon" and all the rest throughout history, are important in making their nations "great," there is a greatness they cannot achieve. True greatness cannot come through government. When the powers of a nation seek to make it great, they ultimately conclude that greatness is revealed through domination of other countries. This makes war inevitable. Neither Donald Trump nor any other man or woman "from Babylon" can accomplish national greatness.

True greatness transcends human nationalism. Jesus Christ, the Lord of History, did not give the keys of His kingdom to government or any other institution. It is the real church—the healthy church that recognizes His lordship—that the "gates of Hades" cannot withstand (Matthew 16:17–19).

There is a true "MAGA" that goes far beyond anything humans "from Babylon" can envision, and that vision requires a healthy church.

TWELVE

THE TRUE MAGA AND THE NEW JERUSALEM

Let divines and philosophers, statesmen and patriots, unite their endeavors to renovate the age, by impressing the minds of men with the importance of educating their little boys and girls, of inculcating in the minds of youth the fear and love for the Deity and universal philanthropy, and, in subordination to these great principles, the love of their country; of instructing them in the art of self-government without which they never can act a wise part in the government of societies, great or small; in short, of leading them in the study and practice of exalted virtues of the Christian system.

—SAMUEL ADAMS, OCTOBER 4, 1790

Since Nimrod at least, "mighty hunters before the Lord" have been promising people some earthly form of the "New Jerusalem." The result usually has not been the heavenly city but hellish Babylon, with all its oppressiveness and cruelty.

Sometimes those "mighty hunters" are on the prowl for votes. American presidential candidates, like those in other nations, have promised again and again to bring in the kingdom, or at least some snippet of it.

John C. Fremont was near-messianic when he campaigned in 1856 under the slogan "Free Soil, Free Labor, Free Men, and Fremont."

"Rejuvenated Republicanism," promised Benjamin Harrison in 1888.

William McKinley, in 1896, was going to bring back "Patriotism, Protection, and Prosperity."

One of the most ironic slogans was Herbert Hoover's in 1928, just one year before the stock market crash of 1929: "A Chicken in Every Pot and a Car in Every Garage."

On the heels of the Great Depression in Hoover's era, Franklin D. Roosevelt promised a "New Deal."

Harry Truman followed with a "Fair Deal."

In 1956 Dwight D. Eisenhower was promising "Peace and Prosperity."

John F. Kennedy followed in 1960 by dedicating himself to take us to the "New Frontier."

In 1964 Lyndon B. Johnson undertook the building of the "Great Society," a not-so-new twist on the welfare state.

Nixon was "The One" in 1968, but, upon the shame of his resignation, Gerald Ford was going to make us "Proud Again."

When he campaigned against Nixon in 1972 as George McGovern's running mate, Senator Thomas Eagleton said their slogan was "Acid, Amnesty, and Abortion for All."[1]

In 1976 Jimmy Carter was going to be "A Leader for a Change."

Ronald Reagan sought our votes in 1984 with the announcement that "It's Morning in America Again."

George H. W. Bush was going to create a "Kinder, Gentler" America.

Bill Clinton, in 1992, intended to go to work "Putting People First" and, in 1996, was going to busy himself "Building a Bridge to the 21st Century."

George W. Bush's slogan was set for him by the Republican National Convention in 2004: "A Safer World and More Hopeful America."

Barack Obama's slogans were terse: "Yes We Can" and "Hope" in 2008, and "Forward" in 2012.

Donald Trump promises to "Make America Great Again."

So it has gone through each election cycle.

If elections had been held in ancient Babylon, Nebuchadnezzar might have run on the slogan "Make Babylon the Great Even Greater!"

"POLITICAL HYPERBOLE"

Edward Murray Hood, a New York citizen, got fed up with all the slogan-eering. He wrote a letter to the *New York Times* in which he characterized campaign slogans as "political hyperbole." The overpromising especially becomes evident when the slogans "meet the realities of government," as Hood pointed out.[2]

When that happens, everything depends on the style and quality of government. It is either government that rules, or government that serves, a rarity. When the slogan thuds into the bureaucracies, something must give. A ruling government will force acceptance, while a serving government will seek negotiation and partnership, and when that fails, legislation within the bounds of the Constitution.

Richard Nixon was as despised by his opponents in his day as Donald Trump is in ours. In the period I was on his staff, there were holdovers within various government agencies from previous Democrat adminis-trations. They were determined to block any proposals that might fulfill Nixon's agenda and realize his vision. (I am sure the same challenge faces a Democrat presidency whose agencies have Republican holdovers.)

One day I was in a meeting with the head of an agency from one of the cabinet departments. The man was refusing to implement a presidential directive in line with a policy goal of the president. Finally, the bureaucrat blew and said, with grim resolution, that he would *never* do anything that might help Nixon.

This shocked me, especially because we were meeting in the Roosevelt Room, directly across from the Oval Office. In a dictatorship the man would have been taken out and shot. In the American constitutional system, he could sit within forty feet of the president and openly defy the wishes of the chief of state.

This tension afflicts Washington because of competing visions. Voters believe that if their candidate is elected president—or governor, or even mayor—the world will change as soon as they are sworn in. The reality is that Inauguration Day is, to return to the Normandy invasion analogy, "D-Day," when the struggle begins on an incremental level.

FROM PARADISE TO PARADISE

Human beings have striven across history to restore the Paradise that was lost, and if they can't bring it in through their sweat and blood, they will try to legislate it into being.

The Bible begins in Paradise in the form of the garden of Eden and concludes in Paradise in the New Jerusalem. In between, as we discussed in chapter 6, according to Jesus, there is the age of "birth pangs." The Lord of History described this in Matthew 24. The restoration period is revealed in Acts 3:20–21, which tells us that "heaven must receive [Jesus] until the period [in the chronological time we inhabit] of restoration of all things about which God spoke by the mouth of His holy prophets from ancient time."

This passage tells us much about Jesus Christ as the Lord of History.

First, the Greek word for "receive" brings to mind a soldier returning to his or her homeland and taking the rightful place, having successfully completed an assigned mission. Thus, upon the successful completion of His mission in the finite world, Jesus ascended to heaven and was seated at the right hand of the Father (Mark 16:19; Hebrews 1:3; 8:1).

But this was only the beginning.

Restoration is from a Greek word signifying the return of things to their original state. The word also carried the idea of qualitative change. The Lord of History will return at some point and restore the cosmos, including earth, to its original, mint condition. The human beings who have been "born again" in Christ will experience a qualitatively new nature as well.

When we receive Christ in the present age, salvation means having a new spirit, and a soul in the process of transformation, while we remain in a mortal body. At the restoration, our salvation will mean as well the transformation of our bodies and the physical environment we inhabit (Romans 8:19–22). In between, Paul prayed: "Now may the God of peace Himself sanctify you entirely; and may your spirit and soul and body be preserved complete, without blame at the coming of our Lord Jesus Christ" (1 Thessalonians 5:23).

The bottom line: Paradise is coming, but it won't be brought by powerful humans, even the "two men from Babylon," but by the Lord of History, Jesus Christ, the Man from the New Jerusalem.

GNAWING PROBLEM OF THE "BETWEEN TIMES"

The gnawing problem in the times between Eden and the New Jerusalem is that we humans are restless and still tinker at transformation. Ecclesiastes 3:11 says that God has "planted eternity" in the human heart, but we are unable to see the "whole scope of God's work from beginning to end" (NLT).

We are impatient and work feverishly and at great cost to crank up "progress," because right at the core of our being we know there is something that transcends and is far greater than the routine world in which we live. So we strive to bring in Paradise before its *kairos*, its appointed time, which is established in the mind of the Creator and known only to Him.

In that struggle to "bring in the kingdom," we will spend a lot of blood and sweat. The New Jerusalem, the ideal civilization, is not *built* but *arrives*, fully constructed by the hands of the Creator. Therefore, humanity is not to focus on *erecting* it but *embracing* it.

The Bible leaves little doubt that there will be a stunning eschatological moment at the coming of Jesus Christ and His kingdom and the New Jerusalem. This is what John saw in the Revelation visions when he declared, "I saw the holy city, new Jerusalem, coming down out of heaven from God, made ready as a bride adorned for her husband" (Revelation 21:2).

Yet, in the "between times" Jesus said that wherever He is and wherever people receive Him as Lord that "the kingdom of God is in your midst" (Luke 17:21). Everywhere there is a critical mass of people who receive Jesus Christ as Lord of their lives and their societies, there is the blessing of the kingdom.

In the meantime, while waiting for the arrival of the kingdom, people are not to sit on their hands and wait passively until it comes. As Daniel showed in the courts of Nebuchadnezzar, such remnant people are to do "the business of the kingdom" until the Lord comes.

Jesus made this point in a parable recorded in Luke 19. There He told about a rich man about to make a journey far from his home. The landowner called in ten of his workers and entrusted each of them with a portion of his wealth. "Do business till I come," he ordered them.

Jesus told His disciples this parable as He was about to enter Jerusalem for the showdown with His opponents that would lead to the cross. Jesus knew His followers had a misconception about what was to come, supposing that "the kingdom of God was going to appear immediately" (Luke 19:11). Thus, the Lord of History sought to prepare His friends for the fact that there would be "between" times before the culminating age when the kingdom would arrive in the world in full form.

First, there would be the "between" of three days after His death on the cross and His resurrection. Then there would be fifty "between" days from the resurrection to pentecost and the coming of the Holy Spirit on these people who would form the first church. Then there would be a long stretch between pentecost and the return (*parousia*) of Christ and His kingdom.

We live now in that period between pentecost and parousia, the age of "birth pangs," as we discussed in chapter 6. We are indeed people "upon whom the ends of the ages have come" (1 Corinthians 10:11).

Jesus had given His followers much through His teaching. They had seen His authority over darkness and chaos manifest in His miracles. They did not know it, but after His resurrection, and through the Holy Spirit, the Lord would fill them personally with His manifest presence by breathing on them individually.

But there would be more: On the day of pentecost, Jesus, the Lord of History, would empower them to go into all the world with the gospel of the kingdom by pouring out His Spirit upon them. Through that event the Holy Spirit would impart and energize spiritual gifts. The totality of abilities Jesus Himself had utilized in His incarnate ministry would be distributed across the church as a whole so that it could carry out its mission of continuing His incarnate ministry in the world.

And in the "between" of His ascension and return, the command would stand for those baptized into His church to take the gifts He had entrusted to them: "Do business with this until I come back" (Luke 19:13).

What, then, is the business of the kingdom?

THE MOST IMPORTANT KINGDOM WORK

The "two men from Babylon" and all like them, Left and Right, immediately think kingdom "business" is building mighty institutions and beautifying and making their nations "great." Those might help facilitate the work of the kingdom in the material world, but the "business of the kingdom" is much deeper than that.

Perhaps it can be understood in light of a tragedy that struck a young North Carolina couple. Daniel Luther was "close to God and an all-around family man." Ashley, Daniel's wife, described him as her "soul-mate" and an exemplary dad to their infant son, Silas. Daniel was the type of person who worked at the business of the kingdom, feeding homeless people and carrying out other Christlike acts. But he wanted no recognition.

Then Daniel died in a car crash.

As Ashley prepared his life celebration service, she wanted "to remember him for who he was, not how he left," said a news report.

Daniel had the gift of giving. It is no surprise that his organs were donated to save the life of another human being. He's "already saved some lives with some kidneys and lungs," said Ashley, "and that's what he would have wanted. No doubt in my mind!"[3]

By receiving something of Daniel Luther into his or her own body, another human being was healed and rescued from death through the healthiness in Daniel's life replacing their dysfunctional organs.

One day after watching Jesus feed five thousand people with a meager amount of food, His followers came to Him with a question: "What shall we do, so that we may work the works of God?"

"This is the work of God," Jesus replied, "that you believe in Him whom He has sent" (John 6:29).

The fundamental work of God's kingdom in an individual is, through believing faith, to receive the healthy life of Jesus Christ into one's own life. All the other kingdom works flow from this. This is the meaning of the "inward-outward" dynamic. When we receive Christ's life, the Holy Spirit fills us and brings us into the "baptism" that is the empowerment of the pentecost church into which we are plunged. The Holy Spirit reminds the authentic church through John that "the anointing . . . you received from Him remains [permanently]" (1 John 2:27 AMP).

The result of Christ's indwelling of our being, and the empowerment of the Holy Spirit, is that we begin by the new nature within us to do the functional work of the kingdom, which is the incarnational ministry of Jesus Christ, the Lord of History.

As we have noted in other chapters, God's kingdom, said Paul, "is not eating and drinking, but righteousness and peace and joy in the Holy Spirit"

(Romans 14:17). "Righteousness" refers to qualitative goodness and also to justice. The Greek word in the New Testament for *peace* is based on *eiro*, meaning to link things in relationship that result in wholeness. Lucifer's aim for individuals and their institutions is fragmentation. Apollyon's goal is de-creation. But the objective of Christ and His kingdom is unity of all the parts that constitute wholeness. This is peace.

Kingdom "joy" is, in biblical Greek, *chara*, a word related to *charis*, referring to God's "grace." The joy the Holy Spirit gives is a state of being based on the constancy of God's love and mercy. It is in direct contrast to the strictly human concept of "happiness," which is conditional, circumstantial, and temporal, an existence we struggle to achieve.

Righteousness-justice, peace, and transcendent joy constitute the state of the ideal society, the "New Jerusalem." When it appears upon the world and creation is returned to its original state, there will be a new kind of

- *human*, fully integrated in spirit, soul, and body, as the Holy Trinity is integrated in Father, Son, and Holy Spirit, rather than fragmented
- *atmosphere* free of pollutants and poisons
- *culture*, characterized by the fullness of the Word, and praise to God
- *society*, full of righteousness, justice, peace, and Spirit-given joy
- *government* resting upon the "shoulders" of Christ, the Lord of History, Prince of Peace, Mighty God, Everlasting Father, leading in the fullness of grace and truth
- *nature* in which lion and lamb lie down together because the predator-nature will be gone

All of this will exist in a new kind of cosmos, set free from its bondage to decline, deterioration, death, decay, and disintegration.

The good news is that when people yield their lives, relationships, and work and all they touch to the Lord of History, they can enjoy some of the blessings of Paradise in the "between" ages we now inhabit. Yet,

"No eye has seen, no ear has heard,
and no mind has imagined
what God has prepared
for those who love him."[4]

The patriarch Abraham had this drive in his spirit and soul, and "went out, not knowing where he was going," but nevertheless "looking for the city which has foundations, whose architect and builder is God" (Hebrews 11:8–10).

In the secular efforts to bring paradise to the world, the vision is split between those who want to look backward, to previous idealized periods, and those who want to abandon the past, and look only to the future.

Both Donald Trump and Joe Biden seem to believe that the best route to the future is through the past.

Again, in Trump's slogan "Make America Great Again," seeks an age when the United States had "greatness" in the eyes of the world. Making America "great" in the eyes of God is much more important than the nation's global standing.

Then there's Biden's aim to get us back "like we used to be." The former vice president wants to lead in a return to "core values" he sees threatened under Trump, to a period Biden characterizes as "ethical" and "straight" as well as truthful and supportive of our allies, an era of "all those good things."

HOW FAR BACK?

My concern is that neither man may understand just how far back into historic ages we must go if we are to get to the bright future they envision.

Maybe Trump and Biden should seek a return to the America that Frenchman Alexis de Tocqueville visited in the early nineteenth century. The chaos of his own country's terror-filled revolution was doubtless much in mind in contrast to what he saw in post-Revolution America.

The French visitor would have recalled the anti-God, anti-religious spirit of the French Revolution. Reflecting on the intense spiritual landscape of early America, Tocqueville wrote: "When religion is destroyed in a people, doubt takes hold of the highest portions of the intellect and half paralyzes all the others. . . . I doubt that man can ever support a complete religious independence and an entire political freedom at once . . . if he has no faith, he must serve, and if he is free, he must believe."

Tocqueville would tell Trump that there is no greatness without a faith that is more than words and mere political expediency. The Frenchman would tell Biden there are no ethics, no truth, no moral straightness, no core values in the secularism that fascinates so many in his party—if not himself. "Been there, done that," Tocqueville might say to Biden.

But the period of Tocqueville's America (1831–32) is not far enough back. The nation was no exemplar of highest values because slavery flourished in many of its states.

What about the crucial age of the formation of the Republic and its founding documents? Tocqueville would have read the Founders' belief that God is the source of the fundamental rights of "life, liberty, and the pursuit of happiness," and the inferred accountability of government regarding the protection of those rights.

But, again, for the slaveholders of that day—some of whom composed and/or affirmed the beautiful expression in the Preamble to the Declaration of Independence—the words were somewhat meaningless in their present moment. For today's supporters of abortion, there is a denial of that basic right to life.

We would need to ask Joe Biden and Donald Trump: "What is your concept of accountability, and to whom are you ultimately answerable for your personal life and moral decisions?"

We must keep traveling back to the past for the sake of the future.

What about the age of John Winthrop, the first governor of the Massachusetts Bay Colony? In 1630, as we saw in chapter 3, he spoke the DNA into fetal America when he expressed the hope it would be a "city on a hill," built on the principles of God's kingdom, through which all nations could be blessed.

But that vision faded in the passion for expansion, exploitation, and wealth. We cannot linger with Winthrop. We must go further into the past.

We must leapfrog centuries.

Some six hundred years before the coming of Jesus of Nazareth, the Christ, a king arose in Judah. Josiah was only eight when he came to the throne. As he grew older, he began to understand the problems in his country.

At the center of the national crisis was the neglect and deterioration of the temple. Josiah ordered and paid for its restoration.

One day Josiah's aide, Shaphan, rushed to bring news to the king. Hilkiah, the high priest, had discovered the holy books of God's law in the refuse. Josiah ordered Shaphan to read the scrolls. Immediately, Josiah began to recognize the nation-healing truth that had been cast aside.

EMBEDDED IN THE "BOOKS"

The king knew that national greatness, ethics, straightness, truth, core values—all the things Trump and Biden call for today—were embedded in those books.

When King Josiah realized the tragic disregard for those inspired writings, he ripped his clothes in a sign of desperate sorrow and said, "The LORD's great anger is burning against us because our ancestors have not obeyed the words in this scroll" (2 Kings 22:13 NLT).

The Lord gave His response through Huldah, a prophetess: "You were sorry and humbled yourself before the LORD when you heard what I said against this city and its people. . . . You tore your clothing in despair and wept before me in repentance. . . . So I will not send the promised disaster until after you have died and been buried in peace" (vv. 19–20 NLT).

Donald Trump and Joe Biden both might consider tearing their clothes in sorrow (figuratively at least) for our losing God's Word in the hidden ruins of decaying institutions and forgetting the Scriptures' vital role in the founding of America.

Such leadership would "make America great again" and get us back to our "core values" and "all those good things."

In God's design, true progress and the ideal society come in a linkage between past and future, impacting the present. The past is the foundational principles and values God has revealed historically. The future is the linkage of the qualitative realities of the coming New Jerusalem with the quantitative, the material world and its finite time.

However, as shown by secular humanist progressivist socialism, Communism, Fascism, and other movements functioning without God, and in Nimrod fashion, in defiance of God, such human utopian efforts wind up in disaster.

THE TRUE "MAGA"

Therefore, the true "MAGA" is "Make America Godly Again."

"Again? When was America ever 'godly'?" a skeptic might ask.

Neither the United States nor any other nation has demonstrated a godly character consistently in the world's history. However, especially in its beginnings, America experienced outbreaks of true godliness that have brought blessing to itself and the world.

The concept of covenant was at the heart of the American founding. Samuel Rutherford, a seventeenth-century Scottish theologian and statesman, brought the notion of covenant into civil governance in his book *Lex Rex, or The Law and the Prince.* Rutherford showed, based on Romans 13, that rulers are in covenant with God because it is He who grants them authority to govern. As that vision has faded, the nation has experienced declines in crucial areas of its national life.

The Mayflower Compact, written on November 11, 1620, is considered "America's first great constitutional document."[5] It brought the covenant concept into functional application for governance.

Andrew McLaughlin (1861–1947) was a historian who probed the worldview of America's Founders. McLaughlin was qualified to dig deeply as a professor of history at the University of Michigan and the University of Chicago as well as serving as president of the American Historical Association. McLaughlin wrote *Foundations of American Constitutionalism*, where he reported that "the word 'covenant' and its significance will appear over and over again as we study American constitutionalism."[6]

McLaughlin noted that the framers of the Declaration of Independence concluded by acknowledging God's sovereignty over history and nations and made a covenant with God in the founding of what would become the United States. They wrote: "And for the support of this Declaration, with a firm reliance on the Protection of Divine Providence, we mutually pledge to each other our Lives, our Fortunes, and our sacred Honor."

Covenant was established in antiquity and is central in the Bible for the type of relationship between God and people and people to people. The Bible is a record of those covenants. The American Founders were familiar with the nature of covenantal relationship because they knew the Bible.

In researching the books, pamphlets, newspapers, and other documents of Colonial times that influenced the worldview of the American Founders, Professors Donald S. Lutz and Charles S. Hyneman discovered that "the source most cited by the founding fathers was the Bible."[7] Thus, they would have known Deuteronomy 7:9, where Moses said, "Know [without any doubt] and understand that the LORD your God, He is God, the faithful God, who is keeping His covenant and His [steadfast] lovingkindness to a thousand generations with those who love Him and keep His commandments" (AMP).

SECULARIZING FRENZY

As I write, there is a secularizing frenzy in Western culture. Transcendence is seen as entrapment. As previously noted, the "Chaldeans" in the establishments that form societal consensus—entertainment, information, academic, political, corporate—want to rid us of the covenantal framework through which society can be safe in its freedoms, assured of justice, secure in peace, and thrive with real joy.

However, the human being is "wired" for transcendence, and when we reject the Lord of History, we attempt to square the circle by making the immanent transcendent. Hollywood gives us Nimrod-like "mighty heroes" as "masters of the universe," technology seeks to create the AI gods, academia strives to provide an intellectual base for the new-think, politicians lasso us with laws that will corral our thought and behavior within the new and restrictive PC fences, and corporations will tease us with the trends because they are wonderfully marketable in the new environment.

Meanwhile, the nations are in turmoil, heaving seas as shown in the book of Revelation. This is the condition most favorable to the rise of Antichrist.

We need the Lord of History, the Christ. Urgently.

Therefore, to "make America great again" cannot be done without *leading* America to be godly again. It is a contradiction to try to "make" the nation godly, for this would result in legalistic, repressive theocracy. Proverbs 21:1 says, "The king's heart is like channels of water in the hand of the LORD; He turns it wherever He wishes."

Leadership, rather than authoritarian force, is the way of God's kingdom. Under God that kind of leadership can be given through men and women who are unlikely and complex but powerful in the best sense under His lordship. If they are to lead nations, they must be led by the Spirit of the Lord of History and the nations within it.

Not even the "two men from Babylon" can transform their nations until they and those who govern with them truly turn their hearts to the Lord of History as the Lord of their lives.

EPILOGUE

PAYDAY SOMEDAY

The knowledge of God and his truths have from the beginning of the world been chiefly, if not entirely, confined to those parts of the earth where some degree of liberty and political justice were to be seen, and great were the difficulties with which they had to struggle, from the imperfection of human society, and the unjust decisions of usurped authority.
—JOHN WITHERSPOON

Sin will take you farther than you want to go,
Sin will keep you longer than you want to stay,
Sin will cost you more than you want to pay.
—R. G. LEE

He looked like Moses without the beard.

That's among my memories fifty-six years after my encounter with Robert Greene Lee, hailed in his day as a "peerless pulpiteer" and "spellbinding" preacher.[1]

I was a student, on the eve of entering seminary. My pastor, John Bob Riddle, had invited Dr. Lee to preach at our church and felt I would benefit from meeting the great preacher personally.

Dr. Lee was a genuine patriarch in the eyes of many of us in that day. I almost trembled as I entered the room where he sat. I saw a big man with a rock-determined face crowned with white hair.

Like a prophet, he warned me not to be taken in by liberal theology that denied biblical inspiration. That would be no danger since I was on my way to a seminary presided over by one of R. G. Lee's soulmates.

On that evening Dr. Lee would preach his most famous sermon, "Payday Someday." From 1919 up to his death in 1978, he would proclaim the message 1,275 times. The sermon centered on evil Queen Jezebel and cowardly King Ahab, and the judgments that fell on them for turning away from God. In a thunderous voice Dr. Lee characterized Ahab as "the vile human toad who squatted upon the throne of his nation—the worst of Israel's kings."

Jezebel was "infinitely more daring and reckless in her wickedness . . . a devout worshipper of Baal, she hated anyone and everyone who spoke against or refused to worship her pagan god." But for Jezebel and her sycophantic husband, "payday came as certainly as night follows day, because sin carries in itself the seed of its own fatal penalty."

Today's culture disdains such preaching, but the principle holds.

Dr. Lee spoke in the style and tradition of the preachers in the First Great Awakening that prepared America's spiritual soil for the nation that would rest upon it.

WITHERSPOON'S WISDOM AND WARNINGS

In 1776, John Witherspoon, considered by some as "the most influential teacher in American history,"[2] shook many through a speech he made in Princeton that was published in Philadelphia and circulated widely. Witherspoon had been invited to the American Colonies from his native

Britain by George Whitefield, the man used by God to ignite the spiritual Great Awakening.

Witherspoon's address at the outset of the revolutionary era was both affirmative for the cause of American independence and full of wisdom and warnings for the definitive season the Colonies were entering.

The title of Witherspoon's sermon was "The Dominion of Providence over the Passions of Men."[3]

In our culturally adolescent mindset, Witherspoon might be too quickly written off. There would be attempts to blot out the memory of the man who was president of Princeton University. However, Witherspoon was taken seriously in his day, as he should be in ours. He was an elected member of the Continental Congress and a vocal advocate of the Declaration of Independence—in fact, an ordained minister of the church who signed it. At the end of the War for Independence and the American victory, Witherspoon was among those who wrote the instructions for peace commissioners who would represent America in negotiating the Treaty of Paris that officially ended the conflict.

In short, Witherspoon had earned the right to speak, and, thankfully, significant leaders heeded his words.

What Witherspoon had to say in those days is strikingly relevant in our own.

"There is no greater evidence of the reality of the power of religion, than a firm belief in God's universal presence, and a constant attention to the influence and operation of His providence," said Witherspoon.

God's providence, Witherspoon declared, "extends not only to things which we may think of great moment, and therefore worthy of notice, but to things the most indifferent and inconsiderable." This was evident, Witherspoon pointed out, when Jesus, in the Sermon on the Mount, said, "Look at the birds of the air, that they do not sow, nor reap nor gather into barns, and yet your heavenly Father feeds them. Are you not worth much more than they?" (Matthew 6:26).

If biblically committed people are going to claim the promises of God for the nation by believing that God providentially and sovereignly established

America for His kingdom purposes in history, then we must take seriously the cautions and warnings that come with appropriating that claim. If one is to assume, presume, or claim the name and authority of God, he or she better be willing to take on the implications in his or her personal life, worldview, and work.

Paraphrased from Witherspoon's warnings given long ago, we can derive important alerts for the age of Trump:

1. When celebrating victories and blessings, don't forget the true Source: "It would be a criminal in attention not to observe the singular interposition of Providence."

2. "Guard against the dangerous error of trusting in or boasting of an arm of flesh. There is no story better known in British history, than that the officers of the French army the night preceding the battle of Agincourt, played at dice for English prisoners before they took them, and the next day were taken by them."

3. Never forget that "the whole course of providence" seems "intended to abase the pride of man and lay the vain-glorious in the dust."

4. "I look upon ostentation and confidence ['boasting' in our deeds, the meaning in Witherspoon's day] to be a sort of outrage upon Providence, and when it becomes general, and infuses itself into the spirit of a people, it is a forerunner of destruction."

5. Whoever has the "countenance" and approval of God has "the best at last."

6. "If to the justice of your cause, and the purity of your principles, you add prudence [union, firmness, and patience] in your conduct, there will be the greatest reason to hope, by the blessing of God, for prosperity and success."

7. Have "zeal for the glory of God and the good of others."

8. Recognize that "when the manners of a nation are pure, when true religion and internal principles maintain their vigour, the attempts

of the most powerful enemies to oppress them are commonly baffled and disappointed."

9. "Exert yourselves, every one in his proper sphere, to stem the tide of prevailing vice, to promote the knowledge of God, the reverence of His name and worship, and obedience to His laws."

10. Rather than an attitude of entitlement, apply yourself "with the utmost diligence to works of industry."

I would add to these concerns my own:

- I would wish that Donald Trump would set a better example of personal morality (as I would have Warren G. Harding, John F. Kennedy, Bill Clinton, and several other presidents);
- that Trump would be less adolescent;
- that he be careful about setting precedent with respect to emergency powers;
- that he not encourage a civil religion;
- that he distinguish between authoritarianism, raw power, and true authority;
- that in his efforts to point out fake news he does not stifle freedom of the press; and
- that he not fall into the trap of overwrought nationalism.

Trump, after all, is a mortal who, like the rest of us, falls into the category Paul described in Romans 3:23—"*All* have sinned and fall short of the glory of God" (emphasis added). The leadership of a nation magnifies shortcomings. Think of King David, who, on the one hand, was "a man after [God's] own heart" (1 Samuel 13:14), while on the other was a womanizer and murderer.

God entrusted Donald Trump in 2016 with a great stewardship. Mere power-seekers want to use their office for domination and exploitation. Real authority is upon those who truly see themselves as public servants. In the Bible, a steward maintains the peace and order of the house until its owner and master returns. Stewardship therefore means there is accountability, a day of reckoning at the arrival *of* the master—or one's arrival *before* the master.

May Donald Trump and those who come after him understand the enormity of that with which they have been entrusted and to whom they must answer ultimately.

ACKNOWLEDGMENTS

"In the end, what makes a book valuable is not the paper it's printed on, but the thousands of hours of work by dozens of people who are dedicated to creating the best possible reading experience for you," said author John Green.

He spoke truthfully.

There are several gifted people who have given their creative abilities and time to help bring *Two Men from Babylon* into reality. I owe them much appreciation.

I am grateful for and to Irene, my wife. She is noted among our family and friends for her wisdom and discernment. Her thoughts and counsel have been crucial to me throughout the writing of this book and our shared journey of more than fifty years.

I also thank Joel Kneedler, a wonderful friend and astute consultant on all things publishing. He initiated ideas that led to the writing of this book and advised me throughout the year it took to bring it to completion.

The team at Thomas Nelson and Emanate Books is made up of seasoned professionals who consistently bring excellence to their projects. That team of editors, designers, and artists for *Two Men from Babylon* includes Tim Paulson, Joey Paul, Janene MacIvor, Lauren Langston Stewart, Kristen Golden, and Kristina Juodenas.

To all these I say: Thank you for the many hours and your dedication to applying your talents and skills to creating hopefully "the best possible reading experience" for our readers.

Above all, I am thankful to Jesus Christ, the Lord of History, who at great sacrifice brings to the world the beautiful kingdom of righteousness, justice, peace, and joy.

There can be no greater cause to which to devote one's life.

—Wallace Henley

NOTES

Prologue

1. C. F. Keil and F. Delitzsch, *Commentary on the Old Testament*, vol. 1 (Grand Rapids: William B. Eerdmans Publishing Company, 1983), 165–66.

2. John MacGinnis, "Herodotus' Description of Babylon," Bulletin of the Institute of Classical Studies 33, no. 1 (December 1, 1986), https://www.deepdyve.com/lp/wiley/herodotus-description-of-babylon-7j0C9SzZCu.

3. "Modern Babylon," *New York Daily Quote*, August 15, 2015, http://www.nydailyquote.com/2015/08/modern-babylon.html. Emphasis added.

4. Cited in Brody and Lamb, *The Faith of Donald J. Trump* (New York: HarperCollins, 2018), 91.

5. Victor Davis Hanson, *The Case for Trump* (New York: Basic Books, 2019), 22.

6. Hanson, 63.

7. Hanson, 275.

8. Daniel Henninger, "The Trump Paradox," *Wall Street Journal*, January 17, 2018, https://www.wsj.com/articles/the-trump-paradox-1516234165.

9. George J. Bryjak, "Sad and Absurd," *Adirondack Daily Enterprise*, May 17, 2019, https://www.adirondackdailyenterprise.com/opinion/guest-commentary/2019/05/sad-and-absurd/.

10. "George Will: Donald Trump Is 'Bloviating Ignoramus,'" *Huffpost*, May 27, 2012.

11. Elaine Wilson-Reddy, "Undying Loyalty to Trump Is Perplexing," *Advocate-Messenger*, April 11, 2019, https://www.amnews.com/2019/04/11/undying-loyalty-to-trump-is-perplexing/.

12. Emily Shire, "Stephen Hawking Solved the Riddle of Donald Trump's Rise in Just a Few Words," *Bustle*, May 31, 2016, https://www.bustle.com/articles/163990-stephen-hawking-solved-the-riddle-of-donald.

13. Shire, "Stephen Hawking Solved."

14. David Brody (@DavidBrodyCBN), November 25, 2019.

15. Christopher Dawson, *Dynamics of World History*, ed. John J. Mulloy (Wilmington, DE: ISI Books, 2002), 311.

16. Christopher Dawson, *The Movement of World Revolution* (New York: Sheed and Ward, 1959), 102.

17. As cited in Bradley Birzer, *Sanctifying the World: The Augustinian Life and Mind of Christopher Dawson* (Front Royal, VA: Christendom Press, 2007), 73.
18. Birzer.
19. Cited in Birzer, 151.
20. Christopher Dawson, introduction to David Mathew, *The Celtic Peoples and Renaissance Europe: A Study of the Celtic and Spanish Influences on Elizabethan History* (London: Sheed and Ward, 1933), xiv. Also cited in Birzer, *Sanctifying the World*, viii.
21. Cited in Wilfred M. McClay, *Land of Hope: An Invitation to the Great American Story* (New York: Encounter Books, 2019), xii.
22. Oscar Cullmann, *Christ and Time: The Primitive Christian Conception of Time and History* (Eugene, OR: Wipf and Stock, 1962), 57.
23. Jonathan Sandys and Wallace Henley, *God and Churchill: How the Great Leader's Divine Destiny Changed His Troubled World and Offers Hope for Ours* (Wheaton, IL: Tyndale House Publishers, 2015). Personal communication from Jonathan Sandys to Wallace Henley.
24. London Baptist Confession of Faith, 1689; chapter 5, paragraph 1, http://www.providentialhistory.org/?page_id=100.
25. Alexis de Tocqueville, *Democracy in America*, trans. and ed. by Harvey C. Mansfield and Delba Winthrop (Chicago: University of Chicago Press, 2000), 6.
26. Cullmann, 49.
27. Al Mohler, "Civilization on the Brink," Christian Headlines, September 16, 2004, https://www.christianheadlines.com/columnists/al-mohler/civilization-on-the-brink-1285151.html.

Chapter I: The Lord of History

1. Christopher Dawson, *The Movement of World Revolution* (New York: Sheed and Ward, 1959), 101.
2. We also discuss this in chapter 9 of this book.
3. Paul Kengor and Robert Orlando, *The Divine Plan: John Paul II, Ronald Reagan, and the Dramatic End of the Cold War* (Wilmington, DE: ISI Books, 2019), 15.
4. As cited in Jonathan Sandys and Wallace Henley, *God and Churchill: How the Great Leader's Divine Destiny Changed His Troubled World and Offers Hope for Ours* (Wheaton, IL: Tyndale House Publishers, 2015), 91.
5. As cited in Sandys and Henley, 93.
6. Sandys and Henley.
7. Whittaker Chambers, *Witness: 50th Anniversary Edition* (Washington, DC: Regnery, 1980), 536.
8. Brooke Berger, "Eisenhower and Nixon: Secrets of an Unlikely Pair," *U.S. News & World Report*, February 15, 2013, https://www.usnews.com/opinion/articles/2013/02/15/eisenhower-and-nixon-secrets-of-an-unlikely-pair.

9. "55 Years Ago—'The Last Press Conference,'" November 14, 2017, https://www.nixonfoundation.org/2017/11/55-years-ago-last-press-conference/.
10. "California: Career's End," *Time*, November 16, 1962, http://content.time.com/time/magazine/article/0,9171,829391,00.html.
11. Jules Witcover, *The Resurrection of Richard Nixon* (New York: G.P. Putnam's Sons, 1970). Witcover's quote is from the acknowledgments.
12. Retrieved from https://www.christianblog.com/blog/revgenlink/god-uses-us-presidents-for-his-purpose-israel-golda-meir-and-nixon/, and also from personal conversations.
13. As reported in Daniel Chaitin, "30 Years Ago Today Richard Nixon Wrote a Letter to Trump Predicting Success in Politics," *Washington Examiner*, December 21, 2017, https://www.washingtonexaminer.com/30-years-ago-today-richard-nixon-wrote-a-letter-to-trump-predicting-success-in-politics.
14. Ron Chernow, *Washington: A Life* (New York: Penguin Press, 2010), 129.
15. Chernow, 128–29.
16. Chernow, 131.
17. From a letter written by Burke to François-Louis-Thibaut de Menonville, a member of the French Assembly, May 1791.
18. James Madison, *The Federalist Papers*, 1788.
19. John G. West Jr., "George Washington and the Religious Impulse," in *Patriot Sage: George Washington and the American Political Tradition*, ed. Gary L. Gregg II and Matthew Spalding (Wilmington, DE: ISI Books, 1999), 272.
20. As cited in William W. Freehling, *Becoming Lincoln* (Charlottesville: University of Virginia Press, 2018), Kindle Loc. 432 of 8338.
21. Amity Shlaes, *Coolidge* (New York: HarperCollins, 2013), 96.
22. Claude Moore Fuess, *Calvin Coolidge: The Man from Vermont* (Boston: Little, Brown, 1940), 500.
23. Cited in Shlaes, 447.
24. Shlaes, 302.
25. Shlaes, 314.
26. Shlaes, 115–116.
27. Victor Davis Hanson, *The Case for Trump* (New York: Basic Books, 2019), 272.

Chapter 2: Perfect God, Imperfect People

1. As cited in William W. Freehling, *Becoming Lincoln* (Charlottesville: University of Virginia Press, 2018), Kindle Loc. 1708 of 8338.
2. Freehling, Kindle Loc. 1731 of 8338.
3. Robert S. McGee, *The Search for Significance: Seeing Your True Worth Through God's Eyes* (Nashville: Thomas Nelson, 1998), 2003.
4. David Brody and Scott Lamb, *The Faith of Donald J. Trump* (NewYork: HarperCollins, 2018), 255.

5. For more information, see Scott Glover and Maeve Reston, "How Donald Trump Sees Himself," CNN Politics, April 1, 2016, https://www.cnn .com/2016/04/01/politics/how-donald-trump-sees-himself/index.html.

6. As listed in Romans 12 and 1 Corinthians 12.

7. Dan P. McAdams, "The Mind of Donald Trump," *Atlantic*, June 2016, https:// www.theatlantic.com/magazine/archive/2016/06/the-mind -of-donald-trump/480771/.

8. Ryne H. Sherman PhD, "The Personality of Donald Trump," *Psychology Today*, September 17, 2015, https://www.psychologytoday.com/us/blog /the-situation-lab/201509/the-personality-donald-trump.

9. This gift is listed in the New Testament as "apostleship." It does not refer to one as holding the *office* of apostle, as did Jesus' original twelve disciples, but a functional character trait.

10. Brody and Lamb, 6.

11. Gwenda Blair, "How Norman Vincent Peale Taught Trump to Worship Himself," *Politico*, October 6, 2015. Also cited in Brody and Lamb, 94.

Chapter 3: The Kingdom Plan and Exceptionalism

1. Seymour Martin Lipset, *American Exceptionalism: A Double-Edged Sword* (New York: W.W. Norton Company, 1996), 14.

2. Kevin Roberts, "Timothy Carney's 'Alienated America' & the Future of the American Dream," *The Imaginative Conservative*, May 16, 2019, https:// theimaginativeconservative.org/2019/05/alienated-america-timothy -carney-kevin-roberts.html.

3. Timothy P. Carney, *Alienated America: Why Some Places Thrive While Others Collapse* (New York: HarperCollins, 2019), 122.

4. Carney, 122.

5. Roberts, "Timothy Carney's 'Alienated America.'"

6. Joshua Zeitz, "How Trump Is Making Us Rethink American Exceptionalism," *Politico*, January 7, 2018, https://www.politico.com /magazine/story/2018/01/07/trump-american-exceptionalism-history-216253.

7. John A. Gans Jr., "American Exceptionalism and the Politics of Foreign Policy," *Atlantic*, November 21, 2011, https://www.theatlantic .com/international/archive/2011/11/american-exceptionalism-and -the-politics-of-foreign-policy/248779/.

8. "President Donald J. Trump's America First Agenda Is Helping to Achieve Peace Through Strength," White House Fact Sheet, September 25, 2018, https://www.whitehouse.gov/briefings-statements/president-donald -j-trumps-america-first-agenda-helping-achieve-peace-strength/.

9. Greg Norman, "Eric Holder Goes On MAGA Attack: 'Exactly When Did You Think America Was Great?'" March 28, FoxNews.com, https://www .foxnews.com/politics/eric-holder-when-did-you-think-america-was-great.

10. Bradley Birzer, *Sanctifying the World: The Augustinian Life and Mind of Christopher Dawson* (Front Royal, VA: Christendom Press, 2007), 9.
11. Birzer, 77.
12. Wilfred M. McClay, *Land of Hope: An Invitation to the Great American Story* (New York: Encounter Books, 2019), 27.
13. The 1619 Project, *New York Times Magazine,* https://www.nytimes.com /interactive/2019/08/14/magazine/1619-america-slavery.html.
14. Russell Kirk, *The Roots of American Order* (Wilmington DE: ISI Books, 2017), 13.
15. Christopher DeMuth, "America's Nationalist Awakening," *Wall Street Journal,* July 20–21, 2019, A-15.
16. From Witherspoon's "Dominion of Providence" sermon.
17. Eric Metaxas, *If You Can Keep It: The Forgotten Promise of American Liberty* (New York: Penguin Books, 2017), 17–19.
18. McClay, 6.
19. McClay, 6.
20. William J. Federer, *Change to Chains: The 6,000 Year Quest for Control,* vol. 1 (St. Louis: Amerisearch, Inc., 2013), 13–15.
21. Raymond T. Bond, ed., *The Man Who Was Chesterton* (Garden City, NY: Image Books, 1960), 125.
22. Alexis de Tocqueville, *Democracy in America,* trans. and ed. Harvey C. Mansfield and Debra Winthrop (Chicago: University of Chicago Press, 2000), 282.
23. De Tocqueville, 281.
24. "Telos," Bible Hub, //biblehub.com/greek/5056.htm.
25. Birzer, 11.
26. David Brody and Scott Lamb, *The Faith of Donald J. Trump* (NewYork: HarperCollins, 2018), Kindle loc. 187 of 6591.
27. Oscar Cullmann, *Christ and Time: The Primitive Christian Conception of Time and History* (Eugene, OR, 1962), 57.
28. This is from Wordpress.com: Bartleby's dictionary of quotations traces the quote to a 1941 book titled *The Kingdom of God and the American Dream,* by Sherwood Eddy, a theologically liberal Christian socialist and missionary, who claimed to be quoting Tocqueville. Wikiquotes has identified an earlier source, a 1922 letter to a Presbyterian magazine called the *Herald and Presbyter* (vol. 93, no. 36, p. 8). According to the letter, an official with the Presbyterian Board of Home Missions, the Rev. John McDowell, included the quote in a Sunday sermon and attributed it to Tocqueville. Where Rev. McDowell got the quote is not known, although this much is certain: he didn't get it from Alexis de Tocqueville.

Chapter 4: Time and the Two Men from Babylon

1. "Cracking the Uncrackable: How Did Alan Turing and His Team Crack the Enigma Code?" December 27, 2015, https://www.scienceabc.com/innovation /cracking-the-uncrackable-how-did-alan-turing-and-his-team-crack-the -enigma-code.html.

2. "Oscar Wilde Quotes," BrainyQuote, https://www.brainyquote.com/quotes /oscar_wilde_378307.

3. Max Lucado, "What Was Meant for Evil, God Uses for Good," faithgateway .com, June 19, 2019, https://www.faithgateway.com/what-was-meant-for-evil -god-uses-for-good/#.Xd6acm5FxPY.

4. Quoted in T. M. Rudavsky, *Time Matters: Time, Creation, and Cosmology in Medieval Jewish Philosophy* (New York: SUNY Press, 2012), 35.

5. "History Doesn't Repeat, but It Often Rhymes," Huffpost, January 19, 2017, https://www.huffingtonpost.com.au/brian-adams/history-doesnt-repeat-but -it-often-rhymes_a_21657884/. The statement is most often credited to Mark Twain, though the exact origin is unknown.

6. Oscar Cullmann, *Christ and Time: The Primitive Christian Conception of Time and History,* trans. Floyd V. Filson (London: SCM Press Ltd., 1951), 43.

7. See, for example, Galatians 4:4.

8. "Hillary Clinton Thinks 'God Put Her on the Earth to Be President,' Says Former Adviser," lifezette.com, October 28, 2019, https://www.lifezette .com/2019/10/hillary-god-earth-president-former-adviser/.

Chapter 5: Where We Are in Time

1. Matthew 24:14, a major Bible text at the heart of the thesis of this book.

2. Revelation 4:1. "These things" refers to the visions John had just been given related to seven churches of Asia Minor in his day, which will also be types of churches appearing all across history. The scriptures that follow in this discussion are from Revelation 4–5 NASB.

3. Cited in Joshua J. Mark, "Nebuchadnezzar II," *Ancient History Encyclopedia,* https://www.ancient.eu/Nebuchadnezzar_II/.

4. "Washington's Inaugural Address of 1789, A Transcription," https://www .archives.gov/exhibits/american_originals/inaugtxt.html.

5. "The Inaugural Address, January 20, 2017," whitehouse.gov, https://www .whitehouse.gov/briefings-statements/the-inaugural-address/.

6. See Isaiah 9:6.

Chapter 6: Birth Pangs!

1. Gary Bauer and Sam Brownback quotes are from Nahal Toosi, "Trump's religious freedom conference creates awkward alliance," *Politico,* July 14, 2019, https://www.progressnews.network/2019/07/14/trumps-religious -freedom-conference-creates-awkward-alliance/.

2. *Jewish Antiquities*, 20:97–98.

3. Jakub Bozydar Wisniewski, "The Uneasy Hiatus of the Infantile Era," December 27, 2018, *The Imaginative Conservative*, https://theimaginativeconservative.org/2018/12/uneasy-hiatus-infantile-era-jakub-wisniewski.html.

4. Chris Matyszczyk, "The New Church of the AI God Is Even Creepier Than I Imagined," November 16, 2017, https://www.cnet.com/news/the-new-church-of-ai-god-is-even-creepier-than-i-imagined/.

5. Jonathan Glover, *Humanity: A Moral History of the Twentieth Century*, 2nd ed. (New Haven: Yale University Press, 2012).

6. "How Many Wars Are Going On Right Now?," *Borgen Magazine*, November 17, 2013, https://www.borgenmagazine.com/many-wars-going-right-now/.

7. https://www.studylight.org/lexicons/greek/1484.html.

8. "Basileia," Bible Hub, https://biblehub.com/greek/932.htm.

9. Samuel Huntington, "The Clash of Civilizations?" *Foreign Affairs*, summer 1993, www.foreignaffairs.com.

10. "The Romans Destroy the Temple at Jerusalem, 70 AD," www.eyewitnesstohistory.com/jewishtemple.htm.

11. Jared C. Wilson, "Christian Persecution Is Intensifying," The Gospel Coalition, January 16, 2019, https://www.thegospelcoalition.org/blogs/jared-c-wilson/christian-persecution-intensifying/.

12. Patrick Wintour, "Persecution of Christians 'Coming Close to Genocide' in Middle East—Report," *Guardian*, May 2, 2019, https://www.theguardian.com/world/2019/may/02/persecution-driving-christians-out-of-middle-east-report.

13. "Persecution of Christians Seen on the Rise in Middle East," *Arab Weekly*, December 5, 2019, https://thearabweekly.com/persecution-christians-seen-rise-middle-east.

14. Michael Brown, "Why So Much Hatred Against Christians in America Today?" Townhall, November 7, 2017, https://townhall.com/columnists/michaelbrown/2017/11/07/why-so-much-hatred-against-christians-in-america-today-n2406028.

15. Samuel Smith, "Only 3 in 10 American Adults Hold 'Positive' Perception of Evangelicals," *Christian Post*, November 22, 2019, https://www.christianpost.com/news/only-3-in-10-american-adults-hold-positive-perception-of-evangelicals-barna-research.html.

16. Roger Kimball, *The Long March: How the Cultural Revolution of the 1960s Changed America* (New York: Encounter Books, 2001), 41.

17. "The Berean Call," 10/97, citing *Christian News*, May 12, 1997, 11.

18. Donald S. Armentrout, "Pike, James Albert (1913–1969)" in the *Dictionary of Christianity in America*, ed. Daniel G. Reid et al. (Downers Grove, IL: InterVarsity Press, 1990).

19. C. S. Lewis, *Mere Christianity* (New York: HarperCollins: 2001), 51–52.

20. Tim Challies, "7 False Teachers in the Church Today," January 31, 2017, challies.com, https://www.challies.com/articles/7-false-teachers-in -the-church-today/.

21. Michael Steinberger, "Joe Biden Wants to Take America Back to a Time Before Trump," *New York Times Magazine*, July 23, 2019, https://www .nytimes.com/2019/07/23/magazine/joe-biden-2020.html.

22. Statistics shown here are from respective organizations as grouped at http://prayerfoundation.org/world_christian_growth_statistics.htm.

23. Paul Kengor and Robert Orlando, *The Divine Plan: John Paul II, Ronald Reagan, and the Dramatic End of the Cold War* (Wilmington, DE: ISI Books, 2019), 33.

24. Alexandra Desanctis, "What Northam's Walk Back Really Means," *National Review*, January 31, 2019, https://www.nationalreview.com/corner /what-northams-walk-back-really-means/.

Chapter 7: Destroyers and Deliverers

1. Abigail Tracy, "Joe Biden Is Worried Donald Trump Might Destroy Western Civilization," *Vanity Fair*, January 18, 2017, https://www.vanityfair.com /news/2017/01/joe-biden-donald-trump-davos.

2. "Your Views: Trump Trying to Save Civilization, as the Left Destroys It," *GazetteXtra*, December 27, 2018, https://www.gazettextra.com /opinion/letters/your-views-trump-trying-to-save-civilization-as-the-left /article_2bb2004f-098c-5782–8415-eb4138a51616.html?utm_medium =social&utm_source=email&utm_campaign=user-share.

3. Alexander Zubatov, "4 Reasons Socialism Is More Popular Among Americans Now than Ever Before," *Federalist*, October 31, 2019, https:// thefederalist.com/2019/10/31/4-reasons-socialism-is-more-popular -among-americans-now-than-ever-before/.

4. Niall Ferguson, *Civilization, The West and the Rest* (New York: Penguin Press, 2011), 1–2.

5. Peggy Noonan, *Wall Street Journal*, July 6, 2017.

6. "The Lights Are Going Out," 1938 speech by Winston Churchill, Nationalchurchillmuseum.org.

7. Malcolm Muggeridge, *The End of Christendom* (Grand Rapids: Eerdmans, 1980).

8. "Arnold Toynbee: A Study of History," https://www.age-of-the-sage.org /philosophy/history/toynbee_study_history.html.

9. John Eberhard, "The Tytler Cycle Revisited," June 16, 2015, http:// commonsensegovernment.com/the-tytler-cycle-revisited/.

10. Ferguson, 2.

11. Saint Augustine, *The City of God,* trans. Marcus Dods (Coterie Classics, 2016), 101.
12. Augustine, 438.
13. Ferguson, *Civilization, The West and the Rest,* 287.
14. Saint Augustine, *The City of God,* trans. by Gerald G. Walsh, S.J., and Daniel J. Honan (Washington, DC: Catholic University of America Press, 1954), 486.
15. Dennis Prager, "Why the Left Loathes Western Civilization," *National Review,* April 26, 2016.
16. Taylor, 470–71. The Duke of Devonshire quote is as it appears in Taylor, 471.
17. James Ostrowski, *Progressivism: A Primer on the Idea Destroying America* (Buffalo, NY: Cazenovia Books, 2014), 1.
18. "Humanist Manifesto II," The American Humanist Association, www.americanhumanist.org.
19. Jordan Peterson, *12 Rules for Life: An Antidote to Chaos* (Toronto: Random House Canada, 2018), viii, xviii, xx, emphasis in original.
20. Ostrowski, 1.
21. Ostrowski, 7.
22. Orestes A. Brownson, *The American Republic* (facsimile edition, Clifton, NJ: A. A. Kelley, 1972), 363–64. Cited also in Russell Kirk, *The Roots of American Order* (Wilmington, DE: ISI Books, 2017), 463–64.
23. Kirk, *Roots of American Order,* 463–64.
24. Kirk, *Roots of American Order,* 11.

Chapter 8: Power and the Clustering of Demons

1. H. R. Haldeman, *The Ends of Power* (New York: Times Books, 1978), 122.
2. Eric F. Goldman, *The Tragedy of Lyndon Johnson* (New York: Alfred A. Knopf, 1969), 511.
3. Goldman, 531.
4. Seymour M. Hersh, *The Dark Side of Camelot* (Boston: Little, Brown and Company, 1997), 2.
5. Henry Fairlie, *The Kennedy Promise* (Garden City, NY: Doubleday, 1973), 7, emphasis added.
6. Fairlie, 7.
7. Nancy Pearcey, *Total Truth: Liberating Christianity from Its Cultural Captivity* (Wheaton, IL: Crossway, 2008), 118.
8. *Strong's Concordance,* #5387.
9. I am indebted to Dudley Hall, an insightful Bible teacher and dear friend, for the four categories of control employed by raw power listed here.
10. David Brody and Scott Lamb, *The Faith of Donald J. Trump* (New York: HarperCollins, 2018), 263.
11. Paul Kengor and Robert Orlando, *The Divine Plan: John Paul II, Ronald*

Reagan, and the Dramatic End of the Cold War (Wilmington, DE: ISI Books, 2019), 23.

Chapter 9: The Z-4 Alliance

1. Lawrence W. Reed, "Why the Pilgrims Abandoned Common Ownership for Private Property," *Foundation for Economic Education*, fee.org, November 25, 2019, https://fee.org/articles/why-the-pilgrims-abandoned-common -ownership-for-private-property/, emphasis added.
2. Paul Kengor and Robert Orlando, *The Divine Plan: John Paul II, Ronald Reagan, and the Dramatic End of the Cold War* (Wilmington, DE: ISI Books, 2019), 12.
3. Nicolai Berdyaev, *The Meaning of History* (Semantron Press, 2009). Review appears at https://www.amazon.com/Meaning-History-Nicolas-Berdyaev/dp /1597312576/ref=sr_1_4?crid=3RLHLWBV4GZY3&keywords =the+meaning+of+history+nikolai+berdyaev&qid=1574182049&sprefix =Berdyaev+the+meaning+%2Caps%2C159&sr=8-4.
4. Peter Osnos and Michael Getler, "Polish Throngs Hail Pope," *Washington Post*, June 3, 1979.
5. Kengor and Orlando, 11, https://www.washingtonpost.com/archive/politics /1979/06/03/polish-throngs-hail-pope/841509c0-f79d-4673-b40e -93e704777353/.
6. Kengor and Orlando, 13, emphasis in original.
7. Kengor and Orlando, 16.
8. Kengor and Orlando, 12.
9. Kengor and Orlando, 12.
10. Mark Thiessen, "Evils of Socialism Must Be Taught to Young People," Fox News, https://www.foxnews.com/opinion/marc-thiessen-podcast.
11. Thiessen, "Evils of Socialism."
12. See 1 Chronicles 12:32.
13. Omar Bradley, "Armistice Day Address," cited in William J. Federer (ed.), *America's God and Country Encyclopedia of Quotations* (Fame Publishing), 68.
14. Zechariah sees only one lampstand, while John sees two. The difference may lie in the fact that in Zechariah's time the church has not emerged. In the New Testament era there is a multiplicity of churches, represented in John's vision by the Seven Churches of Asia Minor. Lampstands in the book of Revelation are symbols of the churches. "Two" indicates the plurality of the churches generally.

Chapter 10: The Strategic Remnant

1. Philippians 4:22, emphasis added.
2. *Strong's Concordance*, Word 652, https://biblehub.com/greek/652.htm.

3. J. R. Benjamin, "Do the Jews Prove God's Existence?," April 23, 2015, https://jrbenjamin.com/2015/04/23/could-the-history-of-the-jews-prove-gods-existence/.
4. All quotes are from J. R. Benjamin, *The Bully Pulpit*, https://jrbenjamin.com/2015/04/23/could-the-history-of-the-jews-prove-gods-existence/.
5. "America & Jewish Values," https://www.simpletoremember.com/articles/a/jewsamerica/.
6. I am indebted to Eddie and Alice Smith, prayer warriors, for pointing out this parallel.
7. Deborah Hamilton, "'Remnant' Key to Spiritual Awakening in America, Says Sam Rohrer," *Charisma News*, charismanews.com, January 26, 2015, https://www.charismanews.com/s/48027-remnant-key-to-spiritual-awakening-in-america-says-sam-rohrer.
8. Brody and Lamb, *The Faith of Donald J. Trump*, 238.

Chapter 11: Healthy Church, Healthy Nation

1. Russell Kirk, *Enemies of the Permanent Things* (Providence, RI: Cluny Media, 2016), 356.
2. Christopher Dawson, *Progress and Religion: An Historical Enquiry* (Washington, DC: Catholic University of America Press, 2001), 180.
3. Angelo M. Codevilla, *The Character of Nations: How Politics Makes and Breaks Prosperity, Family, and Civility* (New York: HarperCollins/Basic Books, 1957), 7.
4. Thomas Carlyle, *The French Revolution: A History* (New York: Clarke, Given & Hooper, 1892), 143.
5. Yuval Levin, *The Great Debate: Edmund Burke, Thomas Paine, and the Birth of Right and Left* (New York: Basic Books, 2014), 28.
6. Mark A. Noll, *The Civil War as a Theological Crisis* (Chapel Hill: University of North Carolina Press, 2006), 27.
7. Quoted in Noll.
8. Quoted in Noll.
9. Jonathan Sandys and Wallace Henley, *God and Churchill: How the Great Leader's Divine Destiny Changed His Troubled World and Offers Hope for Ours* (Wheaton, IL: Tyndale House Publishers, 2015).
10. Leon Poliakov, *The Aryan Myth: A History of Racist and Nationalistic Ideas in Europe*, trans. Edmund Howard (New York: Barnes & Noble Books, 1974), 309.
11. Milton S. Terry, *Biblical Hermeneutics: A Treatise on the Interpretation of the Old and New Testament* (Grand Rapids: Zondervan, 1979), 166.
12. Thom Rainer, "Ten Areas Where Pastors Need to Be Trained for the 21st Century," March 8, 2014, https://thomrainer.com/2014/03/ten-areas-where-pastors-need-to-be-trained-for-the-21st-century/.

Chapter 12: The True MAGA and the New Jerusalem

1. "Novak Outs Eagleton as 'Amnesty, Abortion, and Acid' Source, *Washington Examiner*, July 15, 2007, https://www.washingtonexaminer.com /novak-outs-eagleton-as-amnesty-abortion-and-acid-source.

2. Edward Murray Hood, "When Presidential Slogans Meet the Realities of Government," *New York Times*, April 12, 1992, section 4, 20.

3. Laura Brache, " 'He's Still Doing Work,' Organs of Asheboro Man Struck by Driver Charged with DWI Saving New Lives," November 24, 2019, https:// www.wfmynews2.com/article/features/organs-of-asheboro-man-struck-by -drunk-driver-saving-new-lives/83-ff4c4fb1-ed37–4082-b63f-33a433a99089.

4. Isaiah 6:4, as quoted in 1 Corinthians 2:9 (NLT).

5. Marshall Foster and Mary Elaine Swanson, *The American Covenant* (Thousand Oaks, CA: Mayflower Institute, 1992), viii.

6. Foster and Swanson, viii.

7. John Eidsmoe, *Christianity and the Constitution: The Faith of Our Founding Fathers* (Grand Rapids: Baker, 1987), 51–52.

Epilogue: Payday Someday

1. "R. G. Lee—A Peerless Pulpiteer," *Christian Index*, July 28, 2017, https:// christianindex.org/rg-lee-peerless-pulpiteer/.

2. Wayne S. Moss, "Witherspoon, Madison, Moral Philosophy, and the Constitution," *Princeton Alumni Weekly*, April 23, 2014, https://paw.princeton.edu/article /essay-witherspoon-madison-moral-philosophy-and-constitution.

3. The sermon text can be found at several sites, including http://www .constitution.org/primarysources/witherspoon.html.

ABOUT THE AUTHOR

Wallace Henley was born two days before the attack on Pearl Harbor on December 5, 1941. After serving as a White House aide during the Nixon administration, Henley went on to become an award-winning journalist for the *Birmingham News* in Alabama. He is the author of more than twenty books, including *God and Churchill* with Jonathan Sandys, Winston Churchill's great-grandson. Henley has led leadership conferences around the globe. He has been married to his wife, Irene, for more than fifty years. They have two children, six grandchildren, and four great-grandchildren.